Care of the Newborn

Care of the Newborn

Editor

Richard L. Schreiner, M.D.

Section of Neonatal-Perinatal Medicine
Indiana University School of Medicine
James Whitcomb Riley Hospital for Children
Indianapolis, Indiana

Raven Press ■ New York

Raven Press, 1140 Avenue of the Americas, New York, New York 10036

Made in the United States of America

Library of Congress Cataloging in Publication Data

Main entry under title:

Care of the newborn.

    Includes bibliographical references and index.
    1.   Infants (Newborn)—Diseases. 2.   Infants
(Newborn)—Care and hygiene. I. Schreiner, Richard L.
[DNLM: 1.   Infant, Newborn. WS 420 C271]
RJ254.C37   618.92′01   80-5372
ISBN 0-89004-518-6

Great care has been taken to maintain the accuracy of the information contained in the volume. However, Raven Press cannot be held responsible for errors or for any consequences arising from the use of the information contained herein.

Preface

There are numerous neonatology books and manuals available. One might ask, "Why another book?" Most lengthy neonatology books provide a detailed description of all aspects of neonatology. Shorter manuals usually attempt to abbreviate all of neonatology into fewer pages. *Care of the Newborn* provides a detailed, readable, simple, practical approach to the *common* clinical problems which every physician and nurse caring for newborn infants will face. The book addresses the immediate needs of the clinician and provides a core of essential information, presented in a straightforward fashion. Its focus is on common clinical problems of the newborn and basic laboratory procedures required to evaluate a problem, rather than on diagnostic and therapeutic procedures used chiefly in tertiary centers.

The first section deals with general aspects of neonatal care such as physical examination, assessment of gestational age, temperature regulation, infant nutrition, and care of the normal newborn and family. In addition, common neonatal disorders such as hypoglycemia, jaundice, respiratory distress, apnea, low birth weight, bacterial sepsis, and surgical emergencies are discussed. This is followed by a description of basic diagnostic and therapeutic procedures such as intravenous needle placement, blood transfusions, techniques of obtaining blood, lumbar puncture, and umbilical artery catheterization.

The volume will be of interest to pediatricians, family practitioners, obstetricians; family practice, pediatric and obstetric residents; neonatal nurses and respiratory therapists; and medical students.

Richard L. Schreiner, M.D.

Acknowledgments

I would like to thank those people who have helped to make this book possible. Drs. Morris Green, Edwin Gresham, and James Lemons provided encouragement, suggestions, guidance and review of the manuscript. Craig Gosling and the Medical Illustrations Department are responsible for the excellent illustrations. Most importantly, Miriam Cook assisted and tolerated me throughout the organization of this book and typed all drafts of the manuscript.

This book is dedicated to Dr. Edwin L. Gresham, who died November 1, 1980.
He was our teacher and friend.
We loved him and will miss him dearly.

Contents

Part I: General Aspects 1

1. Prenatal Care and Care of the Newborn in the Delivery Room
   Philip F. Merk 3

2. Care of the Normal Newborn and the Family
   Dennis C. Stevens 9

3. Physical Examination
   Richard L. Schreiner and Edwin L. Gresham 15

4. Assessment of Gestational Age
   Richard L. Schreiner, Rita Sullivan, and Jean Foster 31

5. Temperature Regulation
   Richard L. Schreiner 44

6. Infant Nutrition
   Margaret Blythe, James A. Lemons, and Richard L. Schreiner 48

7. Resuscitation
   Richard L. Schreiner, Patricia A. Keener, and Edwin L. Gresham 59

8. Hypoglycemia, Infants of Diabetic Mothers
   Dennis C. Stevens and Richard L. Schreiner 69

9. Jaundice
   Eric Yancy and Richard L. Schreiner 76

10. Approach to the Newborn with Respiratory Distress
    *Richard L. Schreiner, Edwin L. Gresham, and Marilyn B.
    Escobedo* 86

11. Oxygen
    Janet K. Hilliard and Richard L. Schreiner 100

12. Delivering and Monitoring Oxygen
    Tony Goodrich, Jeffrey A. Kisling, and Richard L. Schreiner 107

13. Persistent Fetal Circulation
    Dennis C. Stevens and Richard L. Schreiner 122

14. Apnea
    James H. Jose and Richard L. Schreiner 128

15. Treatment of Respiratory Problems
    Marilyn B. Escobedo and Richard L. Schreiner 137

16. Neonatal Bacterial Sepsis
    Janet K. Hilliard and Richard L. Schreiner 146

17. Newborn Transport—Stabilization of the Infant Before Arrival
    of the Transport Team
    Richard L. Schreiner and Ralph J. Wynn 154

18. Problems of the Very Low Birth Weight Infant
    James A. Lemons 162

19. Fluid and Electrolyte Management
    James A. Lemons 166

20. Necrotizing Enterocolitis
    Richard L. Schreiner 175

21. Surgical Emergencies in the Newborn
    Jay L. Grosfeld 182

22. Seizures
    Christopher L. Meyer and Richard L. Schreiner 196

23. Caring for the Family Mourning a Perinatal Death
    Carol K. Mahan and Richard L. Schreiner 203

Part II: Procedures 211

    Preface

24. Intravenous Needle Placement
    Richard L. Schreiner and Kusuma Bavikatte 213

25. Blood Cultures
    Dennis C. Stevens 218

26. Suprapubic Bladder Aspiration
    Dennis C. Stevens and Richard L. Schreiner 221

27. Blood Transfusions
    Glen W. Cartwright 226

28. Exchange Transfusions
    James A. Lemons 231

29. Intubation
    Dennis C. Stevens and Richard L. Schreiner 237

30. Techniques of Obtaining Arterial Blood
   Glen W. Cartwright and Richard L. Schreiner 242

31. Umbilical Artery Catheterization
   Dennis C. Stevens and Richard L. Schreiner 250

32. Lumbar Puncture
   Dennis C. Stevens and Richard L. Schreiner 258

33. Treatment of Pneumothorax: Aspiration and Chest Tube
   Placement
   Richard L. Schreiner and Edwin L. Gresham 264

Part III: Appendix 277

Subject Index 301

Contributors

Kusuma Bavikatte, M.D., *Fellow, Neonatal-Perinatal Medicine*
Margaret Blythe, M.D., *Instructor in Pediatrics*
Glen W. Cartwright, M.D., *Fellow, Neonatal-Perinatal Medicine*
Marilyn B. Escobedo, M.D., *Assistant Professor, Neonatal-Perinatal Medicine*
Jean Foster, R.N., M.S.N., *Module Coordinator, Newborn Intensive Care Unit*
Tony Goodrich, C.R.T.T., *Chief Respiratory Therapist*
Edwin L. Gresham, M.D., *Professor of Pediatrics and Director, Section of Neonatal-Perinatal Medicine*
Jay L. Grosfeld, M.D., *Professor of Surgery and Director, Section of Pediatric Surgery*
Janet K. Hilliard, D.O., *Fellow, Neonatal-Perinatal Medicine*
James H. Jose, M.D., *Pediatric Resident*
Patricia A. Keener, M.D., *Director of Nurseries, Community Hospital, Indianapolis*
Jeffrey A. Kisling, R.R.T., *Neonatal Respiratory Therapist*
James A. Lemons, M.D., *Associate Professor of Pediatrics*
Carol K. Mahan, M.S.W., *Perinatal Social Worker*
Philip F. Merk, M.D., *Instructor in Pediatrics*
Christopher L. Meyer, M.D., *Fellow, Neonatal-Perinatal Medicine*
Richard L. Schreiner, M.D., *Associate Professor of Pediatrics*
Dennis C. Stevens, M.D., *Fellow, Neonatal-Perinatal Medicine*
Rita Sullivan, R.N., B.S.N., *Module Coordinator, Newborn Intensive Care Unit*
Ralph J. Wynn, M.D., *Fellow, Neonatal-Perinatal Medicine*
Eric Yancy, M.D., *Chief Resident in Pediatrics*

The contributors are affiliated with the Indiana University School of Medicine, James Whitcomb Riley Hospital for Children, Indianapolis, Indiana.

Part I: General Aspects

1

Prenatal Care and Care of the Newborn in the Delivery Room

Ideally, the care of the newborn infant begins during the prenatal period. If the family practitioner is to deliver and care for the infant, all the suggestions below can be carried out during routine prenatal visits. If an obstetrician is caring for the pregnant woman, his close cooperation with the pediatrician or family practitioner provides optimal care to the mother and the fetus, hopefully resulting in the birth of a healthy infant to a healthy, happy mother. In the following instances, this cooperation must begin early during pregnancy: a history of previous premature births, Rh sensitization, genetic disease, or congenital anomaly; a systemic maternal disease; advanced maternal age; and other significant obstetric complications. In most cases, however, the prenatal visit is ideally scheduled with the pediatrician near the seventh month of gestation.

This visit, which optimally includes the father as well as the mother, offers an opportunity to gain much information about the family and the mother, especially that which relates to the present pregnancy. Additional information may be obtained from the mother's obstetric records (Table 1). The medical history of the mother includes her age, general health, the presence of any chronic or acute systemic diseases, the taking of medications, and if she smokes or consumes alcohol excessively.

In addition, any previous obstetric or gynecologic history is obtained, including gravidity, parity, and outcome of previous pregnancies, e.g., complications, type of delivery, gestational age and weight of infants, and any postnatal problems. Needless to say, data concerning the present pregnancy are imperative. Such information includes the estimated date of confinement (EDC); exposure to communicable diseases; acute illnesses or diseases including gonorrhea, syphilis, and genital herpes; and known complications not already reported, including pre-eclampsia, bleeding, twins, maternal surgery, or other factors thought to place the pregnancy at high risk. The results of pertinent laboratory tests are also necessary. These should include hemoglobin and hematocrit, Rh

3

TABLE 1. *Significant information obtained from parents and/or obstetric records*

I. Maternal history
  A. General health
    1. Age
    2. Presence of systemic disease
    3. Medications
    4. Smoking and alcohol history
  B. Previous obstetric and/or gynecologic history
    1. Gravidity and parity
    2. Complications of previous pregnancies, labor, and deliveries
    3. Outcome of previous pregnancies
      a. Type of delivery
      b. Gestational age and weight of infants
      c. Postnatal complications of the infants
    4. Previous gynecologic problems
  C. Present pregnancy
    1. Estimated date of confinement (EDC)
    2. Exposure to communicable diseases
    3. Illnesses or diseases including gonorrhea, syphilis, genital herpes
    4. Known complications
      a. Pre-eclampsia
      b. Bleeding
      c. Twinning
      d. Maternal surgery
      e. Other complications which make this a high-risk pregnancy
    5. Laboratory and other data
      a. Hemoglobin and hematocrit
      b. Rh and blood type
      c. VDRL
      d. Rubella titers
      e. Tests for fetal maturity
      f. Sonography
      g. Amniocentesis
II. Family history
  A. Paternal
    1. Health of father
    2. Presence of inheritable diseases or conditions
  B. Inheritable diseases in maternal family
  C. Health of other offspring

and blood type, VDRL, rubella titers, and possibly tests for fetal maturity, sonography, and amniocentesis.

The father's health is noted as are any inheritable diseases or conditions in his and the mother's families. The health of any offspring is also explored.

Additional topics for discussion are included in Table 2. The family's feelings concerning this pregnancy are explored and the parents provided the opportunity to express any anxieties and fears they might have.

A general discussion of the routine hospital care of the mother and newborn makes the mother and father much more at ease at the time of delivery and during the hospital stay. Included in this discussion are the father's presence in the labor, delivery, and recovery rooms, rooming-in options, birthing rooms, sibling visitation, and visiting hours.

TABLE 2. *Topics of discussion with parents-to-be*

I. Parents' feelings concerning this pregnancy
   A. Anxieties and fears
   B. Complications of pregnancy
II. Routine hospital care
   A. Maternal
   B. Delivery, including birthing room, father's presence in the delivery and/or recovery room, where permitted
   C. Infant care routine, including rooming-in options
III. Infant feeding
   A. General considerations
   B. Advantages of breast feeding
IV. Circumcision
V. Effect of pregnancy and new baby on the family
   A. Changes in lifestyle
   B. Reaction of siblings
   C. Economic considerations
VI. Your philosophy of child care
   A. General newborn care including any literature or recommendations for parenting classes
   B. Plans made for newborn's care
      1. Sleeping arrangements
      2. Help for the mother
      3. Support of father
   C. Supplies necessary for newborn care
      1. Clothing
      2. Bedding
      3. Items necessary for feedings

This prenatal visit is an appropriate time to discuss infant feeding. The advantages of breast feeding are reviewed and literature on breast feeding made available to mothers who are interested. It is obviously important, however, not to engender guilt in mothers who decline breast feeding. Their decision to bottle-feed their infants needs positive support.

The advantages and disadvantages of circumcision (e.g., a description of the procedure) are also discussed at this time. Note that the American Academy of Pediatrics' statement on circumcision points out that there is no medical indication for circumcision during the newborn period.

It is also important at this time to ask the parents about the effects they project the new baby will have on their family life. The potential reactions of other children to the pregnancy and the birth of a new child are noted. At this time the doctor or nurse may advise the parents about the necessary supplies for the new baby—clothing, bed, bedding, bottles, etc. Inquiry into planned sleeping arrangements and who will help the mother is also important. Literature on care of the newborn may be given to the parents at this time, so they may read the material before the baby arrives. If available in the community, classes on parenting may be recommended to expectant parents.

THE DELIVERY ROOM

The delivery room management of a newborn infant begins with a review of the maternal records (Table 3). Much of this information may be obtained earlier in the third trimester during a prenatal visit.

As soon as the infant is delivered, his mouth and nose are suctioned to remove secretions, blood, or other debris which occlude the airway. The physician then clamps and cuts the umbilical cord, keeping the infant at the perineal level before this is done to prevent infant-placenta or placenta-infant transfusions with their accompanying anemia or hyperviscosity.

The infant is placed under a radiant warmer or other warming device and dried with warm towels. *The importance of drying the infant and keeping his environment warm cannot be overemphasized.* Since newborn infants have a greater surface area/mass ratio than older children and adults, they lose heat rapidly via radiant and evaporative loss. This propensity for heat loss, coupled with the newborn's meager ability to produce heat, may lead to hypothermia if appropriate preventive measures are not taken. Premature infants are at an even greater risk to develop hypothermia and are more susceptible to its complications. Problems encountered with hypothermia include increased metabolic rate, increased oxygen consumption, respiratory distress, apnea, metabolic acidosis, and hypoglycemia.

Next, the infant's status is immediately assessed and the need for resuscitation determined. The infant's respiratory effort and heart rate are the most important parameters. Normally, an infant has a strong, vigorous cry with a respiratory rate of 35 to 60 breaths per minute. The child's heart rate should be greater than 100 per minute—normally 120 to 160 beats per minute. Following this initial assessment, the 1- and 5-min Apgar scores are determined.

After the 5-min Apgar score is determined, the infant's stomach may be suctioned. The delay until after the 5-min Apgar minimizes a vagal reflex causing bradycardia. Normally, there is less than 15 ml fluid aspirated from the stomach. If more than 20 ml fluid is aspirated, a high intestinal obstruction must be considered. Passage of the suction catheter through the nares into the stomach rules out choanal atresia and the majority of tracheo-esophageal fistulas.

A brief physical examination is then performed with an assessment of the cardiopulmonary system, palpation of the abdomen for masses, and examination for congenital anomalies. Congenital anomalies that can be diagnosed in the delivery room include choanal atresia, cleft palate and lip, esophageal atresia with tracheo-esophageal fistula, diaphragmatic hernia, high intestinal and anal atresia, intra-abdominal masses, and major anomalies of the central nervous, skeletal, or muscular systems.

If the infant is preterm by dates, appears preterm by physical examination, or is of low birth weight (less than 2,250 g), the gestational age is estimated in the delivery room and compared with the birth weight.

TABLE 3. *Delivery room management of the normal newborn*

I. Review maternal records
    A. Maternal age
    B. Gravidity and parity
    C. Significant maternal illness
    D. Maternal medications
    E. Known obstetric complications
    F. Maternal Rh and blood type
    G. EDC
    H. Time of rupture of membranes
    I. Fetal presentation
    J. Type of delivery planned
    K. Type of analgesia and/or anesthesia planned
    L. Fetal monitoring records
II. Suction mouth, then nose of infant with bulb syringe
III. Clamp and cut umbilical cord with infant at perineal level
IV. Maintain infant's temperature
    A. Place infant under radiant warmer
    B. Dry infant with warm towels
V. Assess infant's condition and need for resuscitation
VI. Assess Apgar scores at 1 and 5 min
VII. Suction stomach after 5-min Apgar score
VIII. Brief physical examination with diagnosis of congenital anomalies
    A. Cardiopulmonary system
    B. Choanal atresia
    C. Cleft lip and palate
    D. Tracheo-esophageal fistula
    E. Diaphragmatic hernia
    F. High intestinal obstruction
    G. Intra-abdominal masses or organomegaly
    H. CNS anomalies
    I. Skeletal anomalies
    J. Muscular anomalies
IX. Estimation of gestational age and comparison with weight
X. Decision on appropriate continuing care
    A. Infants needing special attention in observation nursery
        1. Infants of diabetic mothers
        2. Infants of pre-eclamptic or eclamptic mothers
        3. Infants who are small for gestational age
        4. Infants born by nonelective cesarean section
        5. Infants who weigh more than 4.5 kg
        6. Infants of mothers with serious medical problems
        7. Infants 35 to 37 weeks' gestational age
        8. Any other infant judged to require special observation
    B. Infants anticipated to require continuing care in a special care nursery
        1. Infants with 1-min Apgar score of 4 or less
        2. Infants with 5-min Apgar score of 7 or less
        3. Infants weighing less than 2,250 g
        4. Infants less than 36 weeks' gestation
        5. Infants of mothers with fever or evidence of amnionitis
        6. Infants born 24 hr or more after rupture of the membranes
        7. Infants with Rh sensitization
        8. Infants with significant congenital anomalies
        9. Infants with the probability of meconium aspiration
XI. Silver nitrate to eyes
XII. Vitamin K_1, 1 mg i.m.

Next, a decision concerning continuing care of the infant must be made. Fortunately, most infants may be sent to the observation room of the nursery. The following infants, however, require special attention in the admitting room or observation nursery: infants of diabetic mothers, infants of pre-eclamptic or eclamptic mothers, infants who are small for gestational age, infants born by nonelective cesarean section, infants whose mothers have had serious medical problems before or during pregnancy, infants who weigh more than 4.5 kg, and any other infants believed to require special observation. Even more importantly, the following infants need continuing care in the special care (intermediate or intensive care) nursery: infants with a 1-min Apgar score of 4 or less or a 5-min Apgar score of 7 or less, infants who weigh less than 2,250 g, infants of less than 36 weeks' gestation, infants of mothers with fever or evidence of amnionitis, infants born 24 hr or more after rupture of membranes, infants with severe Rh sensitization, infants with significant congenital anomalies, infants of addicted mothers, infants with the probability of meconium aspiration, and any infant judged to require intensive care.

Finally, three procedures are performed by the nurse prior to taking the infant to the nursery: (a) A thumbprint is taken from the mother and footprints from the infant to ensure proper identification. (b) Silver nitrate is instilled into the infant's eyes to protect against gonococcal ophthalmia. (c) The infant receives 1 mg vitamin K_1 i.m. to prevent hemorrhagic disease of the newborn.

CAVEATS

1. Ideally, the care of the newborn begins with a prenatal visit to the physician who will care for the infant.

2. The importance of drying the infant and keeping his environment warm in the delivery room cannot be overemphasized.

3. A brief physical examination and estimation of the gestational age are performed in the delivery room.

4. Each hospital must have guidelines for routine admission of high-risk infants to the special care nursery.

Care of the Normal Newborn and the Family

The immediate neonatal period, during which the baby recovers from the stress of labor and delivery, is a time for close observation and the use of selected screening procedures so serious disorders may be recognized early or avoided.

CARE OF THE BABY

Thermal stability is essential for neonatal stabilization. The infant is thoroughly dried and placed under a radiant warmer or in an isolette to maintain the skin temperature at 36° to 36.5°C (97° to 97.7°F). The temperature is determined hourly until stable and every 8 hr thereafter. Once thermal stability is established, the infant may be transferred to an open crib. Rooming-in and early maternal-infant contact do not preclude this process. The infant may be kept warm in the parent's arms by using warmed blankets or a radiant warmer.

In addition to the temperature, the heart rate, respiratory rate, and blood pressure need to be monitored, as often as hourly during the first few hours of life. As soon as the infant is stable in the delivery room or nursery, 0.5 to 1.0 mg vitamin K_1 is given intramuscularly as prophylaxis for hemorrhagic disease of the newborn. Silver nitrate (1%) drops are instilled into the conjunctival sac to prevent gonococcal ophthalmia neonatorum.

A number of useful screening procedures may be utilized during the early newborn period (Table 1). Some of these may be obtained on a sample of cord blood, including the blood type, Rh, and direct Coombs, particularly in infants of O and Rh⁻ mothers who may be at risk for ABO or Rh incompatibility. Serologic screening for syphilis (VDRL) may also be performed on cord blood at this time.

A whole blood glucose determination by test strip (e.g., Dextrostix®, Ames Laboratories, Elkhart, Indiana) which may be performed on one large drop of blood, is obtained on all infants during the first hour of life. Any infant who is jittery, lethargic, premature, large (LGA) or small (SGA) for gestational age, stressed, or born to a diabetic mother is subject to hypoglycemia and therefore

TABLE 1. *Suggested neonatal screening procedures*

Test	Frequency
Dextrostix	Performed at 1 hr of age or sooner if symptoms are present. Repeat every 1 to 4 hr until the infant is stable and feeding.
Serum glucose	Used to confirm Dextrostix glucose.
Hematocrit	Performed during the first 4 hr of life. Values greater than 70% are confirmed by a venous hematocrit.
Bilirubin	Performed as needed for jaundice.
Blood type, Rh, and Coombs Test	Routine on cord blood, especially if mother's blood type is O or Rh$^-$.
Serology (VDRL)	Routine on cord blood.
PKU screen	After feeding for 24 hr.
T$_4$-dot	On discharge.

requires early screening. If hypoglycemia is present (blood sugar less than 40 mg%), the serum glucose is measured and glucose offered either orally or by gavage if the child is asymptomatic and if there is no contraindication to feeding. In symptomatic neonates, parenteral glucose is started immediately. In both situations the infant is examined carefully in an attempt to find the cause.

A hematocrit performed on one microcapillary tube of blood provides valuable information. Ideally this is performed on all infants between 1 and 4 hr of age. A hematocrit is particularly important for twins, infants of diabetic mothers, SGA infants, and those with a history of perinatal blood loss (e.g., abruptio placenta and placenta previa). A hematocrit of 40% or less is abnormal and suggests hemolysis or blood loss with possible hypovolemia. A capillary hematocrit greater than 70% suggests polycythemia, which may require a partial plasma exchange transfusion. The peripheral hematocrit may be considerably higher than the central hematocrit, and therefore a venipuncture determination may be required to assess the need for a partial exchange.

Feedings are traditionally started between 4 and 6 hr of age. Initially, either sterile water or 5% glucose solution is offered. If this is tolerated, full-strength formula may be offered on a 4-hr schedule. The volume of formula is not specified. Breast-fed infants may begin nursing *ad libitum.* Most infants have relatively little interest in feeding during the first 24 hr. Neonates commonly lose 5 to 7% of their body weight during the first days of life; however, after the first 3 or 4 days, weight gain of approximately 250 g per week may be anticipated.

Prior to 24 hr of age, the physician performs a detailed physical examination after a complete review of the perinatal history and the infant's chart. The practice of performing the examination in the mother's room provides the parents the opportunity to ask questions and to be reassured concerning their infant. The physician may also demonstrate to the parents the ability of the infant to respond to the mother's voice and other pleasant environmental stimuli as recently emphasized by Brazelton.[1] It also provides the physician the opportunity to observe the parents' interaction with their new baby.

A number of nursing procedures are routine in the nursery. The temperature is taken and recorded every 8 hr after initial stabilization. The weight is recorded daily and a record kept of daily intake and the number of times the infant voids. The time of the first stool is recorded and the physician notified if more than 24 hr elapse prior to the passage of meconium. Once stable, the baby may be bathed gently, using only sterile water on cotton balls. Currently there is no one recommended method of cord care. Various agents, including triple dye solution, alcohol, and antimicrobials, are utilized.

Generally, infants are observed in the nursery for a period of 48 to 96 hr. If the child is feeding formula well at the time of discharge, a combined phenylketonuria (PKU) and filter paper thyroxine (T_4) dot screen are performed. Otherwise, provisions are made to have these done before the end of the first week of life. Serum bilirubin values may also require checking if the child becomes jaundiced.

Parents frequently ask for advice concerning circumcision. Although circumcision is a common procedure, there are but few medical indications. This procedure has many potential complications while offering little benefit. Circumcision is *always* an elective procedure. When desired, it is performed only on stable, term infants—*never* on premature infants and *never* in the delivery suite because the infant has not had sufficient time to adapt to his extrauterine environment.

During the 24 hr before discharge, a physical examination is performed. The eyes are checked for conjunctivitis. Although this is commonly due to silver nitrate, cultures on either chocolate agar or Thayer Martin plates are performed if there is a history of maternal gonorrhea. The umbilicus and the circumcision are checked for infection or bleeding. The skin is examined for jaundice or a rash and the hips checked for congenital dislocation.

CARE OF THE FAMILY

Consideration of the emotional and psychologic aspects of neonatal and maternal care is essential at this time. Maternal-infant interaction at this time includes a series of adjustments on the part of the mother to prepare herself for nurturing the baby. This preparation begins as early as the time of planning and confirmation of the pregnancy. It continues throughout pregnancy, with its acceptance and with conceptualization of the fetus as an individual at the time of quickening.

The promotion of a close maternal-infant interaction begins in the delivery room through such activities as seeing, touching, fondling, and establishing eye-to-eye contact. This process may be fostered by rooming in. As a caveat, it is important to emphasize that *attention to these psychologic considerations, impor-*

---

[1]Brazelton, T.B. (1973): Neonatal Behavioral Assessment Scale, *Clinics in Developmental Medicine*, #50, Spastics International Medical Publications, London.

tant as they are, must never be at the expense of the infant's physical health. It is possible to simultaneously provide for close maternal-infant interaction and good medical and nursing care of the mother and infant.

Prior to the discharge of the infant from the hospital, the physician takes time to discuss infant care with the parents. This provides an opportunity for the physician to establish rapport with the parents and to continue their relationship begun at the prenatal visit. It also provides the parents a time to ask questions and have their anxieties alleviated. The physician must be understanding and emphasize that he considers no question unimportant. A thoughtful, unhurried discussion at this time may prevent many frantic phone calls after discharge. The format of any such interview must be individualized, and so here we highlight only a few topics.

1. *Feeding* is one of the most important subjects discussed. Current medical opinion advocates the use of breast milk as the preferred mode of feeding for the normal term infant. The physician's approach to the mother who intends to breast feed is extremely important. A thorough discussion of the physiology of lactation, the frequently encountered problems, and the practical means of solving such problems is requisite and may obviate many failures (see Chapter 6). This is not to say, however, that it is inappropriate to use a commercial formula, and mothers who have such a preference must be supported in a positive manner.

Generally, infants are fed on an *ad libitum* basis. As a rule, a formula-fed infant takes 2 to 2.5 ounces per pound per day and requires feedings every 3 to 4 hr. Night feedings may be anticipated until approximately 6 weeks of age. The question of when to begin solid foods has been dealt with variously by physicians and parents. It is currently believed that formula alone is an adequate food source for the first 3 to 4 months. However, regardless of medical opinion, most infants are given solid foods before this time. The introduction of rice cereal at 4 to 8 weeks has become a frequent practice.

2. *Vitamin* supplementation is provided in commercial formulas. Formula with iron is recommended during the first year of life. In the breast-fed baby, supplemental vitamins A, C, and D may be given, but their necessity is controversial. In addition, 0.25 mg fluoride per day is given to breast-fed infants.

3. *Spitting up.* Some infants have a propensity for spitting up. This usually consists of a small volume of regurgitated formula (5 to 10 ml) after feeding, often associated with burping. The mother is instructed to burp the infant at least once during and after the feeding. Overfeeding is a common cause of repeated spitting up. The problems usually resolve without difficulty but sometimes only after a number of months. Persistent, projectile, or bilious vomiting is always abnormal and requires immediate medical evaluation.

4. *Crying* may be very disconcerting, but it is the infant's only form of expression. Occasionally even the normal child exhibits prolonged episodes of crying. A survey of the possible causes may be rewarding: Is the infant hungry, wet, tired, cold, in pain (diaper pin), or ill, requiring a visit to the physician?

5. *Hiccups, sneezing, and yawning* are normal.

6. *Bowel habits* are discussed with the new mother because of the difference in number and consistency of stools from what might be expected. The breast-fed infant is expected to have one to six yellow or golden-colored stools containing seed-like particles per day. These stools are salve-like in consistency. The stools of the formula-fed infant are slightly firmer, more rancid in odor, pale yellow to light brown, and occur with an average frequency of one or two per day. However, the number may be quite variable, and a frequency of one to seven per day may be normal.

7. *Skin care.* Tub bathing is postponed until after separation of the umbilical remnant. Sponge baths are adequate until this time. Bathing is performed with either clear water or a mild soap and water. Skin cream, baby lotion, and petroleum jelly are to be avoided. Decreasing the frequency of bathing does more to retain natural skin oils than attempting to restore them after the drying effect of soap and water. Diaper rashes are best cared for by cleansing the diaper area with water on cotton balls at diaper changes. This is followed by keeping the infant as dry as possible, discontinuing the use of plastic pants or even leaving the diaper off until the rash has subsided. Milia are punctate white vesicles over the nose and cheeks caused by plugged sweat glands. These resolve spontaneously with only mild cleansing.

8. *Umbilicus.* The umbilical stump can be expected to detach by 7 to 10 days of age. It is best to avoid wetting the cord with water prior to this time. Applying alcohol to the cord two or three times a day facilitates the detachment by decreasing bacterial colonization and aiding drying. The small amount of bleeding which may occur when the cord does separate may be stopped with gentle pressure. Folding the diaper down so that it does not rub on the umbilicus also helps alleviate this problem. Purulent drainage and erythema demand more detailed investigation by a physician.

9. The *circumcision* requires only a small amount of petroleum jelly placed around the end of the penis to prevent the skin edges from sticking to the diaper. The remaining foreskin should not be retracted during the initial few weeks because of the possibility of tearing apart the partially healed skin edges.

10. *Health promotion.* This is the time to impress on the parents the need for routine well-baby visits and immunizations. It is currently recommended that the infant be seen initially at 2 weeks of age. This is perhaps a better time to check weight gain than at the traditional 1 month examination. The circumcision and umbilicus also deserve early inspection. This arrangement also gives the mother an early opportunity to ask the questions that did not occur to her in the hospital. Immunizations are not started until the second visit at 6 weeks or 2 months.

11. *Safety* is an extremely important subject, often overlooked by the new parent. Now is the time to start "childproofing" the home in anticipation of the child's crawling and walking in the months to come. Similarly, car safety and the use of protective safety seats are discussed.

12. Finally, at some point the *needs of the parents* are discussed. This will be the first time the new father competes with another individual for his wife's

attention, and the new mother may be unprepared for the *constant* demands of motherhood.

CAVEATS

1. Early maternal-infant contact must not interfere with stabilization of the infant in the delivery room.

2. Each hospital must establish high-risk criteria for admission of infants to the special care nursery.

3. Thermal stability is essential for neonatal stabilization.

4. A circumcision is *never* performed in the delivery room.

5. Consideration of the emotional and psychologic aspects of neonatal and maternal care is essential.

6. A number of screening tests (glucose, hematocrit, blood type and Rh, VDRL, PKU, and T_4) are routine for all newborn infants.

7. Feedings are initiated before 8 hr of age in healthy term infants.

3

Physical Examination

The newborn infant is unable to articulate his cares and woes, if any, to those of us entrusted with his care. Hence we must rely on our intuition and observations to determine variations from normal. It is obvious, therefore, that the newborn examination is of vital importance if we are to recognize potential problems before they reach critical proportions.

As with the examination of any patient, a history is of preeminent importance. A maternal history concerning illnesses, drugs, and obstetric records, including a record of any previous pregnancies and problems occurring during the pregnancy, labor, and delivery, should be obtained. Information is needed concerning Apgar scores and treatment of the infant in the delivery room, as well as any symptoms or signs recognized by the nurse caring for the newborn infant.

Evaluation of the newborn must be gentle, unhurried, and minimally stressful to the child. Most often the baby is sleeping or resting quietly when the examiner arrives. Take advantage of this subdued state to observe those parameters that require a quiet state for evaluation.

THE PHYSICAL EXAMINATION

Observe the child's resting posture and activity in the unstimulated state. Auscultate the heart and lungs while the child is quiet, thereby avoiding the confusion of crying and vigorous muscular activity. Make sure you have warm hands and equipment so the child is not startled. The abdomen is best palpated when the baby is quiet as relaxed abdominal musculature is a prerequisite for an adequate examination. When these areas have been appraised, proceed with the remaining portions of the examination that can be performed on an active child. The following discussion obviously does not include all abnormal findings but, rather, the ones most likely to be seen in clinical practice.

OBSERVATIONS

The observations to be recorded are the vital signs, including temperature, respiratory rate, pulse, and blood pressure; the presence of lethargy or irritability; the time of first urination and passage of first stool; feeding behavior; posture; activity; body proportions; evidence of respiratory distress; color; facial features; and presence of congenital anomalies.

BODY MEASUREMENTS

Certain body measurements (weight, head circumference, and length) are obtained on all newborn babies as baseline criteria for future growth and to identify deviations from normal. These determinations must be performed carefully if they are to be useful.

The head circumference is measured with a flexible tape, preferably metal. The largest measurement with the tape wrapped around the occipital and frontal prominences is the occipital frontal circumference (OFC). In a normal full term infant this is approximately 34 cm.

The length is preferably measured with a measuring board specifically designed for this purpose. Hanging the infant by the feet or simply placing the tape on the bed from the head to the soles is an unreliable means of measuring length. The normal length of a full term baby is approximately 50 cm.

Once obtained, these measurements are plotted on standard growth curves so that deviations from normal can be more readily appreciated and growth followed in a prospective manner. A more detailed discussion of maturity and intrauterine growth is presented in Chapter 4.

SKIN

The skin of the newborn is generally pink and uniform in color. Occasionally, *scaling* of the skin is observed shortly after birth. This may indicate that the child is postmature, i.e., that he has spent a longer than usual time *in utero*.

In order to preserve heat, the newborn responds to cold with peripheral vasoconstriction. Because of the relatively transparent newborn skin, the vascular plexus is easily seen. Vasoconstriction in response to cold may normally result in a *mottled* appearance. However, mottling may also reflect shock or sepsis.

Acrocyanosis (i.e., cyanosis of the distal extremities) is commonly seen in the newborn. This results from decreased perfusion and does not necessarily indicate true arterial oxygen levels. For this reason, the hands and feet are not good indicators of the baby's oxygen status. In contrast to peripheral cyanosis, central cyanosis reflects true arterial hypoxemia. Central cyanosis, best seen by observing the newborn's lips and tongue, is always abnormal and requires evaluation.

Milia are small white papules that result from distended sebaceous glands. They are noted especially over the nose and forehead. At times their distribution is extensive, and it may be difficult to differentiate milia from bacterial infection.

A *nevus flammeus* (sometimes referred to as "stork bite") is a reddish discoloration of an area of skin. This lesion has no clinical significance and usually disappears by 2 years of age. It is frequently seen in the occipital area of the head and supraorbitally.

Vernix is white cheesy material (composed of cellular and other debris) present on the newborn skin at birth and is usually absent in postterm infants. It may provide an immunologic advantage to the infant.

As a result of trauma to the presenting part, the infant may appear *bruised.* When trauma is extensive or severe, infants may develop shock and hyperbilirubinemia.

The *Mongolian spot,* a bluish discoloration of the skin usually noted on the back or buttocks, is frequently seen in the darker pigmented races. It usually disappears after a few months of life.

Shortly after birth the full term newborn often demonstrates skin lesions characterized by white papules surrounded by an area of erythema—*erythema toxicum* of the newborn, or "newborn rash." The name is actually a misnomer since the lesion is not related to infection, although these lesions must be differentiated from a variety of bacterial and viral infections. Although rarely necessary, a Wright's stain of the material within one of these benign papules demonstrates many eosinophils.

Lanugo, or fine body hair, covers the entire body until approximately the 32nd week. Between the 32nd and 37th weeks of gestation it vanishes from the face; between the 38th and 42nd week it is present only on the shoulders; and after 42 weeks' gestation lanugo is absent.

Abnormal skin findings in the newborn include jaundice during the first 24 hr of life, edema, meconium staining, petechiae, pustules, hemangiomas, forcep marks, harlequin sign, scaling, and bullous lesions.

Jaundice in the newborn is common. It can reflect a physiologic increase in red cell breakdown with inability of the newborn liver to conjugate and excrete the increased bilirubin load, or it may represent a serious and life-threatening condition. *Jaundice, especially when noted during the first 24 hr of life, is never taken lightly.* A careful evaluation of its etiology must be pursued.

Edema is seen frequently in premature infants, either as a normal finding or secondary to hypoxia and vascular damage. Edema of the hands and feet may also be seen in Turner's syndrome. Diffuse massive edema of the newborn, or hydrops fetalis, is indicative of severe underlying pathology, e.g., erythroblastosis fetalis, cardiac defects.

Meconium staining of the newborn occurs from *in utero* passage of the infant's first stool or meconium. In a significant percentage of cases, it represents evidence of fetal distress. It is also seen in postmature and small for gestational age

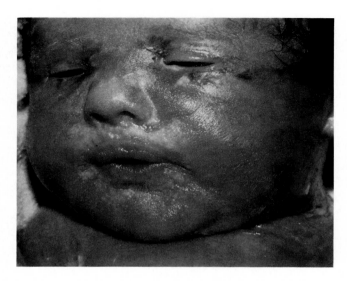

FIG. 1. Newborn infant with congenital ichthyosis. Note scaling and stretching of the skin, especially around the mouth.

(SGA) infants. Aspiration of meconium may cause a severe aspiration pneumonia in the newborn.

Petechiae of the face are commonly noted in the infant born in the cephalic presentation or delivered with the cord wrapped around his neck. Petechiae on the trunk or extremities are abnormal; in such cases platelet or infectious abnormalities should be investigated carefully. *Infectious lesions* of the skin may be secondary to bacteria (e.g., staphylococci) or viruses (e.g., herpes simplex).

Hemangiomas, which may be very small or not noticeable at birth, may increase dramatically during the first 18 months of life. Most hemangiomas are treated conservatively with watchful waiting, as they usually regress during childhood.

Occasionally, especially in premature infants, one side of an infant's body is pink and the other side white. This so-called *harlequin sign* is probably related to a transient abnormal neurologic supply to the blood vessels. This is a benign and transient condition.

Bullous lesions of the skin are always abnormal and may be due to infection or to an inherited disease, e.g., epidermolysis bullosa. *Severe scaling* may represent an early presentation of ichthyosis (Fig. 1).

HEAD

Measurement and evaluation of the contour of the skull are important parts of the newborn examination. The newborn head is large relative to the body. If the baby is born in a cephalic presentation, considerable *molding* of the easily malleable skull bones may take place to facilitate passage through the birth canal. Within 2 to 3 days after birth, most of the molding has usually resolved and the head assumes its normal configuration. Molding is not usually present when the infant is born by cesarean section or breech presentation.

The *suture lines* are often overriding during the immediate newborn period. The major suture lines can be rapidly assessed for premature closure, which could result in later asymmetry of the skull. The area where the metopic, coronal, and sagittal sutures converge is called the *anterior fontanelle.* If it is not palpable in the newborn, premature closure of the sutures is suggested. If the soft spot is bulging and tense, increased intracranial pressure is suggested. The sagittal and lambdoidal sutures converge at the *posterior fontanelle.* This may or may not be open at birth.

A partial list of abnormal findings in the examination of the head include caput succedaneum, cephalohematoma, bulging fontanelle, hydrocephalus, macro- and microcephaly, encephalocele, premature closure of the sutures, and scalp defects.

The *caput succedaneum,* which results from trauma to the presenting part of the head, consists of subcutaneous edema or hematoma. This can be so extensive as to cause anemia and hyperbilirubinemia secondary to hemoglobin breakdown. These lesions must not be aspirated as this predisposes to infection.

Subperiosteal bleeding (i.e., between the bone and the periosteum) results in a *cephalohematoma.* Since this bleeding separates the periosteum from the skull, it does not cross suture lines. Such bleeding may also cause anemia or jaundice. A cephalohematoma most commonly involves the parietal bones. When they occur on both sides, bilateral bulges result—the "Queen Anne" or "Mickey Mouse" sign. A cephalohematoma may subsequently calcify and then slowly resolve as the head grows.

An increasing head circumference with prominent veins, bulging fontanelle, and setting-sun eyes usually is due to *hydrocephalus.* A flashlight with a special rubber adaptor can be useful in determining the amount of transillumination of the infant's skull. With hydrocephalus the transillumination is increased.

Anencephaly (Fig. 2), or absence of part of the brain and skull, is incompatible with life. An *encephalocele* is a defect in the head which allows protrusion of brain tissue outside the skull. If meninges, but no brain tissue, are present outside the defect, the lesion is called a meningocele.

EYES

To induce the infant to open his eyes, gently rock him from an upright to a horizontal position. Note the size of the eyes and pupils, the conjunctivae, the clearness of the corneas, and size of the palpebral fissures. Perform a funduscopic examination, looking for a red reflex and retinal hemorrhages.

The normal newborn has *blue sclerae.* Frequently his *eye movements* are not coordinated. When present, epicanthal folds may give a false impression of strabismus (pseudostrabismus). When the infant has been born in face presentation, mild to moderate edema of the eyelids may be noted, but this subsides quickly.

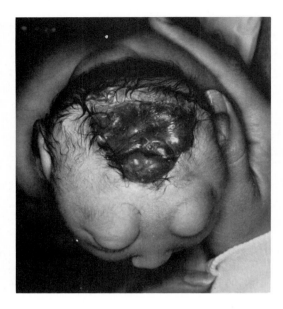

FIG. 2. Congenital anen-cephaly.

Abnormal eye findings include subconjunctival hemorrhages, small eyes, narrow palpebral fissures, conjunctivitis, clouded cornea, and cataracts. The eye may also reflect changes due to trauma at birth. *Subconjunctival hemorrhages* are frequently seen and generally disappear within a few weeks.

Silver nitrate, placed in the infant's eyes at birth as prophylaxis for gonorrhea infections, causes a chemical *conjunctivitis* with edema and is the most common cause of a purulent discharge from the eyes during the first 24 hr of life. It is virtually impossible to differentiate this from bacterial infection; therefore if it persists, appropriate cultures are taken and the exudate is stained. This is extremely important as bacterial infections of the eye may result in permanent blindness. However, most cases of bacterial conjunctivitis do not present until the second or third day of life.

Clouding of the cornea (Fig. 3) may indicate increased intraocular pressure secondary to glaucoma, congenital infection, or trauma. It is extremely important to diagnose congenital *cataracts* early as they may be due to an intrauterine infection or a metabolic disorder. If not treated, they can result in permanent blindness.

EARS

A considerable amount of information can be obtained from an evaluation of the external ear. Its form and elasticity are helpful guides to the maturity of the newborn, as discussed in Chapter 4. Gross anomalies of the exterior aspect of the ear are frequently associated with abnormalities of other body systems, particularly the genitourinary. Otoscopic examination during the immediate newborn period is usually not rewarding because the tympanic membranes are obscured by vernix and other debris.

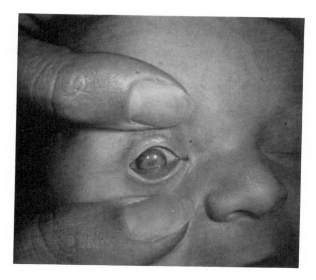

FIG. 3. Newborn infant with clouded cornea.

Abnormalities of the ear include malformation, malposition, preauricular tags, and sinus tracts. *Malformation* of the external ear may be familial, an isolated finding, or part of a congenital syndrome.

In order to determine if an ear is *low-set,* an imaginary straight line is drawn between the lateral epicanthus and the posterior occipital area. If an ear is low-set, the top of the auricle is below this line. This suggests the possibility of other malformations or syndromes. *Preauricular tags* (Fig. 4) may also be familial, be a manifestation of particular syndromes, or represent the opening of a sinus tract.

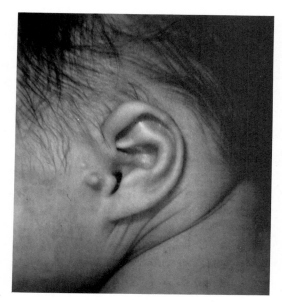

FIG. 4. Preauricular tag.

NOSE

Since newborns are obligate nose-breathers for the first few months of life, any obstruction to the nares may result in respiratory impairment and even death during the newborn period. It is important, therefore, to check the patency of each nostril. This may be performed in a number of ways: (a) obstructing one nostril with a finger and watching for respiratory distress; (b) placing cotton in front of each nostril to detect air movement; or (c) gently placing a soft catheter through each nostril in the delivery room.

Abnormalities of the nose may take the form of gross malformation, choanal atresia, or displaced nasal cartilage. Dislocation of the nasal septal cartilage is not uncommon and should be corrected shortly after birth (Fig. 5).

MOUTH

Besides visual inspection of the mouth, the palate is palpated. Normal findings in the newborn include Epstein's pearls and a lingula frenulum. *Epstein's pearls,* the intraoral counterpart of the facial milia, are discrete, round, pearly, cystic structures in the midline of the palate. Lingula frenulum or "tongue tie" is normal and never requires therapy.

Abnormal findings on the physical examination of the mouth include clefts, high-arched palate, masses, micrognathia, natal teeth, thrush, large tongue, and asymmetry with crying.

Cleft palate (Fig. 6) is not always associated with cleft lip. Palpation of the palate with the finger is necessary to rule out a cleft of the bony palate with intact mucous membranes (submucous cleft).

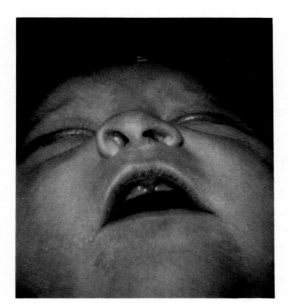

FIG. 5. Dislocated nasal septal cartilage.

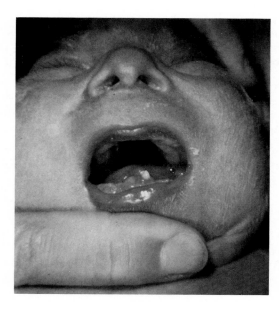

FIG. 6. Cleft palate.

Masses in the mouth include encephaloceles, teratomas, aberrant thyroid, thyroglossal duct cyst, other cysts, and epulis. Congenital epulis is a benign tumor of the upper or lower jaw that requires simple resection.

A *short jaw,* or micrognathia (Fig. 7), is a frequent congenital abnormality. It may be associated with a small posteriorly positioned tongue (glossoptosis) that can cause symptomatic airway obstruction. These findings are frequently seen in the Pierre-Robin anomalad and may be associated with significant feeding problems.

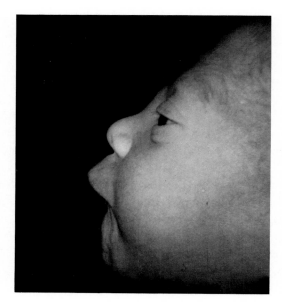

FIG. 7. Severe micrognathia.

Teeth may erupt *in utero* or shortly after birth and interfere with sucking. Since a large percentage of these are normal deciduous teeth, X-ray films are obtained to determine their structure before a decision is made for removal. If the teeth are loose, removal is indicated to prevent their aspiration.

Thrush, or *monilial infection* on the tongue, is characterized by white plaques and can be differentiated from dried milk by scraping the lesions. In cases of oral monilial infection, mild bleeding occurs with scraping.

A large tongue, or *macroglossia,* may cause significant respiratory distress as well as a feeding problem. This lesion may be seen in hypothyroidism, the mucopolysaccharidoses, or Beckwith's syndrome, or it may represent a tumor within the tongue.

Failure of the corner of the mouth to elevate with crying may reflect a congenital absence of the orbicularis oris muscle or a seventh cranial nerve palsy. Early recognition minimizes feeding problems. If the peripheral facial nerve is involved, the child must be observed for adequate closure of the eyelid on the affected side.

NECK

The normal newborn neck is short and broad. Abnormalities of the neck include skin folds, webbing, fistulas, fractured clavicle, torticollis, vertebral anomalies, and goiter. *Skin folds* in the neck may be isolated findings or may suggest syndromes with multiple congenital abnormalities. *Webbing* of the neck usually suggests syndromes with multiple congenital abnormalities.

Anomalous development of the *branchial arches* may be manifested by fistulas or cysts along the anterior border of the sternocleidomastoid muscle. *Torticollis* may be secondary to a number of disorders, most commonly a "fibroma" of the sternocleidomastoid muscle, probably related to birth trauma. *Goiters* may cause respiratory obstruction and are an indication for thyroid evaluation.

CHEST

Enlarged breasts are often observed during the newborn period and are due to maternal hormonal stimulation. A whitish substance may be expressed during the first few days of life. If erythema or tenderness is present, this finding must be differentiated from a breast abscess.

Abnormalities of the chest include wide-spaced nipples, malformation of the rib cage, and supernumerary nipples. Wide-spaced nipples suggest particular syndromes. Malformation of the rib cage may be present in the chondrodystrophies. There may also be failure to fusion of the sternum as well as rib defects. Supernumerary nipples are occasionally observed in the "milk line," which runs from the axillae to the inner thigh.

CARDIORESPIRATORY SYSTEM

The normal newborn is pink and has a respiratory rate of 30 to 60/min and a heart beat of 120 to 160 beats/min. Evaluation of the neonatal chest includes observation and auscultation. Breath sounds are readily referred from one side of the chest to the other, and rales are occasionally heard during the first few minutes of life. Unilateral or bilateral *absence of breath sounds* in infants with respiratory distress suggests serious intrathoracic pathology. Suspected intrathoracic abnormalities require a chest X-ray for evaluation. Early systolic *murmurs* may be heard during the first few hours of life and are due to a persistent patency of the ductus arteriosus. Because of the high pulmonary artery pressure, significant murmurs may not be heard during the first few days of life, and so cardiac auscultation is also performed just prior to hospital discharge.

Abnormal cardiorespiratory signs and symptoms include apnea, tachypnea, bradycardia, tachycardia, grunting, retractions, cyanosis, heart murmurs, and weak or bounding pulses. Because of the poor fixation of the newborn rib cage, airway obstruction or decreased lung compliance results in marked intercostal and sternal *retractions.*

Palpation of the peripheral pulses is important. Generally the femoral and brachial pulses are easily palpated. Absent femoral with good brachial pulses suggest the presence of a coarctation of the aorta. Very weak peripheral pulses may indicate hypotension or other significant heart disease. Bounding peripheral pulses may indicate hypertension, patent ductus arteriosus, or hyperthyroidism.

ABDOMEN

The infant's abdomen is best examined when he is quiet, preferably during the first 24 hr of life. Abdominal palpation of the newborn requires a very soft touch so abdominal organs are not pushed out of the way of the examining finger. The newborn liver is normally palpated approximately 1 to 2 cm below the right costal margin. Occasionally the spleen tip can be palpated, and the kidneys are usually within reach of the examining finger, especially the left kidney. Neonatal abdominal masses may represent a surgical emergency. The most common intra-abdominal pathological mass in the newborn is an enlarged kidney.

Examination of the abdomen includes a close inspection of the umbilical cord. There are normally three vessels present. The two arteries have very small lumina with thick walls, whereas the vein has a large lumen with a very thin wall. If only one artery and one vein are present, there is an associated increased incidence of other congenital malformations.

Abnormal abdominal findings include a distended abdomen, omphalocele, gastroschisis, absent musculature (prune belly syndrome), masses, an enlarged liver or spleen, and a scaphoid or flat abdomen.

Abdominal distention in the newborn is regarded as a surgical obstruction until proved otherwise. Abdominal distention with or without bilious vomiting requires immediate evaluation. When the abdomen is extremely flat and gives the impression of a lack of abdominal contents, diaphragmatic hernia or esophageal atresia without a tracheo-esophageal fistula is suspected.

An *omphalocele* is a defect in the umbilicus, with the bowel and possibly other abdominal contents herniated through the umbilicus. There is also a significant increase of other congenital malformations. *Gastroschisis* is a defect in the abdominal wall musculature, usually to the right and below the umbilicus. Because the peritoneal covering is absent, it is always associated with peritonitis. *Prune belly syndrome,* a condition in which the abdominal muscles are absent, is accompanied by a markedly increased incidence in genitourinary anomalies.

The most common *abdominal mass* in the newborn is an enlarged kidney caused by hydronephrosis, dysplasia, or multiple cysts. Other lesions include Wilm's tumor, renal vein thrombosis, ovarian cyst, hydrocolpos, adrenal hematoma, neuroblastoma, sacrococcygeal teratoma, and gastrointestinal lesions such as a distended loop of bowel.

GENITALIA

When examining the genitalia, the testes, scrotum, clitoris, labia, uretheral meatus, penis, and anus are observed. Normally in the premature infant the testes are undescended. A whitish vaginal discharge is common during the first few days of life secondary to maternal hormones. In some female infants withdrawal vaginal bleeding occurs during this period. Hymenal tags are often noted but should not be removed because they involute shortly after birth.

Abnormal findings on examination of the genitalia include hypospadias, hernia, hydrocele, torsion of the testicles, ambiguous genitalia, imperforate anus, and extrophy of the bladder. The male with *hypospadias* should not be circumcised as the redundant skin may be used for surgical repair. *Hydrocele* is commonly found in the newborn. Transillumination is necessary to rule out a hernia or testicular abnormalities (e.g., torsion). Infants born in the breech presentation may have significant trauma manifested by bruising of the genitalia.

Careful examination of the external genitalia is extremely important. Any child with *ambiguous genitalia* (Fig. 8) requires immediate attention as this may reflect a life-threatening metabolic derangement of steroid metabolism. Masculinization of the female external genitalia can result from maternal medications and congenital abnormalities of adrenal steroid production. Careful examination for testes as well as a sophisticated endocrine and genetic diagnostic assessment is frequently necessary to determine whether an infant with ambiguous genitalia is a female with masculinization or a male with anomalous development of the genitalia. Whenever there is a question about an infant's sex identity, the parents are informed that the sex is not known and the infant is referred immediately to a tertiary center.

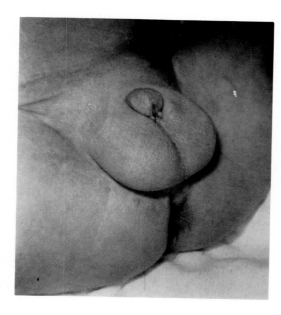

FIG. 8. Female infant with masculinization of the female external genitalia associated with congenital adrenal hyperplasia.

Extrophy of the bladder (Fig. 9) is a serious abnormality in which the bladder is exposed to the skin. There is an associated increased incidence of other genitourinary anomalies.

ANUS

The newborn anus is examined for patency. Either malposition, lack of patency, or failure to pass a meconium stool requires evaluation.

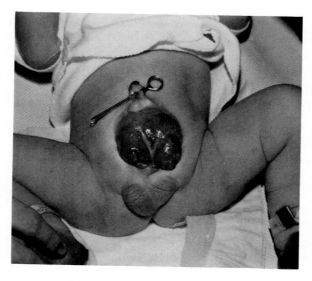

FIG. 9. Extrophy of the bladder.

MUSCULOSKELETAL SYSTEM

The infant's posture is observed, the spine palpated for defects, and the extremities, joints, and hips examined. Normal findings include deformities secondary to intrauterine position, bowing of the legs, and absent arches of the feet.

Intrauterine position may cause temporary distortion of the extremities, especially the feet. An inturned foot must be differentiated from a club foot. Mild bowing of the legs is common in the normal newborn. Normally the newborn foot is flat.

Abnormal findings include scoliosis, spina bifida, polydactyly, syndactyly, clubbed feet, dislocated hips, and deformities of the joints and extremities. *Meningomyelocele* is usually obvious on physical examination. The spine is palpated for body defects. A close examination is necessary to diagnose a *sacral dimple* (Fig. 10). A dimple, especially if surrounded by a tuft of hair, may indicate a communication between the skin and the neural tube.

The extremities are examined for extra digits, fusion of digits, and gross deformities. *Extra digits* of the fifth finger are common. When connected to the fifth finger by a thread-like structure, the supernumerary digits may be removed by ligation. However, if a significant amount of skin connects the extra digit to the fifth finger or if there is a bony connection, orthopedic consultation is advised. *Positional abnormalities* of the feet include equinovarus, calcaneovalgus, and metatarsus varus.

Dislocation of the hips requires early correction if a satisfactory result is to be obtained. Merely examining the hip for range of motion in flexion and abduc-

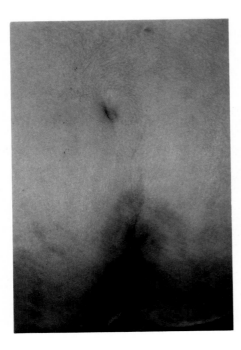

FIG. 10. Sacral dimple.

tion is not an adequate examination for stability of the hip. It may be argued that the most common presenting finding in the dislocated hip is limitation of abduction. This is certainly true but only after the second or third month of life. In the newborn, one must look for stability of the hip and not range of motion.

Almost everyone is aware of the "jerk sign" of Ortolani. This maneuver is positive only when the femoral head is dislocated behind the socket; upon abducting the flexed hip, the sign is produced by the head of the femur sliding over the edge of the acetabulum and snapping into the socket. This gives the palpable, audible, and visible "jerk sign."

A more comprehensive test for stability of the hip is the Barlow maneuver (Fig. 11) to distinguish those hips that are unstable, i.e., capable of being displaced from their acetabulum to a dislocated position and then being reduced back into the socket. These hips are classified as dislocatable. The Barlow maneuver is performed with the pelvis held stabilized with one hand while the other hand holds the hip and leg flexed; the long finger palpates the greater trochanter and the thumb rests in the adductor muscles (not in the femoral triangle). The hip is brought into slight adduction, and gentle downward pressure with the weight of the hand is applied to the hip (Fig. 11A). A normal hip does not dislocate! A dislocatable hip moves very smoothly and subtly out of socket. The second part of the Barlow maneuver is the classical Ortolani test, i.e., abducting the hip and lifting the dislocated femoral head over the rim of the socket with pressure of the long finger on the greater trochanter (Fig. 11B).

Severe deformities of the joints may be due to multiple dislocations, fractures, or *arthrogryposis*. Infants with normal trunk size but extremely *short limbs* may have one of many of the syndromes characterized by short-limbed dwarfism. *Amniotic bands*, or Streeter's bands, are strands of amniotic membranes that

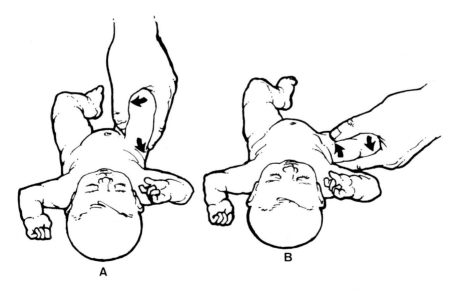

FIG. 11. Barlow maneuver for stability of the hip (see text). (Modified from Ritter: *Am. J. Dis. Child.*, 125:30, 1973.)

may cause constrictions of the extremities. In severe cases, amputation of part of an extremity may occur. *Hypoplastic nails* are seen in certain syndromes or may result from maternal drug exposure, e.g., diphenylhydantoin.

NEUROLOGIC EXAMINATION

The newborn neurologic examination serves many purposes: (a) the detection of abnormalities that might affect subsequent development; (b) the detection of acute disorders such as meningitis, cerebral edema, or nerve palsy; and (c) as an aid in the assessment of maturity. Timing of the neurologic examination is of importance because after the first hours of life the newborn may experience the so-called "physiologic depression," which usually improves after the first 24 hr, or he may be depressed from maternal anesthesia or analgesia drugs.

The routine neurologic examination consists primarily in assessing the child's awareness, use of all extremities, cry, muscle tone, and a variety of normal reflexes. Abnormal findings in the neurologic examination include seizures, failure to move all four extremities in response to stimulus, and abnormal muscle tone (hypo- or hypertonia).

Failure to move one extremity strongly suggests nerve, muscle, or bone damage. A large infant with a history of birth trauma may have a brachial plexus palsy. Whereas hypotonia occurs normally in premature infants, in full term infants it suggests serious abnormalities. Excessive muscle tone, hypertonia, is abnormal in any infant.

CAVEATS

1. The perinatal history is of pre-eminent importance.
2. The first aspect of the physical examination is observation.
3. The second aspect of physical examination is auscultation of the heart and lungs and palpation of the abdomen.

4

Assessment of Gestational Age

It is essential for the physician and nurse who care for infants—whether in a normal newborn nursery, delivery room, premature nursery, special care nursery, or neonatal intensive care nursery—to understand the etiology, problems, and prognosis of small for gestational age (SGA) infants, premature infants, and large for gestational age (LGA) infants. With this knowledge, one can anticipate many of the needs of the patient and can institute the appropriate intervention before long-range consequences develop.

A routine gestational age assessment is performed on every newborn soon after birth. This chapter provides a step-by-step guide to a simple method of determining gestational age.

A variety of intrauterine growth charts have been designed. An ideal intrauterine growth chart would be individualized for the specific age, race, socioeconomic status, and geographic area the patient represents. A practical approach is to use some standard of intrauterine growth to identify the high-risk, inappropriately grown infant. Most nurseries use the Colorado Intrauterine Growth Chart, but one must realize that the infants who comprise the population on which it is based lived at a higher altitude than most and included many medically indigent infants; therefore the weight standards are probably somewhat lower than those that would apply to a middle class population living at sea level. By definition, an infant is premature if born before 38 weeks' gestation, term if 38 to 42 weeks, and postmature if greater than 42 weeks. An infant is said to be "appropriate for gestational age" (AGA) if his birth weight is between the 10th and 90th percentiles when compared with other infants of the same gestational age. An infant is "large for gestational age" if his weight is greater than the 90th percentile for that particular gestational age, and "small for gestational age" if his weight is less than the 10th percentile for all infants at that particular age.

ESTIMATING GESTATIONAL AGE

There are basically three different methods of estimating an infant's gestational age: (a) menstrual dates; (b) obstetric methods; and (c) examination of the infant. Menstrual dates are frequently unreliable, although they should be considered. Obstetric methods include uterine size, auscultation of fetal heart tones, quickening, serial ultrasound measurements beginning early in gestation, and chemical analysis of the amniotic fluid, e.g., measuring creatinine and osmolality. X-rays and single ultrasound measurements during the last half of pregnancy are unreliable.

A reliable method of determining gestational age is examining the newborn with particular attention to breasts and nipples, skin creases on the soles, ear cartilage, development of external genitalia, posture, muscle tone, and reflexes.

The observation of physical characteristics to determine gestational age requires little manipulation of the patient and can be done during the first 12 hr without stressing the infant. Every infant should have a gestational age examination in the delivery room or in the newborn nursery within a few hours after birth. This is most efficiently done by the nurses in the delivery room or in the newborn nursery.

Charts such as those in Fig. 1 help in performing these physical examinations. The examination for gestational age can be divided into nonneurologic and neurologic segments. Optimally, the nonneurologic examination is performed within a few hours after birth so the needs of the infant can be anticipated early.

When first learning the technique of determining gestational age by physical examination, it is recommended that five or six criteria be used, rather than the entire examination. Looking at breasts, ears, genitalia, sole creases, and posture allows the determination of correct gestational age (within 1 to 2 weeks) in almost all cases.

Nipples and Breast

In infants less than 34 weeks' gestation, the areola and nipple are barely visible (Fig. 2). After 34 weeks' gestation, the areola becomes raised. Owing to maternal hormonal stimulation, breast tissue appears in the infant with increasing gestational age. The infant less than 36 weeks' gestation has no breast tissue. However, the amount of breast tissue increases with increasing gestational age so an infant at 39 to 40 weeks' gestation has 5 to 6 mm of breast tissue.

Ears

The infant less than 34 weeks' gestation has a very flat and shapeless ear (Fig. 3). Between 34 and 36 weeks' gestation, there is a slight incurving of the superior part of the ear. In the term infant, there is incurving of the upper two-thirds of the pinna. In an infant greater than 39 weeks' gestation, the incurving continues to the lobe.

If the ear is folded over in a premature infant, it stays folded. Cartilage begins to appear at approximately 32 weeks' gestation and results in the ear returning slowly after being folded. In an infant greater than 40 weeks' gestation, there is

PHYSICAL FINDINGS	WEEKS GESTATION

Weeks scale: 20 21 22 23 24 25 26 27 28 29 30 31 32 33 34 35 36 37 38 39 40 41 42 43 44 45 46 47 48

VERNIX: APPEARS — COVERS BODY, THICK LAYER — ON BACK, SCALP IN CREASES — SCANT, IN CREASES — NO VERNIX

BREAST TISSUE AND AREOLA: AREOLA & NIPPLE BARELY VISIBLE NO PALPABLE BREAST TISSUE — AREOLA RAISED — 3·5 MM / 5·6 MM — 7·10 MM — ?12 MM

EAR — FORM: FLAT, SHAPELESS — BEGINNING INCURVING SUPERIOR — INCURVING UPPER 2/3 PINNAE — WELL-DEFINED INCURVING TO LOBE

EAR — CARTILAGE: PINNA SOFT, STAYS FOLDED — CARTILAGE SCANT RETURNS SLOWLY FROM FOLDING — THIN CARTILAGE SPRINGS BACK FROM FOLDING — PINNA FIRM, REMAINS ERECT FROM HEAD

SOLE CREASES: SMOOTH SOLES ŠĊ CREASES — 1·2 ANTERIOR CREASES — 2·3 ANTERIOR CREASES — CREASES INVOLVING ANTERIOR 2/3 SOLE — CREASES INVOLVING HEEL — DEEPER CREASES OVER ENTIRE SOLE

SKIN — THICKNESS & APPEARANCE: THIN, TRANSLUCENT SKIN, PLETHORIC, VENULES OVER ABDOMEN EDEMA — SMOOTH THICKER NO EDEMA — PINK — FEW VESSELS — SOME DESQUAMATION PALE PINK — THICK, PALE, DESQUAMATION OVER ENTIRE BODY

SKIN — NAIL PLATES: AP·PEAR — NAILS TO FINGER TIPS — NAILS TO FINGER TIPS — NAILS EXTEND WELL BEYOND FINGER TIPS

HAIR: APPEARS ON HEAD — EYE BROWS & LASHES — FINE, WOOLLY, BUNCHES OUT FROM HEAD — SILKY, SINGLE STRANDS LAYS FLAT — RECEDING HAIRLINE OR LOSS OF BABY HAIR SHORT, FINE UNDERNEATH

LANUGO: AP·PEARS — COVERS ENTIRE BODY — VANISHES FROM FACE — PRESENT ON SHOULDERS — NO LANUGO

GENITALIA — TESTES / SCROTUM: TESTES PALPABLE IN INGUINAL CANAL — FEW RUGAE — IN UPPER SCROTUM — RUGAE, ANTERIOR PORTION — IN LOWER SCROTUM — RUGAE COVER — PENDULOUS

GENITALIA — LABIA & CLITORIS: PROMINENT CLITORIS LABIA MAJORA SMALL WIDELY SEPARATED — LABIA MAJORA LARGER NEARLY COVERED CLITORIS — LABIA MINORA & CLITORIS COVERED

SKULL FIRMNESS: BONES ARE SOFT — SOFT TO 1" FROM ANTERIOR FONTANELLE — SPONGY AT EDGES OF FONTANELLE CENTER FIRM — BONES HARD SUTURES EASILY DISPLACED — BONES HARD, CANNOT BE DISPLACED

POSTURE — RESTING: HYPOTONIC LATERAL DECUBITUS — HYPOTONIC — BEGINNING FLEXION THIGH — STRONGER HIP FLEXION — FROG-LIKE — FLEXION ALL LIMBS — HYPERTONIC — VERY HYPERTONIC

RECOIL — LEG: NO RECOIL — PARTIAL RECOIL — PROMPT RECOIL

RECOIL — ARM: NO RECOIL — BEGIN FLEXION NO RE·COIL — PROMPT RECOIL MAY BE INHIBITED — PROMPT RECOIL AFTER 30" INHIBITION

FIG. 1. Gestational age chart. (Modified from Kempe, Silver, and O'Brien: *Current Pediatric Diagnosis and Treatment*, 5th ed., Lange Medical Publications, Los Altos, California, 1978.)

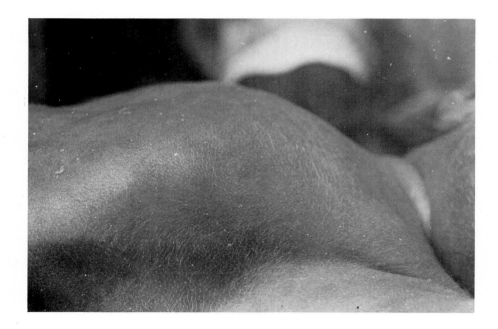

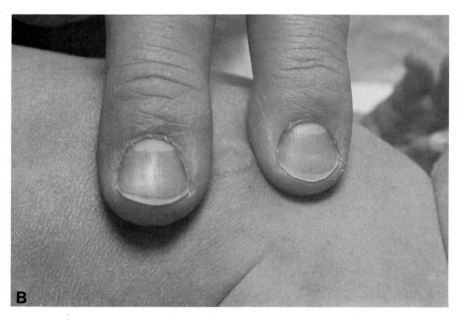

FIG. 2. Premature nipple **(A)** and full term nipple and breast **(B).**

enough ear cartilage for the ear to remain erect from the head. Remember, when folding the ear over to determine gestational age, be certain that the vernix is wiped from the surrounding area or else even a full term ear may not return quickly after being folded.

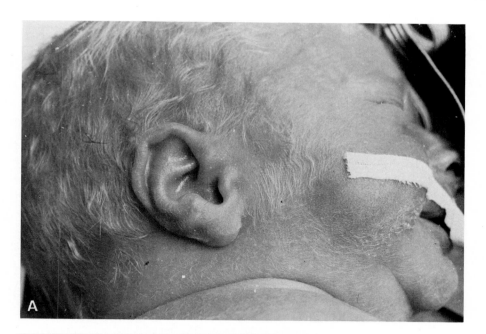

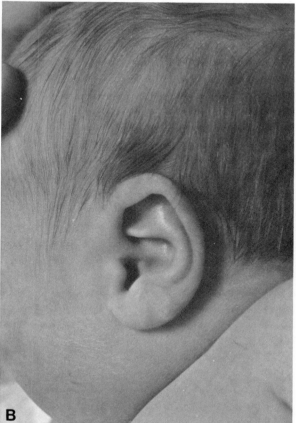

FIG. 3. Premature **(A)** and full term **(B)** ear.

Genitalia

The testes in the premature infant are very high in the inguinal canal, and there are very few rugae on the scrotum (Fig. 4). In the full term infant, the testes are lower in the scrotum and there are multiple rugae.

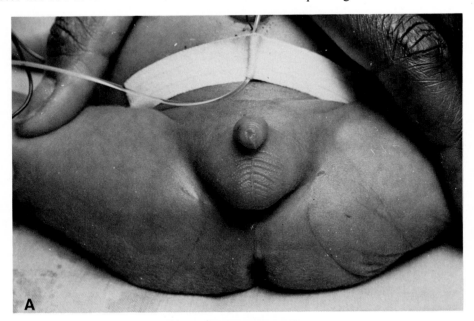

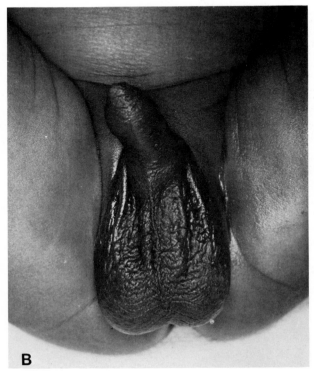

FIG. 4. Male genitalia in premature **(A)** and full term **(B)** infant.

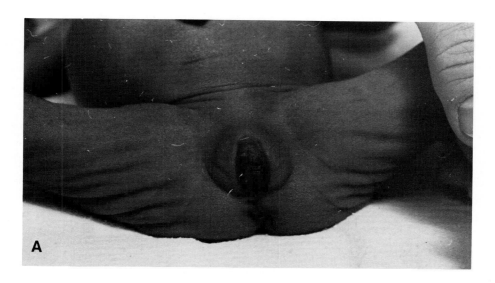

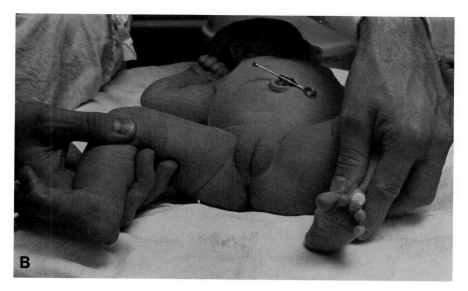

FIG. 5. Female genitalia in premature **(A)** and full term **(B)** infant.

In the premature female infant, the clitoris is prominent and the labia majora are small and widely separated (Fig. 5). In the full term infant, the labia minora and the clitoris are completely covered by the labia majora.

Sole Creases

The sole of the premature infant has no or very few creases (Fig. 6). With increasing gestational age the number and depth of the sole creases increase,

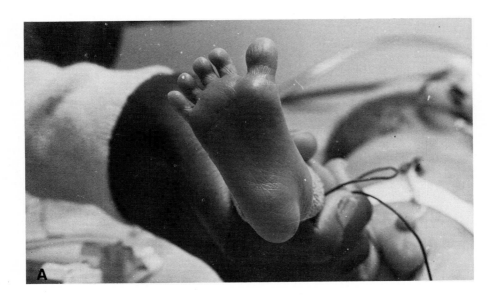

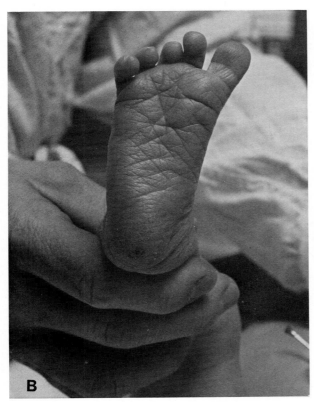

FIG. 6. Sole of premature **(A)** and full term **(B)** infant.

and the full term infant has sole creases involving the heel. Wrinkles occurring after 24 hr of age are sometimes confused with true creases.

Resting Posture

In the premature infant there is little, if any, flexion in the upper extremities, with only partial flexion of the lower extremities. In the full term infant, all four extremities are flexed (Fig. 7).

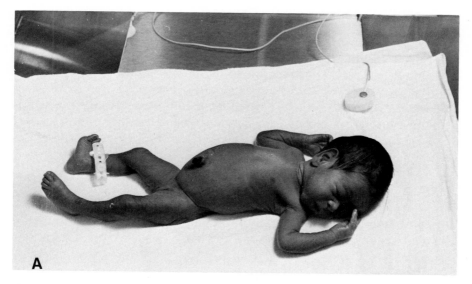

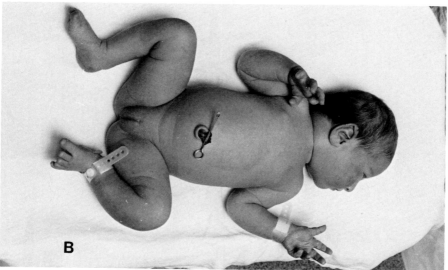

FIG. 7. Resting posture in premature **(A)** and full term **(B)** infant.

Recoil of Extremities

With the infant supine, the legs and knees are fully flexed for 5 sec, and then extended by traction on the feet and released. A maximal response as seen in the full term infant is one of full flexion of the hips and knees. With the infant supine, the forearms are first flexed for 5 sec, fully extended by pulling on the hands, and then released. In the premature infant there is minimal, if any, recoil, whereas in the full term baby the arms return briskly to full flexion (Fig. 8).

Other Neurologic Criteria

The criteria discussed above provide a practical as well as a reasonably accurate (within 1 to 2 weeks) estimation of the infant's gestational age. If a more accurate estimation is desired, a more detailed and of course more time-consuming examination can be performed. One would then examine the heel-to-ear reflex, scarf sign (elbow to opposite shoulder), neck flexion and extensors, horizontal position, ankle flexion, wrist flexion, rooting reflex, grasp reflex, and Moro reflex.

Charting

As you perform the various parts of the physical examination for gestational age, shade in the appropriate box on the chart. When first becoming familiar

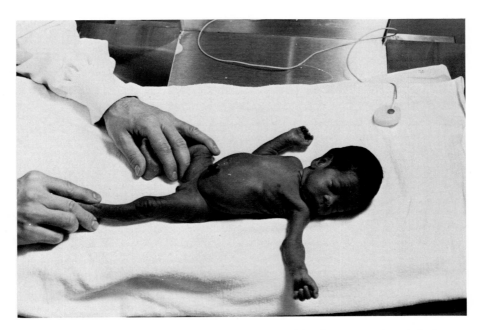

FIG. 8. Testing for recoil of the lower extremities in a premature infant.

with the gestational age examination, concentrate on breast tissue and areola, ears, sole creases, genitalia, and posture. Figure 1 is an example of a physical examination for gestational age. After you have shaded in the appropriate boxes, choose the appropriate week. This is not done by averaging. Rather, it is done by attempting to find that gestational age which most closely approximates most of the findings of the physical examination. In the example in Fig. 1, the individual physical findings could be seen in infants anywhere from 36 weeks' gestational age to a postterm infant. However, all but one of the physical findings agree with a gestational age of 40 weeks—that one finding being the ear form, which correlates with a 39-week gestational age. Hence this infant appears to have a gestational age of 40 weeks. If only one of the aspects of the physical examination markedly disagrees with the others, disregard it.

After determining the gestational age, the intrauterine growth chart is completed to determine whether the infant is appropriate, small, or large for gestational age. Figure 9 is a typical example of an intrauterine growth chart. The gestational age is plotted along the horizontal axis. The weight, length, and head circumference measurements are plotted along the vertical axis. The five dark lines indicate the 10th, 25th, 50th, 75th, and 90th percentiles for each measurement. If an infant were 36 weeks' gestation and weighed 1,600 g, he would be represented by the square; i.e., he would be premature and SGA. However, if he weighed 2,400 g, he would be represented by the triangle, i.e., premature and AGA. If he weighed 3,600 g, he would be represented by the dot, i.e., premature and LGA.

PROBLEMS ASSOCIATED WITH SPECIFIC GESTATIONAL AGE GROUPS

Why be so concerned with knowing the gestational age of a newborn? We have come to realize that an infant's behavior is a function of his age, not just his size. Thus infants who are premature are different than full term infants who are SGA, and they have different problems for which nurses and doctors must be alerted.

Premature infants (Table 1) could be expected to possibly develop hyaline membrane disease, apnea, inability to maintain temperature, hypoglycemia, difficulty feeding, intracranial hemorrhage, hypocalcemia, infections, and jaundice. SGA infants are likely to develop hypoglycemia, hypocalcemia, neonatal asphyxia, meconium aspiration, and polycythemia. In addition, they may have multiple other problems related to the etiology of the infant's poor growth, e.g., congenital anomalies seen in chromosome disorders. LGA infants are likely to develop hypoglycemia and birth trauma.

Infants who are postterm can be recognized by the desquamated skin, meconium staining, and long fingernails. They may develop hypoglycemia, fetal distress, neonatal asphyxia, or meconium aspiration, and they are frequently SGA.

Colorado Intrauterine Growth Charts

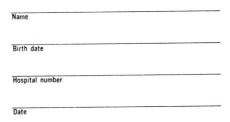

Name

Birth date

Hospital number

Date

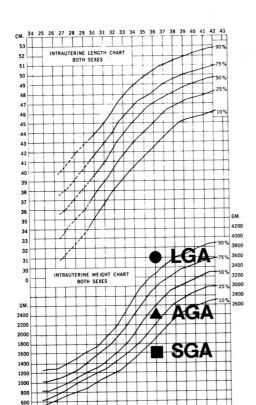

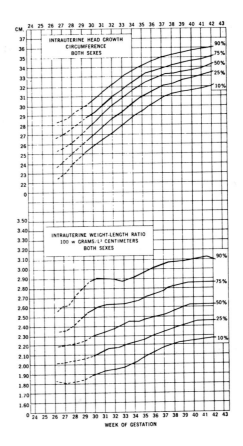

From Lubchenco, L.O., et al.: Pediatrics 37:403, 1966.
Additional copies available from Ross Laboratories, Columbus, Ohio 43216

46901/NOVEMBER, 1971

FIG. 9. Plot of birth weight against gestational age. (Modified from Lubchenco et al.: *Pediatrics,* 37:403, 1966, copyright American Academy of Pediatrics, 1966.)

TABLE 1. *Problems associated with specific gestational age groups*

1. *Premature infants*
   Hyaline membrane disease
   Apnea
   Inability to maintain adequate temperature
   Hypoglycemia
   Difficulty feeding (may need gavaging)
   Intracranial hemorrhage
   Hypocalcemia
   Infection
   Jaundice
2. *SGA infants*
   Hypoglycemia
   Hypocalcemia
   Asphyxia at birth
   Meconium aspiration
   Polycythemia
   Other problems related to the etiology of the infant's poor growth (e.g., congenital anomalies)
3. *Postterm infants*
   Hypoglycemia
   Fetal distress
   Neonatal asphyxia
   Meconium aspiration pneumonia
   SGA
4. *LGA infants*
   Hypoglycemia
   Birth trauma with resultant CNS problems

CAVEATS

1. A routine gestational age assessment is performed on every newborn soon after birth.

2. The technique of determining gestational age by physical examination is accurate within 1 to 2 weeks.

3. Infants who are premature have different problems than SGA infants of the same weight.

4. Premature infants are at risk to develop hyaline membrane disease, apnea, hypothermia, hypoglycemia, feeding problems, hypocalcemia, sepsis, and jaundice.

5. SGA infants are at risk to develop hypoglycemia, hypocalcemia, and polycythemia.

6. LGA infants are at risk to develop hypoglycemia and to experience birth trauma.

Temperature Regulation

Providing newborns a thermoneutral environment and protecting them against excessive heat loss increases their survival rate. Many years ago it was shown that premature infants who are kept warm have a much greater chance of survival than those who are cold. Maintaining the newborn, especially the premature, with the proper temperature control is one of the most important factors in decreasing mortality and morbidity.

METHODS OF HEAT LOSS

Heat may be lost by four methods: (a) Convection involves a flow of heat from the body surface to cooler air currents passing over the body. Examples are air-conditioning and cool oxygen currents. When an infant is in a warm incubator without cold oxygen currents, this loss is kept to a minimum. (b) Radiation involves the loss of heat to cooler solid objects in the environment. Although not directly influenced by room or incubator temperature, radiation is the most significant mechanism of heat loss in the newborn outside the delivery room. Examples are incubator walls, room walls, windows, and cold air-conditioners. (c) Evaporation involves a loss of heat during the conversion of a liquid to a vapor, a process which uses thermal energy. Evaporation of amniotic fluid, water from baths, mists, and "prep" solutions (e.g., alcohol and betadine) from the infant's skin are common examples. (d) Conduction involves the loss of heat during direct contact of the skin with a cooler solid object. Examples are cold mattresses, cold weighing scales, and X-ray cassettes.

THERMAL ENVIRONMENT

The normal skin temperature for an infant is 36° to 36.5°C (96.8° to 97.7°F). Normal axillary and rectal temperature is 36.5° to 37°C (97.7° to 98.6°F). Measurement of temperature with rectal thermometers may be dangerous because of the possibility of rectal perforation. Further, rectal temperatures are less useful than skin or axillary temperature because rectal temperature repre-

TABLE 1. *Neutral thermal environment*

| Age (days) | Optimal temperature (°C) | |
	Birth weight 1 kg	Birth weight 2 kg
1	35.0–35.5	34.0–34.6
5	34.5–35.0	33.0–33.8
10	34.0–34.6	32.5–33.5
15	33.5–34.4	32.3–33.3
20	33.2–34.2	32.1–33.2

Modified from Hey and Katz: *Arch. Dis. Child.*, 45:328, 1970.

sents the core temperature, which may be normal even when the infant is in fact suffering the effects of hypothermia (recognized by a low skin temperature).

The zone of thermal neutrality is the ambient air temperature at which oxygen consumption necessary to maintain the normal body temperature is minimal. Maintaining the environmental temperature (in the incubator) within this range (Table 1) is especially important in premature infants.

THERMAL DISADVANTAGES OF THE NEWBORN

Newborns, especially prematures, are susceptible to hypothermia for a number of reasons: a greater surface-area-to-weight ratio, less brown fat stores, less subcutaneous tissue, and a flaccid posture which increases the surface area exposed to the environment.

Hypothermia is an abnormally low temperature, i.e., a skin temperature less than 36°C (96.8°F) or a rectal or axillary temperature less than 36.5°C (97.7°F). It increases mortality dramatically, as well as oxygen consumption, metabolic rate, and the risk of kernicterus. It may cause apnea, respiratory distress, metabolic acidosis, hypoglycemia, and decreased surfactant production with resultant increased risk of hyaline membrane disease. *Hypothermia must be avoided in the newborn.*

Hyperthermia may be caused by incorrectly adjusted incubators and radiant warmers, improperly placed servo control probes, phototherapy lights, sunlight through the walls of an incubator, infection, and intracranial hemorrhage. It is important also to remember that hyperthermia [i.e., a skin temperature greater than 37°C (98.6°F) or a rectal temperature greater than 37.5°C (99.5°F)] also results in serious problems, including increased metabolic demands, increased oxygen consumption, and apnea in a premature infant. Premature infants, even though they have normal skin temperature, may have apnea secondary to a high environmental temperature. Therefore it is important to maintain the environmental temperature in an incubator within or near the thermal neutral zone as seen in Table 1.

Equipment

The incubator temperature is recorded simultaneously with the infant's axillary or skin temperature as an infant may show indirect evidence of fever if his temperature remains the same when the incubator temperature drops. When using servo control, the probe must be dry and taped securely on the skin on the upright side of the infant. If servo control is unavailable, the temperature in the incubator is set according to the neutral thermal environment, i.e., the environmental temperature at which skin temperature is normal and oxygen consumption minimal (Table 1).

Radiant warmers provide maximum access to the infant and are ideal for exchange transfusions and other minor surgical procedures. A servo control probe is used when procedures are done under the radiant warmer. Evaporative water losses are increased, sometimes dramatically, in a patient under these warmers, and fluid requirements are increased when radiant warmers are used for prolonged periods in very low birth weight infants.

Plastic heat shields or bubble material (see Chapter 18) may be placed over the infant to reduce heat loss by radiation. Also, aluminum foil or a plastic bubble may be used to line the inside of the incubator in order to reduce the radiant heat loss. These methods are especially useful in the small premature infant. Tables 2 and 3 include some other suggestions, guidelines, and important points about thermoregulation in the newborn.

TABLE 2. *Clinical guidelines and suggestions*

1. Keep incubator away from cold walls, windows, and other objects.
2. For small infants use a Plexiglas shield or plastic bubble material over the infant, or else line the inside of the incubator with aluminum foil if there is difficulty maintaining the temperature.
3. Do not place infant on a cold, wet surface.
4. Keep infant and incubator away from air currents (e.g., air-conditioner, window, oxygen line).
5. Use warm, humidified oxygen when given directly to infant.
6. Keep infant dry, especially in delivery room.
7. Provide adequate humidity in incubator (approximately 75%).
8. Use radiant warmer in delivery room and when working with infant.
9. Do not keep infant in delivery room for prolonged periods (e.g., circumcision).
10. When transporting infant, provide adequate thermal control.

TABLE 3. *Other clinical points*

1. Infant's water requirement may increase significantly when under a radiant warmer.
2. High or low temperature may indicate sepsis, asphyxia, intracranial hemorrhage, or meningitis.
3. When using servo control, the use of temperature as a clinical sign is lost. Therefore keep a record of the incubator temperature.
4. A full term newborn in usual room temperature (25° to 27°C) normally does not require an incubator. If he does, something is wrong with him.
5. Even in a normal thermal environment, the stress of a cold air current (e.g., oxygen) to a small area of the body (e.g., face) may trigger increased oxygen consumption and the metabolic rate.

CAVEATS

1. Keeping newborn, especially premature, infants warm increases their chance of survival.

2. In the delivery room the infant is dried and placed under a radiant warmer.

3. Outside the delivery room, radiation is the most significant mechanism of heat loss.

6

Infant Nutrition

Breast feeding, with the introduction of solid foods around 1 year of age, was the norm prior to the 1930s. During the "preantibiotic" era breast feeding was believed to be essential for the health and survival of infants. A 1934 survey of 20,000 babies in Chicago showed a death rate of 1.54/1,000 for breast-fed infants compared with 84.36/1,000 for artificially fed babies. As improved hygienic and sanitary conditions became available in the industrialized countries with refrigeration and uncontaminated water supplies during the 1940s and 1950s, the pendulum swung from breast feeding to the use of commercial formulas, with early introduction of solid foods, often during the first 1 to 2 months of life. The statistics for the bottle-fed infant improved.

Gradually over the past one to two decades, the practice of breast feeding has been re-evaluated, and scientific information acquired during the past 10 years has given impetus to physicians, nurses, and nutritionists to support the mother who expresses an interest in nursing. Marked changes in attitudes of mothers toward breast feeding have also occurred: in 1971, 24.7% of mothers left the hospital breast feeding; by 1978 the number had nearly doubled to 46.6%. Furthermore, the 5.5% of mothers in 1971 who were still nursing at their infant's 6-month birthday had increased to 20.5% by 1978. Moreover, these changes have occurred in the higher-income, better-educated group of mothers as well as the lower-income, less-educated groups.

POTENTIAL ADVANTAGES OF BREAST FEEDING

Human milk is still regarded as the standard for neonatal/infant nutrition. Standard formulas simulate the basic composition of breast milk, although many factors present in human milk have either not yet been identified or cannot be reproduced at this time. Breast milk thus remains unique, providing general and specific advantages to the baby as depicted in Table 1. The major advantages of breast milk for the newborn are believed to reside in: (a) the greater digestibility of the milk; (b) the host defense properties of the milk; (c)

TABLE 1. *Potential beneficial properties of human milk and breast feeding*

1. Nutritional—generally well absorbed and appropriately balanced
   a. Efficient fat and protein absorption
   b. Decreased curd formation with prolonged transit time
   c. Adequate amounts of all known nutrients for term infant
   d. Increased iron absorption
   e. Proper calcium and phosphorus concentrations, and ratio
   f. Increased cholesterol content (? significance)
2. Immunologic—general decreased incidence of gastrointestinal and respiratory infections
   a. Altered intestinal flora *(Lactobacillus bifidus)*
   b. Immunoglobulins (particularly secretory IgA)
   c. Lactoferrin, transferrin
   d. Lactoperoxidase
   e. Lysozyme
   f. Cellular components (macrophages, lymphocytes, neutrophils)
   g. Interferon
   h. Complement (all components)
3. Hypoallergenic
4. Psychologic—may enhance maternal-infant bonding
5. Miscellaneous—convenient (usually), economical, less possibility of overfeeding

the hypoallergenicity of breast milk; and (d) the psychological aspects of maternal-infant bonding.

Since it seems reasonable to assume that the milk of each species is well adapted to the particular needs of that species, commercial formula companies have attempted to duplicate "mother's milk" for human infant consumption. Table 2 summarizes the nutrients found in human milk, "conventional" commercial formulas, and cows' milk.

Immunoglobulins and phagocytic cells are present in human colostrum and mature human milk; their concentration and distributions vary at different times after the onset of lactation. The acquisition of such possible immunity may be important during the early neonatal period when the "secretory immune system" is poorly developed. The significance of these "protective factors" in a clean, urban environment is difficult to evaluate. No study has yet surmounted the difficulties of all the variables involved in determining the presence or absence of a protective advantage of breast feeding.

TABLE 2. *Milk composition*

Milk source	Protein (g/liter)	Fat (g/liter)	Carbohydrates (g/liter)
Human	9	45	68
Formula	15	38	70
Cows	35	37	49

From Hambraeus: *Pediatr. Clin. North Am.,* 24:21, 1977.

In Western countries the estimates for cows' milk allergy run from 0.4% to as high as 7.5%, with an average around 1%. The main allergens seem to be found in cows' milk protein, particularly in the β-lactoglobulin fraction not found in human milk. In a family with a strong allergic history, it seems advantageous to delay not only the introduction of cows' milk but also other food substances until nearly 6 months of age.

Much has been written about maternal-infant attachment. Nursing, whether by breast or bottle, requires intimate touching and frequent handling. However, many mothers find breast feeding a very positive and pleasant experience, possibly enhancing maternal-infant interaction.

DISADVANTAGES AND CONTRAINDICATIONS TO BREAST FEEDING

Although almost all drugs pass into breast milk to some degree, most are not contraindications to breast feeding (Table 3). Currently, the only antibiotics definitely contraindicated include chloramphenicol, tetracyclines, metronidazole (Flagyl®), nitrofurantoin, nalidixic acid, and sulfonamides if G6PD deficiency is suspected. Sulfonamides, which seem to displace bilirubin from its protein binding site, are contraindicated when breast feeding a premature infant who is considered to be at more risk for kernicterus. Since isoniazid (INH) is found in equal concentrations in milk and plasma, the infant whose mother is taking the drug should be monitored for possible toxicity as reflected in peripheral neuropathy, vomiting, and hepatitis. Although other antibiotics such as penicillins and aminoglycosides are found in the milk and may change the flora of the infant's gastrointestinal tract, in general they appear safe. Antibiotics found in negligible amounts in breast milk and considered safe include the cephalosporins, oxacillin, and para-aminosalicylic acid.

TABLE 3. *Drugs in breast milk*

May not be used during breast feeding—Definite Adverse Effects	Probably contraindicated during breast feeding—Possible Adverse Effects
Gold	Indomethacin
Chloramphenicol	Aspirin, high dose
Tetracyclines	Sulfonamides
Nalidixic acid	Warfarin
Antineoplastic agents	Reserpine
Iodides	Corticosteroids, high dose
Antithyroid medications	Sex steroids
Ergot, ergotamine	Diazepam
Lithium	Chloral hydrate
Radioactive drugs	Some stool softeners
Bromides	Marijuana
Prolonged alcohol	Cocaine
	Hallucinogens
	Others

Other drugs contraindicated during breast feeding include anticancer agents, antithyroid drugs, and anticoagulants. Diazepam, meprobamate, and lithium carbonate are also contraindicated, although other tranquilizers (e.g., phenothiazines) seem safe for the infant when given in therapeutic doses to the mother. The tricyclic antidepressants appear in negligible concentrations in breast milk, so their administration during breast feeding is permissible. Oral contraceptives are generally discouraged during breast feeding, although they are not specifically contraindicated. Ideally, however, other means of effective contraception are employed during this period. Steroids such as prednisone are not specifically contraindicated, but data only for short-term, low-dose administration to the breast-feeding mother are available. Indomethacin should not be taken by a breast-feeding mother until additional information regarding its safety can be obtained. Caffeine, alcohol, and salicylates are permissible in moderation. More complete lists with other references and discussions are available (Anderson: *Drug Intell. Clin. Pharmacol.*, 11:208, 1977). Simply stated, a nursing mother should not take a drug unless it has been previously documented as being safe for the infant and mother. If the drug is essential to the mother's health and its safety is unknown, breast feeding should be discontinued.

The only disease processes contraindicating breast feeding are active tuberculosis and sepsis. Whether to allow a mother to breast feed if she has been diagnosed as having viral hepatitis A or B is an unanswered question. Other conditions which contraindicate breast feeding include alcoholism, drug addiction, poor maternal nutrition, and severe emotional disability.

As breast feeding has become more "in vogue," several reports of "failure to thrive" and even hypernatremic dehydration in breast-fed infants have been documented. Other reports comment on the manifestations of vitamin D deficiency (rickets) developing in infants breast fed without vitamin supplementation. All these reports point to the need for proper instruction and close early follow-up and support, particularly for the young, inexperienced mother who wants to breast feed. The physician must also develop the expertise to recognize and then gently guide the mother who "cannot," or chooses not to, breast feed to an alternate method of feeding without evoking guilt feelings.

Breast milk feeding is not related to an increased incidence of jaundice during the first 4 days of life. The nonhemolytic hyperbilirubinemia classically referred to as breast milk jaundice is characterized by an increase in the indirect fraction of bilirubin after the fourth day of life. Several etiologies have been considered, including the effect of steroid derivatives and/or the fatty acid content in breast milk. At this time no clear explanation can be given. The diagnosis becomes one of exclusion, with appropriate consideration and diagnostic evaluation for other potential causes of jaundice. Management of the hyperbilirubinemia is dependent on the clinical situation and is similar to that of any other indirect hyperbilirubinemia. Interruption of breast feedings for 24 to 36 hr usually results in a prompt and rapid decline of the baby's bilirubin. During this time the mother is instructed to pump her breasts and is reassured that her breast milk is not harmful. Resumption of breast feedings usually does not result in a further rise of bilirubin.

PRACTICAL ASPECTS OF BREAST FEEDING

Proper instruction concerning breast feeding is essential if an informed decision is to be made. This is particularly important to the expectant mother of a first child, or where family support is lacking. Ideally, the preparation begins prenatally, 2 to 3 months before anticipated delivery. Instruction may be provided individually at office visits or in groups at prenatal classes. However, it is essential that the instructor be very familiar with the practical aspects and documented facts concerning breast feeding. If an expectant mother expresses a desire to breast feed, it is often helpful to speak with the father or other immediate family as well to generate familiarity and support from those close to the mother. A new father may then anticipate to some degree the needs of the breast-feeding mother at home. Prenatal instruction also permits an opportunity for new mothers to become familiar with their breasts and begin specific preparation if such findings as depressed nipples are present.

During the early postpartum period, the infant is allowed to nurse on a "demand" schedule with the mother, permitting the infant to suckle for approximately 5 min on each side. The colostrum which the infant receives during these sessions varies in amount from 10 to 50 ml and provides approximately 67 kcal/100 ml (20 kcal/oz). If the infant seems hungry after these limited sessions at the breast, his diet can be supplemented with 5% glucose water or sterile water until he seems content. Supplementation with formula during the early newborn period is not generally recommended, as this may decrease the frequency with which the infant demands to be fed and may also decrease the baby's enthusiasm for suckling. This subsequently may decrease stimulus for milk production and create significant problems as the transitional milk "comes in" at 3 or 4 days.

The stimulus for milk production occurs through the action of prolactin on the mammary alveoli beginning 24 to 96 hr postdelivery. Breast engorgement can occur during this time in lactating and nonlactating women and is due to two factors: (a) There is an increase in venous and lymphatic stasis in the surrounding breast tissue; and (b) there is an accumulation of milk within the alveoli and duct system. Early nursing after delivery and flexible feedings during the postpartum days may significantly decrease breast engorgement in lactating women. This is particularly important as breast engorgement is not only painful but is associated with a high rate of breast infection and lactation failure.

The infant is nursed every 2 to 4 hr (5 min per breast) during the immediate postpartum period, when possible, in order to promote milk production and prevent breast engorgement from becoming uncomfortable for the mother. This schedule is continued around the clock. It is a mistake to "allow" the mother who is becoming engorged to sleep through the night if these 6 to 8 hr of nonnursing result in breasts so painfully full of milk that she is unable to put the infant to breast. Pain, anxiety, and tension are all inhibitors of the let-down reflex and may sabotage the mother's nursing experience. If engorgement becomes a problem, it is often advantageous to apply heat (via a shower or warm packs to the breasts) prior to nursing. The use of mild analgesics may be necessary but is avoided when possible. Milk is expressed from both breasts by manual or pump techniques until the infant can grasp the nipples easily. The baby is then permitted to nurse until completion, during which time the mother massages the breasts thoroughly. Reassurance is provided to the mother that breast engorgement is normal and temporary, and does not interfere with the success of the breast-feeding experience.

The mother may increase the time the infant nurses to 5 to 10 minutes per side as her milk production increases, keeping in mind, however, that more frequent and shorter periods at the breast initially are less likely to cause soreness and cracking of the nipples. It is advantageous to air-dry the nipples after each nursing session for 15 to 30 min and then apply some type of lanolin-based, nontoxic breast cream, which is rubbed in gently and need not be washed off before the next nursing session. A daily bath or shower is adequate for breast hygiene. The mother should be careful to avoid harsh soaps or drying agents; in fact, simply rinsing with clean, warm water is usually adequate. It is not necessary to cleanse the nipples prior to a feeding as this merely removes protective oils. However, care is taken to wash the hands carefully before the mother handles her breast.

Positioning the infant to avoid any traction on the nipple is extremely important when placing the infant at the breast. Further, the infant should be able to grasp as much of the areola as possible (milk reservoirs being located behind the nipple). This can be accomplished most easily by first teaching the mother to position herself comfortably. Sitting in bed or on a soft chair with a pillow across her lap is ideal. The environment should be pleasant, quiet, and without interruptions or distractions. The mother may then manually express a few drops of milk onto the nipple to encourage the infant to begin to suckle. She may help him grasp the nipple by using her first two fingers to "scissor" or project it forward. Illustrating the rooting reflex for the mother is also helpful, as it becomes apparent that touching the infant's cheeks may be confusing to the baby. It is best to guide the infant to the breast with gentle pressure on the back of the head.

The key to maximum milk production is adequate emptying of the breasts on a routine basis. To ensure total emptying, the mother is taught to start each feeding with alternate breasts, as the infant is likely to suck more vigorously on the side first offered. Since the breast is emptied after 7 to 8 min, it is preferable to switch the infant at that point to the opposite side and let him finish nursing on the side which still contains a supply of milk. Nursing beyond the 8- to 10-min interval on one side can be emotionally satisfying to the infant but is often nonnutritive. Breast massage in a circular fashion around the breast while the infant is nursing also increases milk production by enhancing milk flow. Care is taken to keep the breasts dry between feedings, as moisture on the nipples may cause excoriation. This can be accomplished by using breast pads that absorb leakage of milk (changing the pads as they become saturated) and air-drying for 15 to 30 min after nursing or washing. A freshly cleaned support brassiere is used each day. Areas of lumps and soreness in the breast that remain after the feeding session need special attention by further massage, milk expression, and/ or moist heat application to prevent the development of mastitis.

Engorgement is a frequent and normal occurrence during the first days of lactation. Prevention of excessive engorgement (which may limit the ability to nurse) is usually possible with proper instruction and care of the breasts. Early, frequent feedings to stimulate milk production and to promote breast emptying are necessary. The infant is fed on demand (every 2 to 4 hr) during the first few days postpartum. Adequate massage of the breasts during nursing is important to maintain patency of milk ducts throughout the gland.

Should a milk duct become obstructed with inspissated milk over the next several days, it may present as an area of localized tenderness, erythema, and swelling. The galactocele thus formed may be treated effectively by frequent massaging during continued nursing, or by milk expression. Occasionally, mild analgesics are required. Should superinfection within the galactocele be suspected, antistaphylococcal antibiotics may be prescribed.

Severe mastitis with generalized infection of the breast parenchyma is a relatively rare complication which usually occurs after the first 2 to 3 weeks of lactation. It is the result of bacterial invasion (usually coagulase-positive *Staphylococcus aureus*) into the breast via cracked or fissured nipples. Some degree of engorgement often precedes the actual infection, which is heralded by acute systemic symptoms. High fever and chills, with hardening and tenderness of the entire involved breast, are characteristic. Appropriate management includes expression of milk for culture and sensitivity tests, and institution of appropriate antibiotic therapy. Continued expression of the milk from the infected breast reduces discomfort and assists drainage. Continued nursing from the opposite breast may be possible, although in severe cases nursing may have to be interrupted or discontinued.

SUPPRESSION OF LACTATION AND WEANING

At present, no medications can be recommended for safely preventing normal breast engorgement and milk production during the postpartum period of the mother who does not breast feed. All medications currently available in the United States either have an inadequate success rate and/or possess significant side effects. The recommended approach during the early puerperium is mechanical and supportive. Withdrawal of any sucking stimulus to the breast in conjunction with a support brassiere and mild analgesics is usually all that is necessary. Occasionally, cold compresses, binders, and intermittent partial emptying of the breasts to alleviate exquisite pain are required. Throughout this process the mother must be supported psychologically as well, reassuring her that artificial formula is suitable and sometimes even the preferred method of infant feeding.

Weaning at the completion of the lactation period is accomplished by a gradual reduction in the frequency of feedings over several days to weeks. Should discomfort and engorgement become problematic, measures similar to those utilized during the early postpartum period for nonnursing mothers are employed. When to wean an infant is a decision to be made by the mother. In our society, the majority of women wean their infants between 3 and 9 months of age, although prolonged breast feeding is becoming more common.

NUTRITION DURING LACTATION

A well-balanced diet is encouraged; fad diets, strict dieting, excessive nonnutritional food intake, or excessive alcohol consumption are to be avoided. Although maternal fluid intake (either excessive or restricted) has little, if any, effect on milk supply, fluids should not be limited. The inclusion of three to four cups of milk or equivalent dairy products ensures adequate protein intake as well. Prenatal vitamins are continued throughout lactation.

SUPPLEMENTATION: VITAMINS, IRON, FLUORIDE, AND SOLID FOODS

Breast feeding or an iron-fortified formula is recommended. If neither is chosen, the diluted, evaporated (not condensed) milk may be used in the following mixture: 1 can milk (13 ounces), 1.5 cans water (19.5 ounces), and 2 tablespoons (1 ounce) corn syrup (Karo). When supplemented with vitamin C and iron beginning at age 2 weeks, the evaporated milk, which is already fortified with vitamin D, provides the infant adequate nutrition. A supplement with a combination of vitamins A, D, and C with iron is usually given.

The breast-fed baby is supplemented with vitamin D beginning around 2 weeks. Some suggest the additional use of iron, but this is controversial. Iron deficiency anemia has not been found to be a problem in the totally breast-fed infant, certainly before the age of 6 months and possibly up to 12 months. Although the concentration of iron in human and cows' milk is similar, the bioavailability of iron in human milk may allow 50% absorption compared to less than 10% from cows' milk. As a pure liquid form of vitamin D is not readily available, a combination of A, D, and C is suggested. The child fed iron-fortified formulas needs no supplements unless he is born prematurely.

The question of supplemental fluoride has received much attention recently. Because of variable amounts of fluoride found in the water of processed formulas and commercial baby food, fluoride is not prescribed for children under the age of 6 months, except for the breast-fed infant. The present recommendation is 0.25 mg daily, to be discontinued when solids or any other form of milk are

TABLE 4. *Summary of recommended daily vitamin, iron, and fluoride supplements during the first 6 months*

Milk	Vitamin D, 400 IU	Vitamin C, 20 mg	Iron, 1 mg/kg	Fluoride, 0.25 mg
Human	Yes	No	No	Yes
Evaporated (D-fortified)	No	Yes	Yes	No
Iron-fortified formulas	No	No	No	No

regularly introduced. Table 4 summarizes the daily vitamin, iron, and fluoride supplement recommendations for the various milk sources during the first 6 months of life.

As suggested before, the age for introducing solid food is shifting back toward a moderate position. Whether breast-fed or bottle-fed, it is recommended to delay giving the infant solid food until about 4 to 5 months of age. The larger child over the 75th percentile in weight and height may seem more demanding when he consumes larger milk volumes at shorter feeding intervals. At around age 3 months, solid foods are added to many of these babies' diets. Cereal is usually introduced first, as a single grain: oatmeal or rice. Whether fruits or vegetables are added next, the recommendation is to "go slow" and avoid solids prepared with extra salt or sweeteners, e.g., sugar and tapioca. Meats and then egg yolk are usually next.

FEEDING THE PREMATURE INFANT

The subject of nutritional support of the premature, especially the very low birth weight (less than 1,500 g) infant, usually stimulates considerable controversy which, in general, is based on anecdotal experience rather than scientific data. There is little or no agreement among experts concerning the ideal formula, technique of feeding, time of initiation of feeding, or the concentration or rate of formula administration. Disadvantages of delayed feeding include hypoglycemia, dehydration if water is not provided by the intravenous route, breakdown of fat and muscle stores, increased incidence of jaundice, and delayed growth. Although prolonged severe malnutrition may result in impaired central nervous system development, there are no data to suggest that short (1 to 4 weeks) periods of suboptimal (40 to 80 cal/kg/day) caloric intake result in any permanent detrimental effects on the central nervous system. Disadvantages of overly vigorous and early feeding include aspiration, abdominal distention, apnea, and necrotizing enterocolitis.

Factors to consider when choosing the appropriate method of feeding premature infants include the gestational age, birth weight, coordination of sucking and swallowing reflex, and the presence of other medical disorders. Each infant must be individually assessed to determine the best method of feeding, the volume of feeding, and the rate of increase in volume. However, certain guidelines and some general principles may be helpful.

Intravenous fluids are administered as soon after birth as possible to all infants in distress and all premature infants less than 1,500 g or 34 weeks' gestation. These infants should probably not be fed on the first day of life; if no medical disorders are present, cautious feedings may be started after 24 hr of age. Infants larger than 1,500 g, in general, can be fed after 4 to 6 hr of age. Infants with significant respiratory distress or other significant medical disorders are treated with intravenous glucose and are not fed enterally.

Most infants less than 1,500 g require gavage feeding, as may many larger infants initially. In addition, infants with respiratory rates greater than 70/min or with labored respiration receive gavage feedings rather than nipple feedings. When deciding on the time to initiate nipple feedings, it must be remembered that coordinated sucking, swallowing, and an effective gag reflex may not be present until a gestational age of 34 to 35 weeks. Continuous gastric and transpyloric feeding techniques are currently being used in some newborn intensive care units, but these are not recommended as routine methods of feeding premature infants.

One may begin feedings with a volume of 4 to 20 ml, depending on the birth weight of the infant. Generally, infants less than 1,000 g receive 4 to 6 ml; 1,000 to 1,500 g, 6 to 8 ml; 1,500 to 2,000 g, 9 to 15 ml; and 2,000 to 2,500 g, 15 to 20 ml. Glucose water is usually given as the first feeding, but sterile water may be used if hypoglycemia is not a problem, especially if the infant is receiving intravenous fluid. Sterile water is preferable if intestinal obstruction is a consideration. Two feedings of the initial volume are given before an increase in volume is considered. When the initial feedings are tolerated, formula is begun in the same amount and increased slowly as tolerated. Increases of 1 ml every other feeding for very small babies and 1 to 2 ml each feeding for larger babies is appropriate for gavage feedings. Nipple feedings may usually be increased more rapidly, limited by the baby's appetite and tolerance. The volume is increased up to an amount calculated to give the infant approximately 120 cal/kg/day. Further increases may be required to ensure weight gain in a small percentage of infants.

The ideal form of nutritional support for premature infants has not been determined. A great deal of controversy exists concerning the use of breast milk or formula for premature infants. Proponents of breast milk claim that it is the optimal form of nutritional support for premature infants and that its immunologic benefits make it superior to commercial formulas. Opponents of breast milk for the premature infant claim that breast milk contains inadequate quantities of protein, calcium, and sodium for very low birth weight infants. To date, most of the controversy has been based on extrapolations from fetal tissue studies, anecdotal experience, and emotion, rather than scientific data; and it appears unlikely that the answers to these questions will be forthcoming in the near future.

Similar controversy exists regarding which formula is optimal for feeding the premature infant. Commercial formulas designed for the full term infant have been used in the past. However, recently, "humanized" formulas designed specifically for the premature infant have been developed. The characteristics of these formulas include higher protein, calcium, and sodium concentrations. In addition, in some of the formulas the protein is more "humanized" with a whey/casein ratio of 60:40, similar to that of breast milk. A portion of the fat is frequently in the form of medium-chain triglycerides, which are more readily absorbed in the premature infant, and the carbohydrate may be provided as glucose polymers rather than disaccharides as in routine commercial formulas. To date, there are few data which strongly support the use of one formula compared to another. Although some newborn intensive care units use soy base formulas for the premature infant, there have been no studies evaluating their efficacy or safety, and so these formulas cannot be recommended for *routine* use in premature infants.

The concentration of formula administered to the patient is also controversial. In infants less than 1,500 g, a dilute formula (5 to 12 kcal/oz) is recommended for 12 to 24 hr followed by gradual increases of the concentration to 20 kcal/oz formula. Some infants, especially those less than 1,500 g, may be unable to tolerate a sufficient volume of 20 kcal/oz to gain weight. In these instances, 24 kcal/oz formula may be used.

Most infants less than 1,500 g require intermittent gavage feeding every 2 hr. In infants weighing 1,500 to 3,000 g, feedings every 3 hr are appropriate.

The above guidelines obviously must be modified to the individual baby. In addition, the feeding plan is re-evaluated if there is regurgitation, abdominal distention, diarrhea, green or bilious gastric aspirate, or gastric residual greater than 5 ml.

CAVEATS

1. Breast feeding is the recommended form of nutrition for full term infants.

2. If a mother decides to bottle feed her infant, she must receive positive support from physicians and nurses.

3. Physicians and nurses must be familiar with the practical aspects and documented facts concerning breast feeding.

4. Normal, healthy term infants are fed within 4 to 6 hr after birth.

5. Coordinated sucking and swallowing and an effective gag reflex may not be present until a gestational age of 34 to 35 weeks.

6. The ideal form of nutritional support for the premature infant has not been determined.

7. To date, there are few data that support the use of any one formula for feeding premature infants.

Resuscitation

The introduction of intensive care for low birth weight and high-risk infants has lowered the mortality rate and the incidence of long-term handicaps such as mental retardation, seizures, and cerebral palsy in these infants. A favorable outcome depends on such additional factors as prenatal recognition of potential risk, appropriate intrapartum management, and proper care at the time of delivery. The finest newborn intensive care unit cannot influence the quality of life if irreversible damage has occurred prior to admission. The importance of proper resuscitation of the sick neonate is well known. Hypoxia, acidosis, and inadequate ventilation constitute an immediate threat to the infant's life. Hypoxia may result in severe central nervous system (CNS) damage or death.

It is mandatory that every physician involved in the delivery of a newborn infant be competent in neonatal resuscitation. Other delivery room personnel must also become familiar with the proper techniques of resuscitation, as a team approach is often necessary. There must be at least one person—physician, nurse, anesthetist, or respiratory therapist—at each delivery who is capable of resuscitating an asphyxiated infant. Likewise, every delivery room must be properly equipped to provide the total support required during such a crisis. Only when this complement of equipment and trained personnel is routinely available in every delivery room will the incidence of neonatal deaths and long-term CNS disabilities due to acute asphyxia be maximally reduced.

A prerequisite to good resuscitation is good equipment. The items in Table 1 constitute the suggested minimum for equipment. Responsibility for the upkeep and periodic inspection of the resuscitation tray must be designated to a specific individual.

Often the need for resuscitation can be predicted before delivery. Some of the factors associated with neonatal asphyxia are presented in Table 2. Whenever any one of these conditions is recognized, advance preparation for possible respiratory support of the infant is indicated.

TABLE 1. *Resuscitation equipment*

Overhead radiant heater
Light source
Heated, humidified oxygen
Stethoscope
Suction
Infant resuscitation bag with face masks (full term and premature)
Laryngoscope with 0 and 1 straight blades
Endotracheal tubes (sizes 2.5, 3.0, 3.5 mm) and stylet
Sterile umbilical vessel catheterization tray
Umbilical catheters, 3.5 and 5 Fr.
Sterile suction catheters
Suction bulb
Medications
Intravenous fluids

TABLE 2. *Factors associated with asphyxia at birth*

Maternal factors	Intrapartum factors	Fetal factors
Maternal disease (renal, pulmonary, cardiac, hematologic, endocrine, infectious, collagen, diabetes mellitus, anemia)	Cephalopelvic disproportion	Multiple births
	Sedative or analgesic drugs	Polyhydramnios
	Prolonged labor	Oligohydramnios
	Precipitous labor	Immature lecithin/sphingomyelin (L/S) ratio
	Difficult delivery	
Maternal drugs (magnesium, ethyl alcohol, barbiturates, narcotics)	Maternal hypotension	Premature delivery
	Cord compression	Postterm delivery
History of previous perinatal morbidity or mortality	Prolapsed umbilical cord	Large for gestational age
	Cesarean section	Small for gestational age
Surgery during pregnancy	Abnormal presentations	Meconium-stained amniotic fluid
Inadequate prenatal care	Forceps delivery other than low elective	Abnormal heart rate or rhythm
Prolonged rupture of membranes (greater than 24 hr)		Fetal acidosis
Abruptio placenta, placenta previa, or other antepartum hemorrhage		
Blood type isoimmunization		
Toxemia of pregnancy, hypertension		

EVALUATION OF THE INFANT

The Apgar score (Table 3) is used as a guide when selecting the resuscitative method required for a particular infant. A score of 0 to 3 indicates severe distress and the need for immediate vigorous resuscitative measures. Infants with Apgar scores of 4 to 7 are in moderate distress and *might* require vigorous resuscitation. If the score is 8 to 10, observation is usually all that is required. However, continued close surveillance is very important even under the most

TABLE 3. *Apgar score*

Sign	Criteria for scores of 0 to 2		
	0	1	2
Heart rate	Absent	Below 100	Over 100
Respiratory effort	Absent	Slow, irregular	Good, crying
Muscle tone	Flaccid	Some flexion of extremities	Active motion
Reflex irritability	No response	Grimace	Vigorous cry
Color	Blue, pale	Body pink, extremities blue	Completely pink

favorable circumstances as delayed respiratory depression may occur as a result of drug administration, anesthetic agents, and a variety of anatomical defects.

The Apgar score provides a good means of communication among personnel, but the need for intervention frequently cannot wait for Apgar scores to be assigned. The urgency of the situation can be assessed more efficiently and rapidly by evaluating two parameters of cardiopulmonary function: respiration and heart rate.

TECHNIQUE

Guidelines for management based on a quick assessment of respiratory effort and heart rate are presented in Fig. 1. Adequate temperature is best maintained by immediately drying the infant and then placing him under a radiant warmer. It is critical, particularly for the very low birth weight infant, to minimize exposure to cool drafts (e.g., air-conditioners) or cold objects (e.g., windows) in order to prevent convective, evaporative, and radiant heat loss. Whenever possible, it is preferable to increase the room temperature immediately before the delivery of a very low birth weight infant as, even with adequate drying and use of a radiant warmer, it is frequently difficult to maintain a normal body temperature.

Upon delivery of the infant's head in a vertex presentation, the nose and oropharynx are cleared by gentle bulb suctioning. If there is meconium in the amniotic fluid or the infant is meconium-stained, the nose, mouth, and pharynx are thoroughly suctioned with a bulb or a DeLee mucous trap before delivering the shoulders. This suctioning must be rapid and not interfere with expeditious delivery of the child.

When respirations are spontaneous with no apparent obstruction of air exchange, and the heart rate is greater than 100/min, close observation is all that is required. If respiratory efforts are inadequate or labored but the heart rate is greater than 100/min, additional measures may be indicated. The nose and oropharynx are gently suctioned with a soft catheter, and warm humidified

RESUSCITATION OUTLINE

Delivery—Quick Assessment

1. Maintain head down position
2. Suction upper airway with bulb
3. Dry with towel and place under radiant heater.

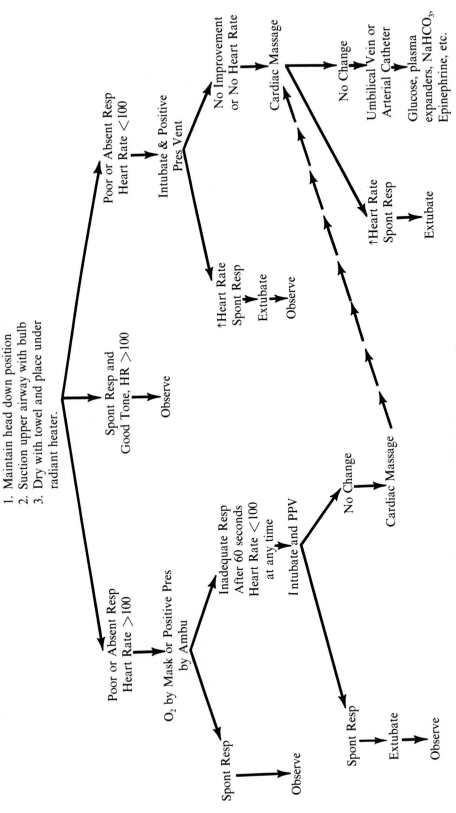

FIG. 1. Resuscitation outline.

oxygen is given by mask. The heart rate must be monitored continuously as a falling rate may necessitate more aggressive intervention.

If these procedures do not result in an improvement in respiratory effort, or if the heart rate deteriorates, bag and mask ventilation with supplemental oxygen is initiated. The infant who has not breathed spontaneously may require large initial ventilatory pressures (occasionally greater than 40 cm water) to inflate unexpanded alveoli. In most cases, after two or three breaths the delivery pressure need not exceed 20 to 30 cm water. The effectiveness of positive-pressure ventilation must be evaluated constantly by observing chest expansion, auscultating air exchange, and monitoring the clinical course. When bag and mask ventilation is used, the tendency to inflate the stomach can be minimized by inserting a nasogastric tube and/or applying gentle abdominal pressure.

If resuscitation by bag and mask does not ventilate the child adequately, the clinical course deteriorates, or the infant is profoundly depressed (i.e., absent respiratory rate and a heart rate of less than 100/min), endotracheal intubation is performed. These severely affected infants are often in shock, as reflected by their pallor and weak pulses.

The most important aspects of resuscitation of the newborn are oxygenation and ventilation. Nearly all infants who require resuscitation can be revived adequately with oxygenation and ventilation. If an infant is not responding promptly to such support, the most frequent reason is that the procedures are not being carried out appropriately. Therefore, whenever an infant is not responding to resuscitation—in which case the cyanosis and depressed heart rate remain—the first thing to recognize is that some error is being made: (a) The infant may not be receiving 100% oxygen because either the resuscitation bag does not deliver 100% oxygen or the oxygen tube has accidentally been disconnected. (b) The resuscitation bag may have a pressure pop-off valve limiting the inspiratory pressure to 40 cm H_2O, whereas the infant requires higher pressures for adequate ventilation. (c) The endotracheal tube may be misplaced, either into the esophagus or down the right mainstem bronchus. These are some of the most common errors made in the delivery room and account for most of the situations in which an infant fails to respond to resuscitative measures. Oxygenation and ventilation, not the use of drugs, are the cornerstones to successful neonatal resuscitation. Although drugs may be indicated, they are the least important aspect of resuscitation.

There is considerable controversy concerning the indication for intubation. Infants can be ventilated and oxygenated adequately with a bag and mask in almost all cases. Unsuccessful prolonged attempts at intubation which result in cyanosis and bradycardia of the infant must be avoided. When ventilating with a bag and mask, it is important to avoid overextension or flexion of the head, either of which may occlude the trachea. In addition, the mask must be tightly sealed over the infant's nose and mouth.

When the heart rate is less than 80 to 100/min and does not respond to 60 sec of assisted ventilation, external cardiac massage is initiated by an assistant. Two fingers are placed over the lower half of the sternum, and sufficient pressure is applied for 1 to 2 cm depression. The massage rate is approximately 100 to 120/min. The assisted respiratory rate should be 40 to 60/min. Because of the compliance of the newborn chest, cardiac massage may be continued at a regular rate while ventilation is being provided. Massage is stopped periodically to determine if there is spontaneous cardiac activity or an improvement in heart rate.

DRUG THERAPY

If a spontaneous heart rate greater than 80 to 100/min is not sustained after 1 to 3 min of adequate ventilation and external cardiac massage, drugs are required. In most cases, however, drugs are not needed to stabilize the patient with acute asphyxia, and they are never a substitute for ventilation and oxygen therapy. Caffeine and other so-called respiratory stimulants must never be used for acute cardiopulmonary support. They are ineffective, and their side effects may further endanger the patient's already precarious state. When drugs are necessary, they are usually administered by an umbilical vein catheter passed into the inferior vena cava, if possible. Table 4 lists the drugs, indications for use, and routes of administration.

Hypotension may be recognized by pallor, mottling of the skin, poor capillary filling, and weak pulses; it is measured by the low blood pressure. The child who is hypotensive because of acute blood loss should receive either whole

TABLE 4. *Drugs used for resuscitation*

Drug	Indication	Route of administration	Dose
Whole blood or 5% protein solution	History of blood loss, shock, hypotension	i.v.	10–20 ml/kg
$D_{10-25}W$	Hypoglycemia	i.v.	2–4 ml/kg over 5 min
Naloxone	Maternal narcotic administration and neonatal depression	i.v.	0.01 mg/kg
$NaHCO_3$ (0.88 or 1.0 mEq/ml)	Severe metabolic acidemia or severe asphyxia not responsive to routine resuscitation	i.v.	1–3 mEq/kg over 5 min—dilute 1:2 with sterile water
Epinephrine 1:10,000	Cardiac arrest, severe bradycardia not responsive to routine resuscitation	i.v. (while performing cardiac massage) or intracardiac injection	0.1–0.3 ml/kg, 1:10,000 solution
Ca gluconate 10%	Severe bradycardia	i.v.	1.0 ml/kg slowly
$CaCl_2$ 10%	Severe bradycardia	i.v.	0.1 ml/kg slowly

blood or other volume expanders (e.g., plasma or a 5% protein solution) in a dose of 10 to 20 ml/kg over 5 to 20 min (as clinically indicated).

It is important to remember that hypotension in the newborn is frequently due to hypoxia. Therefore one's approach includes the immediate treatment of hypoxia with ventilation and oxygenation. When these measures do not immediately improve the hypotension, it is usually assumed that hypovolemia is present, especially when there is evidence of bleeding, as with placenta previa and abruptio placenta. In these situations when an infant is hypotensive, plasma expanders are indicated. Whole blood is preferable but frequently not available; however, in an emergency situation, whole blood may be obtained from either the mother or the placenta (see Chapter 27). It is very important in these situations to avoid overheparinization of the blood, and it is mandatory to maintain absolute sterility. If blood is obtained from the placenta in a heparinized syringe, it is discarded if not used after 30 to 60 min.

Although plasma expanders are indicated for hypotension in the delivery room, care must be taken to avoid overadministration as this may result in fluid overload with congestive heart failure and pulmonary edema. In addition, the overuse of plasma expanders may alter cerebral blood flow, especially in the neonate whose autoregulatory mechanisms are probably impaired, and might predispose to intracranial hemorrhage. Therefore if hypotension in the neonate does not respond to ventilation, oxygenation, and plasma expanders (10 to 20 ml/kg), considerable thought should be given before repeating the dose of plasma expanders.

Stressed infants have an impaired ability to maintain glucose homeostasis. To avoid this complication, a 10% glucose solution is started intravenously. In the severely depressed baby, it may be necessary to administer 10 to 25% dextrose in water (2 to 4 ml/kg) by slow-push infusion.

When narcotic analgesics given to the mother may be contributing to the respiratory embarrassment, naloxone may be beneficial. Naloxone is preferred over nalorphine because of the latter's potential respiratory depressant effects.

Nearly all asphyxiated infants have respiratory and metabolic acidosis. The treatment of acidosis in the neonate is directed primarily at the underlying cause, i.e., asphyxia. Thus respiratory acidosis (low pH and increased pCO_2) is treated with ventilation and oxygenation. Metabolic acidosis (low pH and normal or low pCO_2) is also initially treated with oxygenation and ventilation. The cornerstones to resuscitation and the treatment of asphyxia and acidosis in the newborn are oxygenation and ventilation, not the liberal use of alkali (sodium bicarbonate) solutions. If resuscitation is being carried out appropriately with proper ventilation and oxygenation, and the infant is still not responding, or if the blood gas shows a significant metabolic acidosis (base deficit greater than 10 mEq/liter), sodium bicarbonate may be administered. In cases of severe or prolonged asphyxia, sodium bicarbonate (2 to 3 mEq/kg) diluted with sterile water to 0.3 to 0.5 mEq/ml is given by slow infusion, i.e., over 5 min. Faster infusion rates or use of more concentrated solutions may result in hyperosmolar damage. Subsequent bicarbonate therapy should be administered more precisely based on quantitative serum acid-base studies.

The indications for aqueous epinephrine include cardiac arrest and severe bradycardia not responsive to routine resuscitation. It is administered either intravenously or by the intracardiac route. When given intravenously in the presence of compromised perfusion, it may be necessary to initiate cardiac massage to hasten the pharmacologic effect. A 1:10,000 dilution is given in a dose of 0.1 to 0.3 ml/kg after the bicarbonate injection. Calcium gluconate or calcium chloride may be necessary in cases where severe bradycardia persists despite the previous therapeutic measures.

UMBILICAL VEIN CATHETERIZATION

Umbilical vein catheterization is used for rapid accessibility to the vascular system during resuscitation of the newborn in the delivery room. *Cardiopulmonary resuscitation, especially pulmonary resuscitation (oxygen and ventilation), is the most important aspect of resuscitation in the newborn.* An intravenous line (umbilical venous catheter) is of secondary importance and is used only after appropriate cardiopulmonary resuscitation has been instituted.

Umbilical venous catheterization is relatively easy to perform but carries with it significant major complications, especially when performed by inexperienced personnel. Because of the high complication rate of umbilical venous catheters, the only indications are exchange transfusion and emergency access to the vascular system for resuscitation of the newborn. Complications with umbilical venous catheters include hemorrhage, infection, injection of sclerosing substances into the liver with subsequent hepatic necrosis, air embolism, vessel perforation, and possible electrical hazards. Strict technique for insertion and maintenance of catheters must be followed in order to minimize complications. Catheters are removed as soon as resuscitative efforts have been completed.

MANAGEMENT OF THE MECONIUM-STAINED INFANT

The meconium-stained infant with respiratory distress presents a special problem in resuscitation. A brief guide to the emergency care of this disorder is presented in Table 5. When confronted with a cyanotic, apneic, or flaccid new-

TABLE 5. *Management of meconium staining in the delivery room*

1. Before delivering shoulders, thoroughly suction the nose, mouth, and pharynx.
2. Immediately after delivery of the infant, repeat suctioning of upper airway, dry rapidly, and place under radiant warmer.
3. If baby is depressed or shows signs of respiratory difficulty, aspirate trachea with mouth-to-endotracheal tube suction.
4. Repeat suction until trachea is clear of meconium (not to exceed 60 sec).
5. Ventilate and resuscitate.
6. Aspirate meconium from stomach.

born infant, our first inclination is to provide ventilatory assistance. This tendency must be modified when meconium aspiration is suspected, for ventilation without clearing the airway may result in death. Whenever there is meconium- or blood-stained amniotic fluid, the physician or nurse rapidly, but carefully, suctions the mouth and nose upon delivery of the head (before delivery of the chest in vertex presentations). Immediately after delivery the upper airway is aspirated again; and if there is any indication of respiratory depression (low Apgar) and/or thick meconium is present in the oropharynx, deep suctioning of the trachea is performed under direct laryngoscopy. This can be accomplished within 30 to 60 sec by means of a DeLee catheter or via mouth-to-endotracheal tube suction and is repeated until the aspirate is clear.

Ten to 20% of all deliveries are complicated by meconium-stained amniotic fluid. Most of these infants do very well, and we do not believe that all of them need tracheal suction. Whenever the infant is depressed, as indicated by a 1-min Apgar score of less than 5 to 7 *or* there is thick meconium present, direct visualization and suction of the trachea are mandatory. On the other hand, if there is a small amount of thin meconium in the amniotic fluid, no meconium in the upper airway, *and* the infant is vigorous and crying immediately after birth, direct tracheal suction is probably not warranted. Because the child may deteriorate during prolonged tracheal suction, the entire procedure should take no more than 60 sec. Only after the meconium has been cleared from the trachea is ventilation by bag and mask or by endotracheal tube begun. Aspirating the stomach of all babies who are meconium-stained is also important to minimize the risk of repeated aspiration of regurgitated material.

Care of the resuscitated infant does not end after emergency resuscitation. Continued close monitoring of temperature, respiratory rate, heart rate, blood pressure, glucose, pO_2, pH, pCO_2, hematocrit, etc. is required in every infant severely depressed at birth. Appropriate attention to the stability of vital functions and metabolism is essential for early recognition and correction of the many sequelae which may follow periods of significant stress. Only with structured programs which provide training of adequate personnel and maintain proficiency in acute and convalescent management of neonatal asphyxia can the ultimate goal of eliminating preventable causes of psychomotor retardation be achieved.

CAVEATS

1. Every physician involved in the delivery of a newborn must be competent in neonatal resuscitation.

2. When high-risk factors predicting the need for resuscitation are present, advance preparation in the delivery room is indicated.

3. The need for resuscitation can be best assessed by evaluation of the respiratory and heart rates.

4. The most important aspects of resuscitation of the newborn are oxygenation and ventilation.

5. The most common reasons for an infant failing to respond to resuscitative efforts are technical problems in oxygenation and ventilation.

6. In almost all cases, infants may be adequately ventilated and oxygenated with a bag and mask.

7. In most cases, drugs are not needed to stabilize the patient with acute asphyxia in the delivery room.

8. Severe hypotension, if not responsive to oxygenation and ventilation, usually requires the administration of plasma expanders (5% protein or blood).

9. Respiratory acidosis is treated with ventilation, not drugs.

10. Metabolic acidosis is best treated by correcting hypoxia and hypotension.

11. Thorough suctioning of the oro- and nasopharynx (before delivery of the chest) in the meconium-stained infant prevents most cases of severe meconium aspiration.

8

Hypoglycemia, Infants of Diabetic Mothers

Hypoglycemia is frequently observed in the neonate. With proper screening and therapy, much of the associated morbidity and mortality is preventable.

SIGNS AND SYMPTOMS

Clinical manifestations of hypoglycemia (Table 1) include apnea, cyanosis, jitteriness, limpness, high-pitched cry, poor feeding, seizure, coma, sweating, and irregular or rapid respiration. Essentially, any abnormal clinical finding in the newborn is compatible with hypoglycemia. Therefore always include a blood sugar test in the evaluation of any abnormal infant.

DIAGNOSIS

The criteria for diagnosing neonatal hypoglycemia (Table 2) are different than those for the adult. In the premature infant, hypoglycemia has been defined as a whole blood sugar level of less than 20 mg% during the first 3 days of life and less than 30 mg% thereafter. In the full term infant, hypoglycemia has been defined as a whole blood sugar level of less than 30 mg% during the first 3

TABLE 1. *Clinical manifestations of hypoglycemia*

Apnea
Cyanosis
Jitteriness
Limpness
High-pitched cry
Poor feeding
Seizure
Coma
Sweating
Irregular respirations

REMEMBER: Whenever a neonate appears sick, always include a blood sugar test in the immediate workup.

TABLE 2. *Definition of hypoglycemia*

1. Premature: Blood sugar less than 20 mg% during the first 3 days of life; less than 30 mg% after 3 days.
2. Term infant: Blood sugar less than 30 mg% during the first 3 days of life; less than 40 mg% after 3 days.
3. Usually we attempt to keep the blood sugar level greater than 40 mg%.

days of life and less than 40 mg% thereafter. These values were established many years ago in fasting infants, and arguments can be advanced that they do not represent optimal levels. Blood glucose studies in healthy infants who nurse at delivery might provide this information, but these are not currently available. The effect of a blood sugar level of 20 or 30 mg% on an infant of any size or gestational age is not known. In addition, the tests used for screening for hypoglycemia are not as accurate as the usual laboratory chemical determinations. Therefore it is preferred to maintain a blood sugar level of greater than or equal to 40 mg% in the premature and the full term infant at all times.

The blood sugar level can be determined in a number of ways. The usual laboratory chemical determination (a specific glucose oxidase method) is the most accurate but requires 1 to 2 hr for completion in most clinical facilities. This delay is unacceptable if a baby has symptomatic hypoglycemia. Many hospitals therefore utilize the Dextrostix® (Ames Laboratory, Elkhart, Indiana) or similar commercially available screening tests for determining the blood sugar. In this simple method, whole blood is applied to the glucose oxidase-impregnated filter paper and washed with water after 60 sec. The color of the strip can be matched with the reference on the bottle and an approximate glucose value assigned. The Eyetone Reflectance Colorimeter or Ames Reflectance Meter may also be used. There are many potential problems with the Dextrostix and the reflectance meters which may affect the reliability of the glucose measurement, including delay in reading the strip, overwashing, inaccurate timing, too thin a film of blood, and improper storage of the Dextrostix. Moreover, substances in the blood such as uric acid and bilirubin occasionally result in underestimation of the glucose level.

Fortunately, the Dextrostix more often underestimates, rather than overestimates, the blood sugar level and is acceptable as a screening tool. An abnormally low blood glucose value by Dextrostix is checked by laboratory methods, although treatment should not be delayed until the results of the laboratory test are obtained. It seems reasonable to consider any infant with a Dextrostix less than 40 mg% as having hypoglycemia. Therapeutic modalities are discussed below.

CAUSES OF HYPOGLYCEMIA

A number of factors predispose the newborn to hypoglycemia. The most common associations (Table 3) include: infants of diabetic mothers, infants who

TABLE 3. *Cause of hypoglycemia*

1. Common causes
   a. Infants of diabetic mothers (IDM)
   b. Infants small for gestational age (SGA), especially premature SGA infants
   c. Infants large for gestational age (LGA)
   d. Prematurity
   e. Sepsis, asphyxia
   f. Hyaline membrane disease (HMD)
   g. Erythroblastosis (hemolytic disease)
   h. Low temperature
   i. Other illness
2. Less common causes
   a. Inborn errors of metabolism (galactosemia, amino acid disorders, fructosemia)
   b. Adrenal insufficiency
   c. Beckwith syndrome (macrosomia, macroglossia, omphalocele)
   d. Pancreatic tumors (increased insulin)
   e. Idiopathic

are small for gestational age (below the 10th percentile for weight for that particular gestational age), those large for gestational age, those who are premature, and those who exhibit infection, asphyxia, low Apgar scores, respiratory distress, erythroblastosis, and hypothermia. *Any sick infant is at significant risk to develop hypoglycemia.*

Other less common causes or associations include inborn errors of metabolism (amino acid disorders), adrenal insufficiency, Beckwith-Wiedemann's syndrome (omphalocele, large tongue, hypoglycemia, and macrosomia), islet cell tumors of the pancreas, and nesidioblastosis.

It is important to know which infants are most likely to develop hypoglycemia and to institute routine screening in all infants at risk before symptoms occur. The infants described above should have frequent screening tests from the first hours or minutes of life. One test per day is inadequate screening for infants at risk for hypoglycemia.

TREATMENT OF HYPOGLYCEMIA

Infants with asymptomatic hypoglycemia, hopefully the largest group of infants, are fed as soon as possible if they can tolerate the feeding (Table 4). If the infant is premature with a poor suck, feeding is not appropriate, and the infant is given an intravenous infusion; however, if the infant has a good suck and is vigorous, early feeding may be instituted with follow-up screening. Usually D_5W or formula is given. Oral $D_{10}W$ is avoided as a routine feeding as it is a hyperosmotic solution which may cause gastrointestinal disorders, particularly in premature infants.

Prevention is much better than treatment. Symptomatic hypoglycemia is prevented by screening high-risk infants. Most infants who develop hypoglycemia are in one of the high-risk categories discussed above. If the infant is symptoma-

TABLE 4. *Treatment of hypoglycemia*

---

1. *Prophylactic:* In infants likely to develop hypoglycemia, feed early, if possible.
2. *Asymptomatic infants:* If alert and sucking, begin feeding with D_5W. If not sucking, start IV with $D_{10}W$. Glucagon 1 mg i.m. may be used as a temporary measure while attempting placement of an IV.
3. *Symptomatic infants:* $D_{10-25}W$ 2 to 4 ml/kg i.v. push. Then $D_{10-15}W$ 75 to 150 ml/kg/day i.v. by infusion pump to maintain normal blood sugar. Always decrease intravenous glucose *slowly*, in steps. Do not stop intravenous $D_{15}W$ suddenly or hypoglycemia will probably recur.
4. *Intractable hypoglycemia:* Occasionally steroids (cortisone acetate 5 mg/kg/day in three divided doses) may be necessary if normal blood sugar cannot be maintained with intravenous $D_{15}W$ or $D_{20}W$ 100 to 200 ml/kg/day.

---

tic with a Dextrostix test indicating a blood sugar level of less than 40 mg%, a blood sample is sent to the laboratory immediately for further testing. As soon as this is done (within minutes after the Dextrostix), an intravenous infusion is started in a peripheral vein and $D_{10}W$-$D_{25}W$ (2 to 4 ml/kg) is given over a few minutes. $D_{10}W$ to $D_{15}W$ is then started by continuous intravenous drip through the peripheral infusion. Usually 75 to 150 ml/kg/day is required. This is given by a constant infusion pump to avoid dramatic fluctuations in the glucose level.

In some situations it is difficult to place a peripheral intravenous apparatus (IV), or the physician may not be readily available. (Nurses who work in newborn nurseries should learn the technique of inserting the peripheral IV needles.) If the infant is alert, active, and vigorous with a good suck, early feedings may be instituted until an IV can be placed. Glucagon (1 mg i.m.) may be used as a *temporizing* measure to increase the blood sugar. However, in infants who have low liver glycogen stores (e.g., SGA infants), glucagon is probably contraindicated. Again, this is temporizing, not definitive, therapy.

Hypoglycemia may persist even in infants receiving intravenous $D_{10}W$-$D_{15}W$; these infants should continue to have frequent glucose monitoring even though they are receiving intravenous glucose.

Hyperglycemia must also be prevented. Hyperglycemia, especially in a premature infant, results in osmotic diuresis and possible dehydration. When an infant spills sugar in his urine, water may be lost with the sugar. In addition to blood sugar measurements, the urine from the infant on intravenous glucose is checked frequently (at least once per nursing shift) for glucose. If the infant is spilling glucose in the urine at more than 0.5 g%, the amount of glucose infused intravenously is decreased (if blood sugar levels are adequate or high). Osmotic diuresis secondary to hyperglycemia is especially common in infants under 1,500 g.

If an infant has severe hypoglycemia that does not respond to intravenous $D_{10}W$ or $D_{15}W$ at 100 to 200 ml/kg/day, further treatment is necessary. This may include placement of a central venous catheter in the inferior vena cava for administration of $D_{20}W$. Refractory hypoglycemia may rarely require steroid therapy. If intravenous therapy or steroids are required for more than 1 or 2 weeks, further diagnostic evaluation is necessary.

When decreasing the intravenous glucose dose, it is important to do so gradually. An abrupt withdrawal of intravenous $D_{10}W$ may produce rebound hypoglycemia. If an infant is receiving intravenous $D_{15}W$, for example, this should be changed to D_{10}, then to D_5, and then the rate gradually decreased over several days before it is discontinued.

PROGNOSIS

Infants who develop seizures secondary to hypoglycemia have a guarded prognosis, with perhaps 50% demonstrating permanent neurologic sequelae. Infants who have asymptomatic hypoglycemia or jitteriness secondary to hypoglycemia but no seizures usually have an excellent prognosis. This is a clear message that symptomatic hypoglycemia, or at least seizures from hypoglycemia, must be prevented when at all possible. Infants who are predisposed to hypoglycemia require frequent blood sugar screening and early treatment before seizures occur, thereby preventing permanent neurologic damage.

INFANTS OF DIABETIC MOTHERS

Diabetic pregnancies are common, as reflected by the fact that 1% of babies are the product of a diabetic or a gestational diabetic mother. With proper care of the mother, the fetus, and the newborn, almost all of these infants will be normal. However, management of the mother and neonate may present complex problems and usually requires collaborative efforts from the obstetric, internal medicine, and pediatric departments as well as the laboratory. Pregnant diabetic women are ideally managed in a high-risk obstetric center with a neonatal intensive care unit.

The appearance of the infant of the diabetic mother (IDM) as classically described includes: large for gestational age, obese, plethoric, and cushingoid with a large liver, spleen, umbilical cord, and placenta. However, many infants appear normal or may even be small for gestational age (usually in association with severe maternal diabetes with generalized vascular involvement).

Table 5 lists the complications that may occur in IDMs. The management of an IDM with respiratory distress is similar to that of other infants with this problem. If preventive measures are not taken, approximately 50% of IDMs will have hypoglycemia; of these, approximately half will be symptomatic if they are not treated appropriately.

Approximately 25% of IDMs have hypocalcemia as diagnosed by a serum calcium less than 7.5 to 8 mg%. This is thought to be due to an impaired responsiveness of the parathyroid glands. The treatment is the same as in other infants with hypocalcemia—calcium gluconate or calcium lactate. We usually screen each infant of a diabetic mother daily for the first 4 days. If the infant has symptomatic hypocalcemia, intravenous calcium with electrocardiographic monitoring is suggested. If the infant is not symptomatic, additional calcium

TABLE 5. *Problems of infants of diabetic mothers*

Respiratory distress
Hypoglycemia
Hypocalcemia
Hyperbilirubinemia
Congestive heart failure
Congenital malformations
Polycythemia
Renal vein thrombosis
Hypercoagulability
Sepsis
Prematurity

may be added to his daily intravenous fluids, or supplemental oral calcium provided.

Approximately 30% of IDMs have hyperbilirubinemia. The pathogenesis of hyperbilirubinemia in the IDM is not well understood but may be secondary to a number of factors, e.g., increased red cell mass, bruising or trauma secondary to the large birth weight, and a higher incidence of prematurity.

Approximately 10% of IDMs have congestive heart failure. These infants frequently have large hearts secondary to a cardiomyopathy, the etiology of which is not well understood. The symptoms of congestive heart failure are the same as in other infants—cardiomegaly, tachypnea, tachycardia, rales, hepatomegaly, and gallop. The therapy for the congestive heart failure may be different from that in other infants, as in many instances an obstructive cardiomyopathy (with septal hypertrophy) may be present; in these cases digoxin may be contraindicated. Most IDMs with cardiomegaly do not have structural heart lesions, and the cardiomegaly resolves over a few weeks. However, to complicate the issue there is also an increased risk of congenital heart defects in IDMs.

Although the literature is controversial, it appears that the incidence of congenital malformations is increased in infants of diabetic mothers. Examples include cardiac and skeletal malformations, although many other anomalies seem to have an increased incidence in infants of diabetic mothers. One of the classical congenital anomalies in IDMs is sacral agenesis, or the caudal regression syndrome. This syndrome demonstrates a wide spectrum, from mild sacral abnormalities to total fusion of the lower extremities (sirenomyelia).

Polycythemia, or an elevated hematocrit, is also common in infants of diabetic mothers. Polycythemia is diagnosed by a central (venous) hematocrit reading greater than 60 to 65%. Infants who have polycythemia and are symptomatic (respiratory distress, neurologic symptoms, hypoglycemia) are treated with a partial plasma exchange transfusion to lower the hematocrit (see Chapters 22 and 28). It is important to remember that a hematocrit obtained by a heel or finger stick may be as much as 10 hematocrit points higher than a venous stick. It is not known if a partial exchange transfusion is of benefit to an infant who has a central venous hematocrit value greater than 60 to 65% and is asymptomatic with no respiratory distress, cardiomegaly, or neurologic manifestations. However, if the infant is symptomatic, a partial exchange transfusion is performed.

Renal vein thrombosis also appears to occur with increased frequency in infants of diabetic mothers. The high incidence of this problem in the past may be related to a number of previously unrecognized factors including polycythemia and dehydration. Renal vein thrombosis presents with an enlarging renal mass, proteinuria, and gross microscopic hematuria. The treatment is controversial, but most experts advocate heparinization rather than surgery.

Hypercoagulability is also seen in infants of diabetic mothers. The incidence of major vessel clots (e.g., renal vein and major arterial thrombosis) is increased. Again, this may be related to polycythemia, although the etiology is not known.

Infection is more common in infants of diabetic mothers, possibly secondary to their more frequent prematurity. Any IDM is considered a possible candidate for sepsis. If the infant has any symptoms or signs suggestive of sepsis, blood, urine, and spinal fluid cultures are obtained and the appropriate antibiotic therapy instituted.

The care of the diabetic mother and her fetus and infant may be complex. These mothers and infants should be cared for in centers where there are high-risk obstetric intensive care units with obstetricians experienced in the care of high-risk pregnancies and where there are sophisticated neonatal intensive care units staffed with neonatologists. With the proper care of the mother, fetus, and newborn, most IDMs will be healthy children.

CAVEATS

1. Always perform a rapid glucose measurement in any sick neonate.

2. Infants at risk to develop hypoglycemia should have *frequent* glucose screening tests to prevent symptomatic hypoglycemia.

3. Attempt to maintain the serum glucose level at greater than or equal to 40 mg%.

4. Symptomatic hypoglycemia is treated immediately with intravenous glucose.

5. If hypoglycemia is treated before seizures occur, the prognosis is excellent. However, if seizures occur, perhaps 50% of infants will have permanent neurologic damage.

6. Management of the diabetic mother and her infant may present complex problems requiring the expertise available in high-risk obstetric centers with neonatal intensive care units.

7. The major acute problems of the infant of a diabetic mother include hypoglycemia, respiratory distress, hypocalcemia, congestive heart failure, and polycythemia.

9

Jaundice

Jaundice occurs in almost all newborns and usually causes no serious problems. However, if it is not treated appropriately, hyperbilirubinemia may result in serious brain damage in a small percentage of infants. It is more difficult to diagnose jaundice visually in the neonate than in adults. Usually the bilirubin level reaches 4 to 6 mg% before the jaundice becomes obvious. Jaundice may be less obvious at levels of 4 to 6 mg% in the black infant, and examination of the sclerae may be helpful in these infants.

METABOLISM

There are two types of bilirubin in the blood—unconjugated and conjugated. Unconjugated bilirubin (indirect) normally comprises more than 90% of all the bilirubin in the serum in newborn infants. Conjugated (direct bilirubin) should comprise no more than 10% of the total serum bilirubin, and the concentration should be less than 1 to 1.5 mg%.

The newborn produces between 8 and 9 mg bilirubin/kg/day—two to three times as much as the adult. The serum bilirubin concentration is related to the difference of bilirubin production and clearance. Any disorder that increases production or interferes with metabolism or excretion causes an elevation of the serum bilirubin.

Seventy-five percent of the bilirubin produced in the newborn comes from the breakdown of red blood cells (Fig. 1). One gram of hemoglobin, when metabolized to bilirubin, yields 35 mg bilirubin. Twenty-five percent of the bilirubin produced in the newborn results from ineffective erythropoiesis and the breakdown of other heme proteins. "Ineffective erythropoiesis" refers to red blood cells that undergo formation in the bone marrow but are destroyed before maturation to normal red blood cells.

The indirect bilirubin formed from the hemolysis of red blood cells is bound to albumin in the blood. It is then taken up by the liver cell and bound to Y and Z proteins. This unconjugated, or indirect, bilirubin is then conjugated in the liver by the enzyme glucuronyl transferase, which changes the bilirubin to the

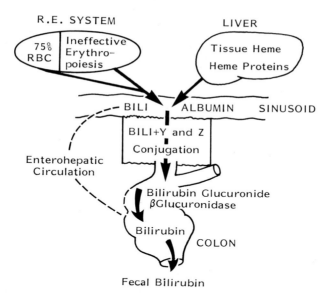

FIG. 1. Bilirubin metabolism in the newborn. (Modified from Maisels: *Pediatr. Clin. North Am.,* 19:452, 1972.)

direct or conjugated form. The conjugated bilirubin is then excreted in the bile. In the adult most of the bile is excreted in the stool after being metabolized by the normal intestinal bacteria. In the newborn, however, much of the bilirubin may be reabsorbed (in the enterohepatic circulation). This is the result of two characteristics peculiar to the newborn: (a) there are relatively few bacteria in the newborn's stool to break down the bilirubin; and (b) there is an enzyme in the newborn intestine called bilirubin glucuronidase that deconjugates the bilirubin, which enables it to be reabsorbed into the blood.

DIAGNOSTIC APPROACH TO THE JAUNDICED NEONATE

Table 1 lists some of the common causes of jaundice in the newborn. Hemolytic disease is most often due to Rh or ABO incompatibility. However, hemolysis may be secondary to other, more unusual immune or nonimmune hemolytic problems, e.g., hereditary spherocytosis. Liver disease is an unusual cause of jaundice during the immediate newborn period. Metabolic diseases such as hypothyroidism, galactosemia, and amino acid disorders are considered in the differential diagnoses of neonatal jaundice. Breast feeding may also be associated with jaundice *after* the first 3 to 4 days of life. The bilirubin level may remain elevated above normal levels for several weeks. The burden of proof of the diagnosis of breast milk jaundice is on the physician. Just because a breast-fed infant is jaundiced, one cannot conclude that the jaundice is secondary to the breast feeding. In these infants we recommend an approach to the diagnosis of jaundice, as described below, and discontinuation of breast feeding for 1 or 2 days. If the jaundice is secondary to the breast feeding, the bilirubin level de-

TABLE 1. *Most common causes of jaundice*

Physiologic jaundice
Hemolytic disease (usually Rh or ABO incompatibility)
Infection (congenital infection and postnatal sepsis)
Hematomas and bruising
High hematocrit (polycythemia)
Breast feeding
Liver disease (neonatal hepatitis, bile obstruction)
Metabolic disease (hypothyroidism, hypoglycemia, galactosemia)
Diabetic mother
Bowel obstruction

---

creases quickly, usually permitting prompt reinstitution of breast feeding without further problems.

Infants of diabetic mothers also have an increased incidence of jaundice. This may be secondary to the increased red blood cell mass, the bruising and trauma that occur because many of the infants are large, or the prematurity often associated with infants of diabetic mothers. Infants with high bowel obstruction may also have jaundice. Polycythemia, or an elevated hematocrit (venous hematocrit greater than 60 to 65%), can result in jaundice. Certain drugs that the mother receives may result in jaundice in the newborn. The most recently described drug suspected of causing neonatal jaundice is oxytocin.

Every time an infant presents with jaundice, the physician should mentally run through this differential diagnosis rather than assuming the cause to be physiologic jaundice. Physiologic jaundice is a diagnosis of exclusion made after other causes of jaundice have been ruled out. The correctable causes of jaundice (e.g., infection, hemolytic disease, bruising, hyperviscosity, bowel obstruction, and metabolic disorders) are especially considered in *all* infants.

When jaundice persists for a longer than normal period, one always considers hypothyroidism. Since persistent jaundice may be a presenting symptom of hypothyroidism in the newborn, a thyroxine (T_4) and/or thyroid-stimulating hormone (TSH) level is determined in any infant with a prolonged elevated indirect bilirubin.

The laboratory evaluation of the infant with jaundice comprises a basic or minimal workup for all infants and a more elaborate workup appropriate to selected infants. If an infant has jaundice to the degree that the physician is considering treatment (phototherapy or exchange transfusion), a basic minimal laboratory evaluation must be performed (Table 2). A complete history and physical examination—looking for signs of sepsis, congenital infection, bowel obstruction, hypothyroidism, and hepatosplenomegaly—are mandatory. The bilirubin level is measured, including a fractionated bilirubin (direct and indirect), in each infant. A blood type and Rh of the mother is also done. If there is a possibility of ABO incompatibility, an indirect Coombs test with A or B cells (anti-A or anti-B titer) is also done on the infant. The hematocrit and a peripheral blood smear are obtained. The blood smear is examined for abnor-

TABLE 2. *Laboratory evaluation of jaundice*

1. Minimal workup for all infants with significant jaundice (bilirubin more than 10 to 15 mg%, or more than 7 to 10 mg% if less than 24 hr old)
   a. Meticulous examination of infant for lethargy, cyanosis, large liver and spleen, signs of sepsis
   b. Direct and indirect bilirubin
   c. Blood type and Rh of mother
   d. Blood type, Rh, direct Coombs of infant (also indirect Coombs if ABO incompatibility suspected)
   e. Complete blood count (CBC) including examination of blood smear, reticulocyte count
2. Other studies sometimes indicated
   a. Blood and urine culture
   b. Spinal tap
   c. Urine for reducing substances (galactosemia)
   d. T_4
   e. Titers and cultures for congenital infection (syphilis, toxoplasmosis, cytomegalovirus, rubella)
   f. Further hemolytic workup
   g. Further hepatic workup
   h. Reserve albumin binding capacity
   i. "Free" serum bilirubin (Sephadex column)

mal red cells, which might suggest hemolysis from congenital spherocytosis or other red blood cell defect. A reticulocyte count greater than 7 to 10% also suggests a hemolytic disease.

Sepsis must also be seriously considered in any infant with jaundice. If the infant has any other symptom or sign suggestive of infection, blood, urine, and spinal fluid cultures are obtained and appropriate antibiotic therapy instituted.

The direct Coombs test (Fig. 2) measures antibodies that are attached to red blood cells. This test does not determine the type of antibody. That is, it is impossible to tell from a positive direct Coombs alone whether the finding is due to Rh, ABO, or some other immune hemolytic process. If this information is desired, an indirect Coombs, or antibody titer, must also be performed.

The indirect Coombs (Fig. 3), or antibody titer, tests for plasma antibodies that are not attached to red blood cells. With this test one may look for specific types of antibodies. For example, an indirect Coombs with A cells (also called anti-A antibody titer in some laboratories) tests specifically for anti-A antibody in the patient's plasma.

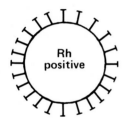

FIG. 2. The direct Coombs test for antibodies attached to red blood cells.

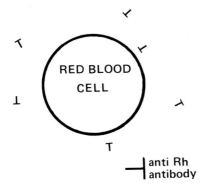

FIG. 3. The indirect Coombs test for antibodies in the plasma, not attached to red blood cells.

The above examinations include those obtained for every infant with a bilirubin considered high enough to warrant therapy. Table 2 lists other tests to be considered in selected infants. If sepsis is a possibility, blood and urine cultures, as well as a spinal tap, are performed. A urine specimen positive for reducing substances but negative for glucose suggests galactosemia. If a prolonged elevated indirect bilirubin suggests hypothyroidism, a T_4 and TSH are done. If there is evidence of congenital infection, cultures and titers for toxoplasmosis, rubella, and cytomegalovirus are performed. If the blood smear or reticulocyte counts suggest hemolysis, red blood cell tests for hereditary spherocytosis, pyruvate kinase deficiency, etc. are done. If hepatosplenomegaly of unknown etiology is present or the direct bilirubin is elevated, sepsis and hepatic disease are considered.

PHYSIOLOGIC JAUNDICE

The major problem with physiologic jaundice is that the burden of proof is on the physician to establish that it is in fact physiologic. The only way of doing this is to rule out all other etiologies. Physiologic jaundice is defined as an elevation (2 to 12 mg% in a full term infant and 2 to 15 mg% in a premature) of unconjugated bilirubin during the first week of life, with no other demonstrable cause. In the premature infant the bilirubin value reaches its peak at day 5 or 6. In the full term infant this occurs at day 3 or 4. *An elevated bilirubin, greater than 10 mg%, on the first day of life is never physiologic* (Fig. 4). A bilirubin greater than 15 mg% is probably not physiologic. A bilirubin less than 15 mg% may or may not be physiologic jaundice. The point is that in every infant with clinical jaundice the physician should seriously think of other causes of jaundice before diagnosing physiologic jaundice.

Physiologic jaundice is not considered when clinical jaundice persists beyond the eighth day of life in the full term infant or the 14th day in the premature. Also, physiologic jaundice is *never* the cause of direct hyperbilirubinemia (direct bilirubin greater than 1.5 mg%).

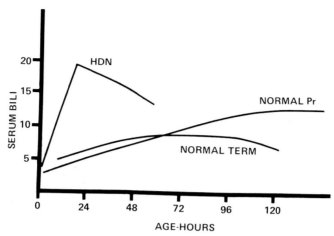

FIG. 4. Physiologic jaundice peaks at a later age in premature than in full term infants. Hemolytic disease of the newborn (HDN), e.g., Rh disease, usually presents with jaundice during the first 24 hr of life. (Pr) premature.

Rh AND ABO INCOMPATIBILITY

With Rh incompatibility, the Rh-negative (Rh⁻) mother may be sensitized by receiving mismatched blood (Rh⁺), aborting an Rh-positive (Rh⁺) fetus, or, as is usually the case, carrying her first Rh⁺ fetus. It is fortunate that most Rh⁻ mothers who have Rh⁺ fetuses never have problems with hemolytic disease. The severity of the disease, when it occurs, increases with each subsequent pregnancy with an Rh⁺ fetus. During the first pregnancy the red blood cells from the Rh⁺ fetus enter the Rh⁻ mother's circulation late in gestation or near the time of delivery. Fetal-maternal transfusion occurs in the majority of pregnancies. The mother then becomes sensitized to the Rh⁺ red blood cells and synthesizes anti-Rh antibodies, which may result in hemolysis and hyperbilirubinemia in the next Rh⁺ offspring. The severity of the disease increases with each successive Rh⁺ fetus.

ABO hemolytic disease is more common but much less severe than that resulting from Rh incompatibility. ABO hemolytic disease may occur during the first pregnancy as these are naturally occurring antibodies. Usually the mother is type O and the infant A or B. If a mother has one infant with ABO hemolytic disease, the chance of the disease becoming worse with the next ABO-incompatible pregnancy is approximately one-third—the same ratio that applies for the same or lesser degree of severity.

The management of a pregnancy complicated by Rh sensitization is extremely complex and is ideally supervised by a perinatal obstetrician in a center that has an obstetric intensive care unit and a neonatal intensive care unit staffed by neonatologists. Pregnancies following previous ABO hemolytic disease are managed as normal pregnancies.

The prevention of Rh disease is important. Rho Gam®, or anti-D antibody, administered to the Rh⁻ mother after the first Rh⁺ pregnancy or abortion (spontaneous or other) prevents most cases of Rh sensitization. If a delivery is traumatic and involves manipulation of the placenta, a larger amount of fetal blood may cross into the mother, and consideration is given for using a larger dose of Rho Gam. One of the more common causes of Rh sensitization and Rho Gam failure is improper administration of Rho Gam. Rho Gam is not necessarily contraindicated for a mother who is O Rh⁻ and has an A Rh⁺ fetus with a positive direct Coombs. It is important to remember that the direct Coombs tests for antibodies on the red blood cells but does not determine which antibody is present. In the case described above, the positive direct Coombs may be due to either ABO or Rh incompatibility, and therefore it would be important to do an anti-Rh titer on the mother or baby. If the Rh titer is negative, then Rho Gam is indicated. In addition, the positive direct Coombs could be due to the presence of some other unusual antibody, rather than anti-D, anti-A, or anti-B.

THERAPY OF HYPERBILIRUBINEMIA

There are basically three modes of therapy: (a) exchange transfusion; (b) phototherapy; and (c) drugs to induce enzyme production. Phenobarbital has been administered to mothers to induce glucuronyl transferase enzyme and decrease the level of jaundice, but the routine use of phenobarbital in pregnant women or neonates cannot be recommended because the potential harmful effects of phenobarbital are not known.

Table 3 presents guidelines and indications for exchange transfusions. Phototherapy might be instituted at a bilirubin concentration of 5 mg% less than (or one-half) the exchange level. It is most important to remember that these are only guidelines. In all instances, "bilirubin" in Table 3 refers to the indirect bilirubin level. The decision as to when to perform an exchange transfusion is a very difficult one. In a healthy full term infant at 3 days of life, an indirect bilirubin of 20 mg% is an adequate indication for an exchange transfusion; whereas in a 1,000-g critically ill infant on a respirator, a bilirubin of 10 mg% may justify an exchange transfusion. Also, if the jaundice occurs very early, during the first 24 hr of life, and is due to Rh incompatibility or other hemolytic disease, an exchange transfusion may be indicated.

We emphasize again that Table 3 provides guidelines, not rules. At this time the best criteria for deciding whether to "exchange" a patient is the indirect bilirubin level and the clinical situation. Currently, laboratory tests such as a Sephadex test (Kernlute®, Ames Laboratory, Elkhart, Indiana) to predict the risk of kernicterus by measuring the "free" (loosely bound) serum bilirubin level have not been proved effective. If such tests are used to increase one's suspicion of the risk of kernicterus and to exchange a patient earlier, they may be helpful;

TABLE 3. *Serum levels of indirect bilirubin and exchange transfusion* [a]

Birth weight (g)	Serum bilirubin level for exchange transfusion (mg/100 ml)	
	Normal infants [b]	Abnormal infants [c]
<1,000	10.0	10.0 [d]
1,001–1,250	13.0	10.0 [d]
1,251–1,500	15.0	13.0
1,501–2,000	17.0	15.0
2,001–2,500	18.0	17.0
>2,500	20.0	18.0

Data from *Standards and Recommendations for Hospital Care of Newborn Infants,* p. 95. American Academy of Pediatrics, 1977.

[a] These guidelines have not been validated.

[b] Normal infants are defined for this purpose as having none of the problems listed in footnote c.

[c] Abnormal infants have one or more of the following problems: (a) perinatal asphyxia; (b) prolonged hypoxemia; (c) acidemia; (d) persistent hypothermia; (e) hypoalbuminemia; (f) hemolysis; (g) sepsis; (h) hypoglycemia; (i) elevated free fatty acids or presence of drugs which compete for bilirubin binding; (j) signs of clinical or central nervous system deterioration.

[d] There have been case reports of basal ganglion staining at levels considerably lower than 10 mg.

if they delay an exchange transfusion in a patient whom you otherwise would "exchange," they may be dangerous indeed.

Exchange transfusions are major, dangerous procedures. They should be performed only by pediatricians who do many—not one or two—per year. Exchange transfusions, especially when done by inexperienced personnel, are associated with significant morbidity and mortality.

Phototherapy appears to work by breaking down bilirubin. However, the breakdown products and the possible effects of these products are not well understood. Possible harmful effects of phototherapy include loose stools, skin rashes, tanning of the skin, and cholestasis. Another important concern is that it may obscure the diagnosis. For example, in an infant with prolonged hyperbilirubinemia due to hypothyroidism, the bilirubin level decreases if the infant is subjected to phototherapy, obscuring a clinical sign that would otherwise be available to the physician as a "red flag" that something is wrong and thereby raise the possibility of hypothyroidism. The phototherapy lights may overheat the infant and dramatically increase water requirements. If infants with hemolytic disease are treated with phototherapy rather than exchange transfusion, hemolysis may continue for many weeks, resulting in late anemia.

Phototherapy is considered a drug and is not used unless clearly indicated. It should not be used prophylactically to prevent jaundice, and it should not be used routinely in full term infants. A bilirubin of 10 to 15 mg% in full term infants is probably not an indication for the use of phototherapy. Table 4 lists some guidelines for the use of phototherapy. Remember, *phototherapy is not used without serious deliberation.*

TABLE 4. *Guidelines for use of phototherapy*

1. Etiology of jaundice must be evaluated.
2. Do not use light therapy prophylactically.
3. Use light therapy in infants in whom risk of hyperbilirubinemia outweighs risks of light.
4. Infants for whom exchange is indicated do not have their transfusion delayed for trial with light therapy.
5. Light therapy is not started until an abnormal rise in bilirubin has been demonstrated.
6. Check irradiance of lamps or replace lamps regularly.
7. Eyes are patched and corneal ulceration guarded against. Examine frequently for conjunctivitis.
8. Body temperature is monitored closely.
9. Follow-up is essential.
10. Rebound may occur when therapy is discontinued.
11. Delayed severe anemia is common with hemolytic disease.
12. Do not use with elevated direct (conjugated) bilirubin.

KERNICTERUS

Kernicterus is characterized pathologically by yellow staining of the brain, particularly the basal ganglia and hippocampus, secondary to deposits of indirect bilirubin. The early manifestations of kernicterus include lethargy, poor feeding, high-pitched cry, vomiting, and hypotonia. Late manifestations appearing after weeks, months, or years include irritability, hypertonia, opisthotonus, seizures, impaired mental function, deafness, and movement disorders (athetosis).

Indirect bilirubin is the fraction that enters the brain and causes kernicterus. To cross the brain, it must be *free* indirect bilirubin, not bound to albumin in the blood. Only a very small percentage of the bilirubin in the blood (less than 0.01%) is free (Fig. 5). At this time there are no reliable clinical tests available to measure free bilirubin, although many tests to evaluate free bilirubin or to assess the saturation of serum bilirubin have been devised (2-[4-hydroxy-benzeneazo] benzoic acid dye binding, salicylate saturation index, Sephadex, red

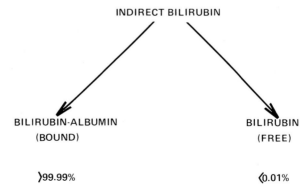

FIG. 5. Most of the indirect (unconjugated) bilirubin is bound to protein. Only free bilirubin (not bound to protein) can cause kernicterus.

cell or mitochondrial bilirubin content, hematofluorometry, peroxidase enzymatic determination of free bilirubin, and fluorescent quenching method for measuring free bilirubin). None of these have been proved to be clinically useful for managing patients with jaundice.

Therefore the physician must still use the indirect bilirubin level and the clinical situation to decide when to institute therapy for jaundice. Although it is not known what level of bilirubin is safe in the various clinical situations, factors such as prematurity, acidosis, hypothermia, hypoalbuminemia, hypoglycemia, infection, and certain drugs (sulfa, aspirin, and caffeine benzoate) increase the risk of kernicterus. Premature infants with indirect bilirubin values no greater than 9 mg% have developed kernicterus.

CAVEATS

1. Jaundice (bilirubin greater than 10 mg%) during the first 24 hr of life is always pathologic, never physiologic.

2. Physiologic jaundice is a diagnosis of exclusion made after other causes of jaundice have been considered.

3. Physiologic jaundice is never the cause of direct hyperbilirubinemia.

4. When jaundice persists for a longer than normal period, hypothyroidism is considered.

5. When a breast-fed infant becomes jaundiced after 4 to 5 days of age, the burden of proof of the diagnosis of breast milk jaundice is on the physician.

6. One of the common causes of Rho Gam failure is improper administration.

7. Routine use of phenobarbital in pregnant women or neonates to decrease the level of jaundice cannot be recommended.

8. Prematurity, asphyxia, hypoxia, acidemia, hypothermia, hypoalbuminemia, sepsis, and certain drugs increase the risk of kernicterus.

9. Phototherapy is not used without serious deliberation and is never used prophylactically to prevent jaundice.

10. Laboratory tests to predict the risk of kernicterus by measuring "free" (loosely bound) serum bilirubin have not been proved effective.

11. The physician must still use the indirect bilirubin level, the clinical situation, and ancillary laboratory data to determine when to initiate therapy for jaundice.

10

Approach to the Newborn with Respiratory Distress

The main clinical findings in a neonate with respiratory distress are cyanosis, tachypnea, grunting, flaring, and retractions (Table 1). Central cyanosis with bluish discoloration of the mucous membranes indicates a level of reduced hemoglobin of 5 g/liter or more. The normal infant may require 10 to 20 min to be relieved entirely of central cyanosis after he is born. Central cyanosis must be differentiated from peripheral cyanosis (acrocyanosis). Acrocyanosis (cyanosis of the hands and feet) commonly seen in full term newborn babies, is thought to reflect sluggish peripheral blood flow in response to a cool environment. Peripheral cyanosis may persist for days in the normal newborn and is *not* considered a sign of difficulty. Central cyanosis, on the other hand, is *always* regarded as a pathologic sign and *always* requires immediate evaluation. Cyanosis does not occur in newborns (who have a high percentage of fetal hemoglobin) until the oxygen tension is much lower than it is in an adult. In adults, cyanosis occurs at oxygen tensions of 45 to 55 mm Hg, whereas in the newborn cyanosis may not be evident until the pO_2 is less than 30 to 40 mm Hg. Because of the steepness of the oxyhemoglobin dissociation curve at this pO_2, further decreases in the pO_2 may be life-threatening for the infant.

A number of factors may interfere with prompt recognition of cyanosis. In a dark room, cyanosis may not be recognized as quickly as in a room that is brightly lighted. Thus babies under observation during the first few hours after birth should always be kept in a well-lighted room. In black babies one must be careful to look at the tongue and mucous membranes. The recognition of central cyanosis also depends on the hemoglobin level. Cyanosis requires the presence of at least 5 g of *unsaturated* hemoglobin. Note that in some cases the anemia may be profound and the baby has a markedly reduced oxygen tension, but there is an inadequate amount of unsaturated hemoglobin for cyanosis to be clinically evident.

Tachypnea in the newborn is defined as a respiratory rate of greater than 60/min. Normal babies establish an efficient respiratory rate of 40/min within a

TABLE 1. *Signs of respiratory distress*

Cyanosis
Tachypnea (greater than 60/min persistently)
Tachycardia (greater than 160/min persistently)
Retractions
Grunting
Nasal flaring

few hours after birth. A respiratory rate above 50/min is suspicious, and a respiratory rate above 60/min requires evaluation. It is impossible to recognize tachypnea unless one counts the respiratory rate. Vital signs are taken at regular intervals for every baby upon entering the nursery. A baby suspected of having difficulty has vital signs measured every 15 min during the first hour.

Because the baby's thoracic cage is very compliant, he depends almost entirely on the diaphragm to increase his chest volume. As the compliance of the lung decreases owing to increased severity of pulmonary disease, the retractions increase and a see-saw respiration pattern develops. As the diaphragm descends to increase thoracic volume, the abdominal contents are pushed down and therefore raise the abdominal wall. The baby's attempt to increase thoracic volume by contracting the diaphragm, coupled with the decreased compliance of the lung, produces severe retraction.

Expiratory grunting is seen typically in hyaline membrane disease but may also be noted with other respiratory problems. The grunting, produced by expiration against a partially closed glottis, is an attempt by the baby to increase his intrathoracic pressure during expiration in order to increase his lung volume at the end of expiration. Grunting with mild respiratory distress may be audible only with a stethoscope. As the baby becomes more severely affected, the grunting may be heard with the unaided ear.

HISTORY AND PHYSICAL EXAMINATION

Optimal care of the newborn infant depends to a great extent on anticipating problems. Once a problem has developed, we may never retrieve the initial advantage available with prevention or early treatment. For care of the newborn, just as in general pediatric and adult medicine, we depend on the history and physical examination. We often fail to think of the newborn as having a significant history, but he does (Table 2). Has the mother had premature infants previously? Has she had cervical incompetence? Has she had babies with hyaline membrane disease? Has she had previous small for gestational age infants? What was her estimated date of confinement, and how was it determined? Answers to these questions help assess how premature the baby may be and the possible etiology of the respiratory distress. What medications was the mother taking? Was she a diabetic receiving insulin that might cause the baby to develop hypoglycemia and other related problems? Was she on drugs (e.g., heroin,

TABLE 2. *Important points in the history*

1. Previous obstetric performance of mother
2. Length of pregnancy
3. Maternal medications (e.g., reserpine, hypnotics, antibiotics)
4. Maternal medical disease (e.g., diabetes, hypertension, heart disease, infection)
5. Complications of pregnancy (e.g., toxemia)
6. Maternal serology for syphilis
7. Abnormalities of monitoring during labor
8. Time of rupture of the membranes
9. Nature and amount of amniotic fluid (e.g., meconium, pus)
10. Prepartum or intrapartum bleeding
11. Infant's presentation (e.g., breech, face)
12. Route of delivery
13. Apgar scores
14. Details of resuscitation
15. Placental abnormalities (e.g., pallor, abruption, infarction)
16. Feeding history (e.g., excessive salivation, vomiting, lethargy)
17. Pattern of vital signs

methadone, Darvon®, or phenobarbital) that might cause withdrawal symptoms in the baby? Did she have any signs of toxemia that predispose the baby to be small for gestational age? Did the mother receive large doses of magnesium sulfate leading to high magnesium levels in the baby that may interfere with respiration? Did the mother have any infection (e.g., of the urinary tract) that might predispose the baby to sepsis? What was the mother's serology?

The events of labor and delivery are even more important. Was the labor spontaneous or induced? Was it prolonged? Was the fetal heart monitored frequently or electronically? If so, were there signs of fetal difficulty? When were the membranes ruptured, and did this happen spontaneously or artificially? What was the nature of the amniotic fluid? Was it meconium-stained or clear? Was the amount of amniotic fluid normal? Prolonged rupture of membranes, particularly with maternal fever, makes us very suspicious of infection in the baby with respiratory distress. If the amniotic fluid is meconium-stained, meconium aspiration becomes much more likely. Polyhydramnios makes us suspicious of esophageal atresia or some other bowel obstruction. Scanty amniotic fluid makes us think of those syndromes that are related to poor renal output, e.g., Potter's syndrome and its associated hypoplastic lungs and respiratory distress. Placenta previa or any vaginal bleeding suggests anemia and hypovolemia in the newborn infant with respiratory distress. As one can see, prior to the baby's birth there are many clues as to what his problems might be.

Observations at the delivery are also important. What was the baby's presentation? If the baby was breech, he is more likely to have asphyxia and head trauma or, more rarely, spinal cord damage with paralysis of the respiratory muscles. Because the latter damage usually occurs below C-5, this baby would have only diaphragmatic breathing. After breech or vertex deliveries in which the baby may sustain a brachial plexus injury or clavicular fracture, an ipsilateral phrenic nerve paralysis is suspected. The paralyzed diaphragm secondary to such injury can often be diagnosed only by fluoroscopy. The Apgar score also helps determine whether the baby was asphyxiated, how severe the asphyxia might have been, and how quickly he recovered. Whether meconium was aspirated from the hypopharynx, as well as the quality and quantity of the meconium, may help evaluate the baby in whom meconium aspiration is suspected. Difficulties in the resuscitation may lead us to suspect a pneumothorax.

The placenta should not be omitted. The appearance of the placenta is an essential part of the history of every newborn. If the placenta is infarcted or small, or if the umbilical vessels have an abnormal placental insertion, placental insufficiency or blood loss in the baby may be suspected. A blood clot on the maternal surface of the placenta may be indicative of partial abruptio, making hypovolemia and anemia more likely in the infant.

What was the baby's history in the nursery? What were the initial temperature, pulse, respirations, and blood pressure? Excessive salivation or regurgitation of feedings may indicate esophageal atresia. Lethargy and refusal to feed suggest infection or central nervous system damage. Repeated and careful nursing observations during the first minutes and hours after the baby's arrival in the nursery are highly valuable.

The physical examination of the newborn is as important as an adequate and careful history. The vital signs are indeed vital. A low temperature may be the tip-off to an infected baby. On the other hand, a hyperthermic baby may develop significant respiratory distress in an effort to supply the extra oxygen demands that hyperthermia creates. A rapid heart rate suggests shock or pulmonary edema from congestive heart failure. A blood pressure determination (usually by Doppler technique) is essential. Hypovolemia and shock may be the sole, or a contributing, cause of respiratory distress. The careful estimation of gestational age using the appearance of ears, skin, nipples and breast tissue, genitalia, and sole creases makes the etiology of respiratory distress easier to determine. Meconium aspiration rarely occurs in a very premature baby, and hyaline membrane disease is rare in a term or postterm infant. Examination of the nose for patency is indicated. The mouth and tongue are examined to ensure that the patient does not have micrognathia accompanied by posterior displacement of the tongue and resultant respiratory distress. A feeding tube is passed through the mouth into the esophagus to ensure that the esophagus is patent to the stomach. The most common type of tracheo-esophageal fistula is the blind esophageal pouch with the lower esophagus connected to the trachea. The configuration of the chest is noted. An increased anterior-posterior (AP) diameter is usually associated with meconium aspiration or transient tachypnea of the newborn. A very small chest may be associated with other congenital anomalies. Auscultation of the chest should not be overlooked. A generalized decrease of breath sounds is typical of hyaline membrane disease. Inequality of the breath sounds heard on one side compared to the other may be associated with pneumothorax or diaphragmatic hernia. If bowel sounds are heard on the side of the chest in the absence of good breath sounds, the diagnosis of dia-phragmatic hernia is nearly assured. Rales may be heard in hyaline membrane disease and pulmonary edema. Coarse rhonchi and adventitious sounds are usually associated with foreign matter in the airways, especially meconium aspi-ration. Auscultation of the heart and observation of the precordium can help establish the diagnosis of congenital heart disease, particularly if a murmur is present.

Examination of the abdomen can help in the diagnosis of respiratory disease. If the abdomen is scaphoid, diaphragmatic hernia must be suspected. If the kidneys are not palpable, Potter's syndrome (renal agenesis with pulmonary hypoplasia) becomes a possibility. An enlarged liver and spleen may make us suspect erythroblastosis, a congenital viral infection, or that the mother is dia-betic.

The staining of skin and nails with meconium is noted, as are the peeling of the skin and the long nails characteristic of the postmature infant especially susceptible to asphyxia and meconium aspiration. A baby's tone and movement may be a clue to central nervous system difficulties. Are the peripheral pulses strong and equal? Is there a difference in pulses between the upper and lower extremities suggestive of coarctation of the aorta? Are the pulses uniformly weak, suggestive of hypovolemia or septic shock?

LABORATORY WORKUP

The minimum laboratory workup (Table 3) of the infant in respiratory diffi-culty includes a chest X-ray, hematocrit, white blood count, blood glucose de-termination, measurement of arterial blood gases, blood cultures, and possibly a shunt study (see *Disorders of the Heart,* below). The chest X-ray is the single most useful diagnostic test for determining the etiology of a baby's respiratory distress. If there has been a question of esophageal atresia, an orogastric feeding tube is left in place while the X-ray is being taken. If the baby requires oxygen, he remains in oxygen during the X-ray procedure. Under no circumstances is any newborn baby in respiratory distress removed from the nursery to the X-ray department for diagnostic chest X-rays. Chest X-rays are taken with the infant in his incubator and with a minimum of manipulation, without exposing the infant to cold or hypoxic stress.

TABLE 3. *Minimal diagnostic workup for infant in respiratory distress*

Chest X-ray
Arterial pO_2, pCO_2, pH
Hematocrit, white cell count
Blood glucose
Cultures (especially blood)
?"Shunt study" (arterial pO_2 in 100% O_2)

DIFFERENTIAL DIAGNOSIS

Upper Airway Obstruction

Newborns with upper airway obstruction (Table 4) frequently have inspiratory stridor. If the obstruction is secondary to a congenital malformation, the infant usually has a good Apgar score immediately after delivery, but within minutes he shows signs of upper airway obstruction (e.g., inspiratory stridor, nasal flaring, and severe retractions with very poor breath sounds on auscultation). Choanal atresia can be suspected by auscultating expired nasal air with a stethoscope and confirmed by carefully inserting a No. 5 or 8 French catheter through each nostril. Patients with severe laryngeal or tracheal obstruction usually require immediate endotracheal intubation.

Micrognathia, or small chin, is most commonly associated with a Pierre-Robin-like defect. The respiratory distress is secondary to the posterior displacement of the tongue, which obstructs the airway. This can be treated in a number of ways: placing the infant in the prone position, pulling the tongue forward, instituting endotracheal intubation, or, as we prefer in our nursery, using a nasopharyngeal tube (a 3.0 or 3.5 mm endotracheal tube).

The diagnosis of tracheo-esophageal fistula (TEF), most commonly associated with a blind proximal esophageal pouch, is suspected if polyhydramnios is present. After the infant is stabilized in the delivery room, we routinely pass a feeding tube through the mouth into the stomach. If obstruction is met, the diagnosis of esophageal atresia with TEF is immediately considered. Rarely, a soft catheter becomes coiled in the blind proximal esophageal pouch, and the diagnosis is delayed until an X-ray can be obtained.

Disorders of the Lung

The most common causes of respiratory distress in the newborn are pulmonary disorders. Hyaline membrane disease (HMD), or idiopathic respiratory distress syndrome, seen almost exclusively in premature infants, increases in incidence with shorter gestational ages. This disorder is associated with 30% of all neonatal deaths and 50 to 75% of the deaths of premature infants in the United States. Its prevention or proper management is of utmost importance.

HMD is due to surfactant deficiency. There are two factors which may lead to a decreased availability of surfactant. The first is a decreased number of surfactant-producing cells as seen in very immature infants; the number of type II pneumocytes decreases with decreasing gestational age. The second factor is some kind of stress that damages or kills the surfactant-producing cells. We know that for any gestational age group some infants are more likely to have HMD than others. In the case of twins, the firstborn twin is less likely to have it than the second. Hence, as these infants are of the same gestational age and have had approximately the same intrauterine environment until the time of labor and delivery, there must be another factor besides immaturity in the

TABLE 4. *Differential diagnosis of respiratory distress in the newborn*

1. Upper airway obstruction
   a. Choanal atresia
   b. Masses (encephalocele, tumor), large tongue
   c. Micrognathia
   d. Nasal stuffiness
   e. Cleft palate
   f. Laryngeal obstruction (paralysis, web, tumor, stenosis, atresia, malacia)
   g. Tracheal obstruction (mass, web, stenosis, atresia, malacia, cleft, vascular ring, goiter)
2. Pulmonary
   a. Hyaline membrane disease
   b. Transient tachypnea (wet lung, RDS II)
   c. Aspiration (meconium, gastric fluid, ?amniotic fluid)
   d. Pneumonia
   e. Pneumothorax, pneumomediastinum
   f. Persistent fetal circulation syndrome
   g. Tracheo-esophageal fistula
   h. Pulmonary hemorrhage
   i. Hypoplasia, agenesis
   j. Cystic disease (emphysema, cysts)
   k. Mikity-Wilson syndrome
   l. Pleural effusions (e.g., chylothorax)
3. Cardiac
   a. Cyanotic congenital heart disease
   b. Acyanotic congenital heart disease
   c. Arrhythmia (paroxysmal supraventricular tachycardia, block)
   d. Increased intravascular volume (iatrogenic fluid overload)
   e. High output failure (hyperthyroidism, A-V malformation)
   f. Pneumopericardium
   g. Cardiomyopathy (infection, endocardial fibroelastosis)
   h. Noncardiac causes of congestive heart failure (CHF): hypoxia, hypoglycemia, sepsis
4. Thoracic
   a. Chest wall deformities (chondrodystrophies, rib deformities)
   b. Masses (tumors, cysts)
5. Metabolic
   a. Hypoglycemia
   b. Infant of diabetic mother
6. Diaphragmatic
   a. Hernia (foramen of Bochdalek)
   b. Paralysis (phrenic nerve)
   c. Eventration
7. Neuromuscular
   a. CNS damage (trauma, hemorrhage)
   b. Medication (maternal sedation, narcotic withdrawal)
   c. Muscular weakness (myasthenia)
   d. Congenital defects
8. Infectious
   a. Sepsis
   b. Pneumonia (viral, bacterial)
9. Hematologic/vascular
   a. Hyperviscosity, hypervolemia
   b. Anemia
   c. Abnormal hemoglobin
10. Other
   a. Asphyxia
   b. Acidosis
   c. Hypothermia
   d. Hyperthermia

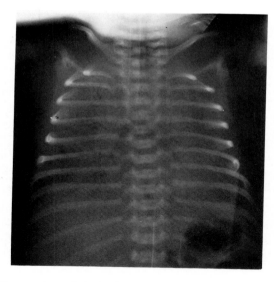

FIG. 1. Chest X-ray of a newborn infant with HMD. Note the ground-glass appearance, air bronchograms, and hypoaeration.

development of the surfactant system. Such factors include maternal bleeding, asphyxia, hypovolemia, acidosis, hypothermia, and oversedation.

Surfactant deficiency allows the lung to collapse at the end of each expiration. This lack of lung stability interferes with maintenance of arterial blood oxygenation and results in increased respiratory work by the patient.

The typical infant with HMD is a premature who experienced a problem during labor and delivery (e.g., placenta previa), some type II dips, or obstetric problems that required analgesia; or he is the second of twins. He may have had a moderately good Apgar score but was subjected to some stress in the delivery room (e.g., hypothermia or a circumcision) during which he was allowed to become cold, hypoxic, and hypoglycemic.

Respiratory symptoms usually appear very early. In the delivery room or within a very few hours, the baby develops a rapid respiratory rate and progressively worsening grunting, flaring, retractions, and cyanosis. The baby requires oxygen in increasing amounts. His respiratory rate rises until it is often over 100/min. The infant becomes progressively more obtunded and flaccid as all his efforts are concentrated on the work of breathing. He may become peripherally vasoconstricted with a pale color as well as cyanosis. He progressively develops edema, particularly of the hands and feet. Auscultation of the chest reveals decreased breath sounds. The chest X-ray in HMD (Fig. 1) is characterized by the reticular granular pattern of microatelectasis with air bronchograms beyond the heart border and, if the disease is severe enough, obliteration of heart borders, or a "white out." The chest X-ray also shows a generalized decrease of intrathoracic volume. By the third or fourth day, if other intervention has not been necessary, the baby's oxygen requirements may start to decrease, at which time ductal murmurs are frequently heard. In most infants the ductus closes spontaneously. With the decrease in respiratory rate, the baby may begin to feed and may recover within a week of the onset of the disease. Less fortunate infants require additional therapy, e.g., continuous positive airway pressure (CPAP) or respirator support.

Transient Tachypnea

Transient tachypnea of the newborn (TTN) or respiratory distress syndrome (RDS) type II typically occurs in the term or near-term baby. There are many similarities between transient tachypnea and HMD, but the course is quite different and the outlook much better in the former. Cesarean section seems to be particularly associated with RDS type II. These infants are nearly always appropriate for dates and either moderately or slightly depressed. They respond well to initial suctioning and minimal resuscitative efforts, and usually arrive in the nursery in good condition. However, when left alone and unstimulated, there may be some depression of cough, gag, and swallowing reflexes, with aspiration of secretions. The infant's initial respiratory efforts during these first few hours may be insufficient to clear all the fluid from the lungs. At a few hours of age, the baby is usually found to have respiratory symptoms almost identical to those of HMD: grunting, flaring, and retracting. Respiratory rates may reach very high levels. Supplemental oxygen is required. The respiratory distress and increased oxygen requirement usually last 24 to 48 hr, in contrast to the infant with HMD, who generally requires additional oxygen and does not improve until the third or fourth day of the disease. The chest X-ray with RDS type II, or TTN (Fig. 2), shows an increase in thoracic lung volume and clear, if not hyperlucent, peripheral lung fields. Sometimes a slight bulging of the pleura is seen between the ribs. Central markings are accentuated, and patchy infiltrates may be present. The AP diameter is increased, and the diaphragm tends to be flat.

Therapy of RDS type II, or TTN, is the same as for other respiratory diseases—primarily oxygen to relieve hypoxia and maintain the arterial blood gases so that the pO_2 is 50 to 70 mm Hg, the pH 7.25 to 7.40, and the pCO_2 at less than 50 to 55 mm Hg. As with other respiratory problems, supportive care of the infant is important. The infant with RDS type II, or TTN, usually does not require additional therapy such as CPAP or respirator therapy. However, some infants who present with a clinical picture similar to TTN progress to severe persistent fetal circulation (PFC), and so these infants must be treated carefully and skillfully.

Infection

Pneumonia with or without concurrent sepsis may occur in premature, term, or postterm babies and mimics HMD. This is particularly true for group B streptococcal sepsis. There may be a history of premature or prolonged rupture of the membranes and perhaps a slight maternal fever prior to the delivery. The

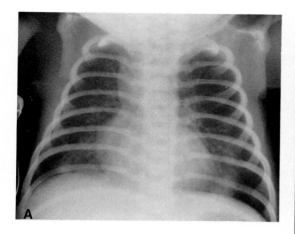

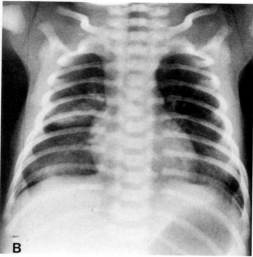

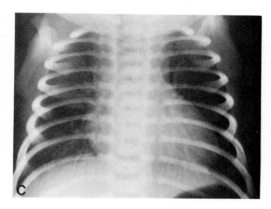

FIG. 2. Chest X-rays of newborn infants with TTN (wet lung syndrome). Note the hyperexpansion, bilateral infiltrates, and fluid in the fissures. All three infants had normal X-rays and were asymptomatic at 24 hr of age. However, these X-rays are also compatible with pneumonia, especially that caused by group B streptococcus; therefore blood, urine, and spinal fluid cultures were done and antibiotic administration instituted until cultures were proved negative.

infant may be born in excellent condition but within a few hours appear sick with significant respiratory distress. He may demonstrate grunting, flaring, retraction, and varying degrees of cyanosis, pCO_2 retention, or apnea. He may rapidly progress into septic shock. White blood counts are often ominously low—less than 5,000/mm³. X-ray films can be helpful in making the diagnosis. Since this syndrome is not easily distinguished from HMD or RDS II, one must be careful to obtain the appropriate cultures (blood, urine, cerebrospinal fluid). Antibiotics are started immediately and continued for at least 3 to 5 days, pending the results of the cultures.

Meconium Aspiration

In order to develop meconium aspiration, the infant must pass meconium sometime prior to birth. This may be a variable length of time. The presence of meconium in the amniotic fluid must be regarded as abnormal and appropriate individuals alerted to the possibility of fetal or neonatal complications. Although the great majority of infants who have meconium-stained amniotic fluid are normal at birth, the passage of meconium into the amniotic fluid indicates that an episode of asphyxia has occurred. Very premature infants seem not to pass meconium, however severe the asphyxia. The passage of meconium is so common in breech deliveries that it has been considered normal; however, the frequency with which meconium is passed in breech deliveries may also be related to the frequency with which asphyxia occurs in these babies.

The typical case of meconium aspiration, then, is a term or postterm infant. These infants often appear as if they had been fatter at some time prior to the delivery. The nails, cord, and skin are stained yellowish; and the cord, which often has very little Wharton's jelly, appears thin and dry. Vernix may be absent. The AP diameter of the chest is increased, and the chest barrel-shaped. The baby often breathes shallowly and rapidly. Rales and rhonchi are common. Hypoxia is often severe, complicated by a persistence of fetal patterns of circulation. The infant with meconium aspiration often does better during the first few hours after birth than he does at the end of the first day and into the second day. Often meconium aspiration is complicated by an episode of asphyxia with resultant seizures, bleeding diathesis, cardiomyopathy, and renal failure.

With meconium aspiration the chest X-ray tends to have a hyperinflated picture similar to that of RDS type II or TTN. The AP diameter is increased; the diaphragm is flat; the ribs tend to be elevated; and there may be some bulging in the intercostal spaces. The infant needs to be watched very closely for pneumomediastinum and pulmonary interstitial air which may progress to a pneumothorax. Because meconium is a good culture medium and because the baby has usually undergone a great deal of manipulation of his airway with suctioning and intubation, blood is obtained for cultures and the baby is given antibiotics. Skilled nursing care is essential. Pulmonary physiotherapy and postural drainage are indicated to help remove the foreign matter from the baby's lungs, except in the infant in whom interstitial air or pneumomediastinum is already present. In this event, further manipulation of the baby may cause vigorous crying and induce a pneumothorax or wide fluctuations in arterial oxygenation and resultant hypoxemia.

Infants with severe meconium aspiration have a significant mortality—up to 50% in many series. Much progress has been made in prevention. After the head is delivered either vaginally or by cesarean section and prior to delivery of the thorax, the baby's oropharynx and hypopharynx are carefully suctioned with the DeLee mucous trap or wall suction to remove all the meconium from the airway. If this cannot be done because of precipitous or breech delivery, the physician or nurse must do the same kind of careful suctioning prior to the onset of breathing. Some of the worst cases of meconium aspiration have been induced by the use of bag and mask resuscitation on an infant who is asphyxiated and meconium-stained. These infants respond very well to suctioning prior to respiration because they are not usually initiating their respirations spontaneously.

Other Pulmonary Disorders

Pneumothorax and pneumomediastinum are frequent in the newborn, occurring in as many as 0.5 to 1% of normal deliveries. Often this complication is asymptomatic and requires no therapy. Infants with HMD and meconium aspiration syndrome, as well as those on CPAP or respirators, are predisposed to this problem. Increasing the ambient oxygen concentration for a few hours for *full term*, mildly symptomatic infants may relieve the pneumothorax by the principle of nitrogen washout. Premature infants, babies with moderate to severe respiratory distress, and those with a tension pneumothorax usually require aspiration of the pneumothorax and/or placement of a chest tube (see Chapter 33).

Persistent fetal circulation syndrome (see Chapter 13) associated with prolonged elevation of the pulmonary artery pressure usually presents with severe hypoxemia and is often confused with cyanotic heart disease.

Disorders of the Heart

Congenital heart disease (CHD), either of the cyanotic or acyanotic type, often presents with respiratory difficulty. The most common causes of cyanotic heart disease recognized during the newborn period are transposition of the great vessels, hypoplastic right ventricle with tricuspid or pulmonary stenosis and atresia, total anomalous pulmonary venous return, truncus arteriosus, and single ventricle. When cyanotic heart disease is suspected, it is diagnostically helpful to obtain an arterial pO_2 on 100% oxygen ("shunt study"). In most infants with cyanotic heart disease the arterial pO_2 increases very little with the administration of 100% oxygen, whereas the increase is more dramatic when a primary lung disorder is present.

The most common cardiac causes of congestive heart failure in the newborn are patent ductus arteriosus, hypoplastic left ventricle, aortic stenosis and atresia, and coarctation of the aorta. These disorders usually present with congestive heart failure (Fig. 3). Cardiac arrhythmias, especially paroxysmal supraventricular tachycardia and congenital heart block, are also observed in the neonate. Other causes of cardiac failure in the newborn infant include hyperthyroidism, cerebral and hepatic arteriovenous (A-V) malformations, myocarditis, the cardiomyopathy of infants of diabetic mothers, endocardial fibroelastosis, hypoxia, hypoglycemia, and sepsis.

Disorders of the Thorax

Any disease which interferes with development of the thorax may interfere with respiratory function. Severe bone disorders (e.g., osteogenesis imperfecta and asphyxiating thoracic dystrophy) that present with respiratory distress are usually suspected clinically and confirmed radiographically.

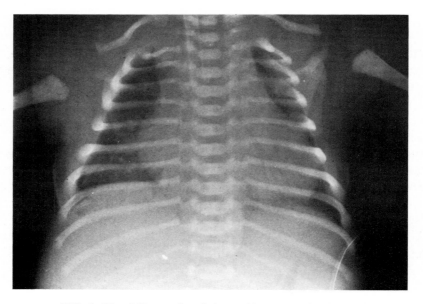

FIG. 3. Chest X-ray of an infant with congestive heart failure.

Metabolic Disorders

Hypoglycemia associated with significant respiratory distress is most commonly seen in infants with intra- or extrauterine stress; small for gestational age, postmature, or premature infants; and infants of diabetic mothers. The latter may have significant respiratory distress with increased pulmonary vasculature, pulmonary infiltrates, and cardiomegaly.

Disorders of the Diaphragm

Diaphragmatic disorders result in a wide spectrum of respiratory problems. Infants with phrenic nerve paralysis or eventration of the diaphragm frequently respond to conservative supportive therapy but may require surgical intervention. A diaphragmatic hernia (foramen of Bochdalek), usually on the left side, may present immediately after birth with severe respiratory distress. An increased AP diameter of the chest and a scaphoid abdomen suggest a diaphragmatic hernia in an infant with respiratory distress. An immediate chest X-ray is diagnostic. Therapy includes placement of a nasogastric tube for intermittent suction to decompress the stomach, endotracheal intubation, intravenous fluid, oxygen, acid-base correction, and emergency surgical intervention.

Neuromuscular Disorders

A variety of neuromuscular disorders—including birth trauma, intracranial hemorrhage, and the sequelae of maternal medications—may be associated with respiratory distress.

Infections

In addition to pneumonia, bacterial or viral septicemia is suspected in every infant with respiratory distress. Whenever the diagnosis of sepsis is considered, cultures are obtained and antibiotics started immediately.

Hematologic Disorders

Polycythemia (venous hematocrit above 60 to 65%) in the newborn may cause respiratory distress, neurologic disorders, and hypoglycemia. Appropriate therapy includes partial exchange transfusion in 10 to 20-ml increments with fresh frozen plasma or a 5% protein solution. Hypervolemia secondary to markedly delayed cord clamping or administration of fluids, as well as severe anemia secondary to erythroblastosis, fetal-to-fetal or fetal-to-maternal transfusions, obstetric complications at delivery, or iatrogenic causes, should be considered.

Miscellaneous

Respiratory distress may be seen in infants with metabolic acidosis, hypothermia, or hyperthermia.

CAVEATS

1. Central cyanosis is always abnormal and requires immediate evaluation.
2. The history and physical examination are helpful when evaluating and determining the etiology of neonatal respiratory distress.
3. The minimal laboratory workup of the neonate in respiratory distress includes a chest X-ray; determination of the hematocrit, white blood cell count, serum glucose and arterial blood gases; and a blood culture.
4. The etiology of HMD is surfactant deficiency, which in turn may be caused by prematurity or stress factors, e.g., hypoxia, hypotension, and hypothermia. These conditions must be prevented in order to decrease the risk of development and/or the severity of HMD.
5. Although TTN is normally a benign, self-limited disorder, some infants who present with a clinical picture similar to that of TTN progress to severe persistent fetal circulation.
6. Because neonatal sepsis and/or pneumonia are not easily distinguished from HMD or TTN, a blood sample for culture is obtained from each infant with respiratory distress and antibiotic administration instituted.
7. Most severe cases of meconium aspiration can be prevented by aspiration of the nasopharynx and oropharynx after the head is delivered.

11

Oxygen

PHYSIOLOGY

We usually do not consider that a person may be hypoxic with a normal arterial pO_2. However, hypoxia is defined as inadequate oxygenation to tissues, which may be effected by a variety of factors (Table 1). In general, those factors result in either (a) a decrease in the delivery of oxygen to tissues requiring the oxygen or (b) an increase in the oxygen requirement beyond the ability of the infant to meet these needs. For example, for oxygen to reach the periphery so that it can be consumed, it needs a carrier (i.e., hemoglobin) and a pump (i.e., the heart). Cardiac output is determined by the rate and the stroke volume. If something should interfere with either of these parameters (e.g., a pneumothorax impinging on the return of blood to the chest, a congenital complete heart block, or obstruction to output as may occur in congenital heart disease), cardiac output may be diminished. The result may be a decrease in delivery of oxygen to the periphery, even though oxygen may be present in the blood in high concentration.

Another factor which may compromise the delivery of oxygen to tissues is the amount of hemoglobin available to carry the oxygen. One gram of fully saturated hemoglobin carries 1.34 ml oxygen. (The amount of dissolved oxygen in plasma is generally negligible.) If a baby has a hemoglobin level of 15 g/100 ml blood, there is 20 ml oxygen/100 ml of blood. If his hemoglobin level is only 10 g/100 ml, the oxygen content of his blood when maximally oxygenated is reduced by 33%. In the face of pulmonary disease, an infant may not be able to completely oxygenate his blood and the resulting mild anemia may become a significant factor in his inability to deliver adequate oxygen to his tissues.

A related factor of importance in oxygen delivery is the oxyhemoglobin dissociation curve. There are a number of factors which decrease the amount of oxygen that hemoglobin takes up as it goes through the lungs (i.e., shifting the curve to the right), including acidosis, hyperthermia, and an increased pCO_2. These are avoided or treated when present, particularly in the infant with respi-

TABLE 1. *Factors affecting oxygen transport*

1. Amount of oxygen in the blood
   Hemoglobin concentration
   Partial pressure of oxygen (pO_2)
   Oxygen-hemoglobin affinity (P_{50}) (temperature, pH, pCO_2, 2,3-DPG, ATP, abnormal hemoglobin)

2. Delivery of oxygen
   Blood pressure and volume
   Cardiac output and distribution of flow
   Peripheral circulation
   Viscosity

3. Abnormalities in cellular metabolism
   Increased oxygen requirements (increased or decreased temperature, increased activity)

ratory distress, by correcting acidosis, preventing hyperthermia, and treating hypercapnia.

The second major group of problems to be avoided includes any stress which may increase oxygen consumption. Thermal stress is the principal cause of increased oxygen consumption in the newborn baby. Oxygen consumption may increase by 300% in the presence of either hyper- or hypothermia. Hypothermia is very common but can be minimized by attention to the details of basic newborn management. During resuscitation in the delivery room, a baby is wet, so he loses heat by evaporation. If he is put on a cold metal table, heat is lost by conduction. Air-conditioner drafts cause heat loss by convection. If the room is cold, the baby loses heat by radiation as well. All of these are avoided by prior preparation of a radiant warmer, a warm delivery room, heated towels, and a padded mattress on the radiant warmer. In the nursery, a sick infant is likely to be taken out of his isolette for emergency procedures such as X-rays and intubation. These actions with a sick, compromised infant put him at risk for an increase in the oxygen consumption he is unable to supply. Any baby who requires such procedures should be kept under an overhead warmer or have the procedures done inside the incubator if possible. Since muscular activity also increases oxygen consumption, a sick baby should be kept as quiet and comfortable as possible so he does not waste energy crying or reacting to unnecessary manipulation.

OXYGEN EXCESS AND DEFICIENCY

The hazards of oxygen excess or deficiency are varied and may be extremely serious. An increased pO_2 may be a factor in retrolental fibroplasia. An increased FiO_2 (inspired oxygen concentration) causes bronchopulmonary dysplasia or lung toxicity, decreases surfactant production, increases utilization of surfactant, and decreases mucous flow in the trachea. Hypoxia, or decreased

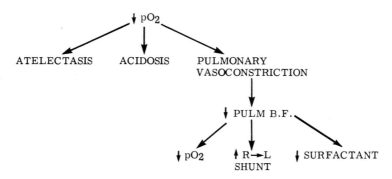

FIG. 1. Cardiopulmonary effects of hypoxia. A decreased pO_2 causes pulmonary vasoconstriction with decreased pulmonary blood flow and increased right-to-left shunting. These, in turn, cause further hypoxia.

oxygen supply to the tissues, can cause systemic vasodilation, pulmonary vasoconstriction, metabolic acidosis, tissue damage (particularly of the brain and kidney), increased risk of kernicterus, and impairment of surfactant production. As shown in Fig. 1, a low pO_2 in an infant with respiratory distress causes atelectasis, metabolic acidosis, and pulmonary vasoconstriction. This in turn decreases pulmonary blood flow, resulting in further hypoxia, increased right-to-left shunting, and decreased surfactant production.

It is worth re-emphasizing the importance of preventing hypoxia in all newborns. Hypoxia results in brain damage, mental retardation, and cerebral palsy. The morbidity and mortality from hypoxia is much greater than that resulting from excessive oxygen administration. Whenever there is a question concerning the amount of oxygen required, one should always err on the side of too much, rather than too little, oxygen until blood gas studies can be performed.

Retrolental Fibroplasia

Table 2 shows the dramatic history of retrolental fibroplasia (RLF). During the 1940s it was found that 50 to 100% oxygen relieved the periodic breathing of premature infants. This resulted in the routine use of oxygen in all premature infants. In 1942 the first description of RLF was published, and in 1952, after many studies and theories, oxygen usage was accepted as its cause. During the late 1950s the pendulum swung the other way and most infants were restricted to less than 40% oxygen. A dramatic increase in mortality and morbidity in prematures with respiratory distress was observed, in part due to the high incidence of hypoxia secondary to restricted oxygen use; of course, the incidence of RLF also decreased. Throughout this period, microtechniques for blood gas analysis were not available. Not until the late 1960s and 1970s was it technically feasible to monitor the arterial pO_2 intermittently, after which time there was another dramatic decrease in the incidence of RLF with an improvement in mortality and morbidity. Subsequently, the improvement in survival statistics in

TABLE 2. *History of retrolental fibroplasia*

Year	Event
1940	Routine, indiscriminate use of 50 to 100% O_2 for premature infants
1942	First description of RLF
1950	RLF the most common cause of blindness in institutions for the blind (infants and young children)
1952	Oxygen administration generally accepted as the etiology of RLF
1958	Period of O_2 restriction (FiO_2 less than or equal to 0.4), markedly decreased incidence of RLF, increased mortality and morbidity of respiratory distress
1960s	Monitoring of pO_2 and FiO_2 gradually becoming established practice; incidence of RLF low but still present
1970s	Increased survival of infants less than 1,500 g with increased incidence of RLF

infants less than 1,500 g during the 1970s was again accompanied by an increase in the incidence of RLF in these small babies.

It is important to know that RLF is still a common disorder and remains a frequent cause of blindness in children. Although some cases can be prevented by proper oxygen monitoring, even in the best newborn intensive care centers some infants less than 32 weeks' gestational age who have the most advanced oxygen monitoring still develop permanent RLF. A serious question that remains is whether with current modes of treatment it is either theoretically or practically possible to prevent all cases of RLF, especially in the very low birth weight infant.

The primary treatment of RLF is prevention with constant (transcutaneous) or frequent monitoring of the arterial pO_2 to maintain levels of 50 to 80 mm Hg. The small (less than 1,000 g) infant who is receiving high oxygen concentrations must have blood gas measurements *at least* every 4 hr during the acute changes in the first few days of life. Sometimes a very low birth weight infant may require 20 or more arterial blood gas assays in 24 hr. Most of the methods of treatment for RLF, once it has developed, have been unsuccessful. Evaluating the methods of treatment is difficult since most cases of RLF improve spontaneously. It is impossible to predict which infant is going to improve and which will become worse. The early stages of RLF frequently resolve with normal vision.

There are two known (and probably some that are not known) factors involved in the pathogenesis of RLF. (a) The most important factor is prematurity—hence the term "retinopathy of prematurity," which many authorities prefer to RLF. Babies who are less than 32 weeks' gestation are the most likely to develop RLF. RLF rarely occurs in full term babies, and then usually in the temporal region of the retina. (b) Although it is not known how high the pO_2 must be before RLF results, and there are many cases of RLF in infants who have never received supplemental oxygen, one should certainly strive to keep the pO_2 under 100 mm Hg, and probably less than 80 mm Hg. It is also not known how long the pO_2 must remain high before RLF results. Is resuscitation with 100% oxygen in the delivery room resulting in pO_2 values as high as 100 to 200 mm Hg for a few minutes enough to cause RLF? What about infants with apnea? If they are given 100% oxygen and their pO_2 reaches 200 to 300 mm Hg and stays there for a few minutes, is this sufficient to cause RLF? The answers to these questions are not available. In general, the baby is treated with only the amount of oxygen necessary to keep the pO_2 at 50 to 80 mm Hg. For this reason, premature infants with recurrent apnea should have their resuscitation bag connected to an oxygen blender that provides the same amount of oxygen the baby is receiving in the incubator. Most infants with apnea can be ventilated by bag and mask with the same amount of oxygen they are breathing in the incubator. Of course, if the infant does not respond to this mixture, the blender can be immediately turned up to a higher oxygen concentration. Umbilical artery blood samples do not necessarily measure the pO_2 in the blood supply to the eye. If there is a large right-to-left shunt across the ductus arteriosus, the pO_2 in the umbilical artery may be much lower than the pO_2 going to the eye and therefore may not be a good indicator of possible retinal hyperoxia.

Bronchopulmonary Dysplasia

Oxygen may also damage the lung, resulting in bronchopulmonary dysplasia (BPD). Newborns generally need to breathe greater than 40 to 60% oxygen for a number of days before they develop BPD. Barotrauma from positive-pressure respirators and the degree of prematurity are other important factors. Whereas RLF is best related to the prematurity and the arterial pO_2, the likelihood of a patient developing BPD is most closely related to the FiO_2 (inspired oxygen concentration), as well as prematurity and barotrauma. Because of this, there is no good means of preventing BPD. One possible approach is to ventilate the patient with as low a peak inspiratory pressure as possible. Increasing the respiratory rate or the inspiratory/expiratory ratio in order to decrease the peak inspiratory pressure has been advocated by some investigators. Data proving whether these methods are efficacious are yet to come.

OXYGEN ADMINISTRATION

Table 3 presents a few *incorrect* statements, or frequent misunderstandings. Some clinicians still think that it is always safe to give an infant 40% oxygen. *This is absolutely wrong.* If the infant does not need oxygen, the resultant high pO_2 may cause RLF. On the other hand, some think that you should never give

TABLE 3. *O_2 in the premature infant—false statements*

Below 40% is safe—*wrong*
Greater than 40% is dangerous—*wrong*
Measuring O_2 in liters per minute is adequate—*wrong*
Clinical examination is adequate for monitoring oxygen—*wrong*
Vitamin E decreases the incidence of RLF and BPD—*not known*

more than 40% oxygen to an infant. This belief is also wrong. If a baby is cyanotic, he needs more oxygen, sometimes up to 100%. Lack of oxygen may cause harm, i.e., brain damage or death.

Measuring the oxygen in liters per minute is totally inadequate. If oxygen at 10 liters/min is vented into a large room, the oxygen concentration stays at 21%, i.e., the same as room air. If oxygen at 10 liters/min is supplied directly into an oxygen hood, the concentration approaches 100%. Oxygen must be measured in percent concentration.

Some clinicians believe they can look at a baby and tell how much oxygen he requires. Again, this practice is wrong. If the baby is cyanotic, he certainly needs more oxygen, but the arterial pO_2 must be monitored to determine how much oxygen the baby requires. It is usually possible to determine if an infant is cyanotic and requires more oxygen, but it is impossible to differentiate between a pO_2 of 80 mm Hg and one of 250 mm Hg by physical examination. The arterial pO_2 must be measured.

Some recent literature suggests that vitamin E may prevent RLF and BPD. These studies suggest a correlation between vitamin E therapy and a decreased incidence of RLF and BPD. Controlled studies are necessary for more accurate conclusions. Fortunately, vitamin E is probably a benign drug; only a few complications resulting from large doses have been reported. A natural antioxidant, vitamin E may protect the red blood cell membrane as well as capillary membranes from damage caused by hyperoxygenation. Because vitamin E is probably benign and because it is used for the treatment and prevention of other disorders in the newborn, especially the premature infant, one might argue, "What is the harm in giving all premature infants vitamin E to prevent RLF and BPD?" Because of the many occasions in which a mode of therapy considered benign has turned out to be pathogenic, no drug should be used in any patient unless it is of proved efficacy. One possible harm from the routine use of vitamin E in the premature infant to prevent RLF and BPD might be less-vigilant monitoring of oxygen therapy and arterial partial pressures (pO_2) of oxygen in all infants receiving supplemental oxygen.

Oxygen is cold and dry; therefore it must be humidified and warmed. In addition, oxygen therapy to the infant must never be interrupted. If a newborn infant requires oxygen, he must never be taken out of the oxygen, even for a minute. Procedures are done while the infant remains in the oxygen. If the infant must be moved, then the move is accomplished with an oxygen mask and tank. Taking the baby out of oxygen for a few minutes may be enough to cause hypoxia, resulting in pulmonary vasoconstriction, decreased pulmonary blood flow, increased right-to-left shunt, metabolic acidosis, and further hypoxia, which may eventually result in his death. He may not succumb immediately because of the 1 min of hypoxia, but he may die 24 to 36 hr later because of the problems precipitated by it.

When an infant is to receive oxygen in an incubator, it is supplied through an oxygen hood. If a baby is in an incubator without a hood and the portholes are

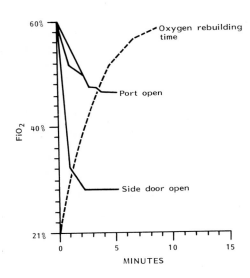

FIG. 2. If the portholes of an incubator are opened, the environmental O_2 drops dramatically unless the infant is receiving O_2 via a hood. (Adapted from Ahlgren: *Int. Anesthesiol. Clin.*, 12, No. 4, 1974.)

opened (Fig. 2), the oxygen is rapidly lost out the portholes and many minutes are required to increase the oxygen concentration back to normal after the portholes are closed.

CAVEATS

1. Hypoxia may be secondary to an inadequate amount of oxygen in the blood or an inability to deliver oxygen to the tissues.

2. Oxygen is carried to the tissues by hemoglobin; therefore a decreased hemoglobin concentration results in decreased oxygen-carrying capacity of the blood.

3. Hyper- and hypothermia increase oxygen consumption.

4. Prematurity and a high arterial pO_2 are the two most important factors in the pathogenesis of retrolental fibroplasia.

5. Premature infants with recurrent apnea should have their resuscitation bag connected to an oxygen blender to prevent hyperoxia during bagging.

6. If a large right-to-left shunt across a patent ductus is present, the pO_2 in the umbilical artery is lower than the pO_2 in the arterial blood supplying the eye.

7. Oxygen toxicity to the lungs (bronchopulmonary dysplasia) is related to prematurity, inspired oxygen concentration, and barotrauma (ventilator).

8. When an infant has central cyanosis, the ambient oxygen is increased to the concentration necessary to relieve the cyanosis.

9. Oxygen must be measured in percent, not liters per minute.

10. Clinical examination alone is inadequate for monitoring oxygen requirement except in emergencies.

12

Delivering and Monitoring Oxygen

This chapter discusses the equipment used to deliver and monitor oxygen in the newborn. Each hospital involved in the care of newborns should have equipment similar to that discussed below, with the personnel familiar with that specific equipment.

Each type of equipment discussed is available from many manufacturers. Although the equipment described here is usually that preferred at the James Whitcomb Riley Hospital for Children, this in no way constitutes an endorsement or recommendation that the particular brand name of equipment is necessarily the best available. The most important consideration when deciding the type of equipment to buy is the service provided by the vendor.

Whenever delivering oxygen to the newborn, the oxygen supply must never be interrupted. If the infant must be removed from the incubator or hood to be weighed or to have an X-ray taken, the oxygen supply must be continued by using an oxygen mask during the procedure.

Whatever method is used to administer oxygen to the patient, the concentration should be stable and easy to regulate. The patient's face should be visible so the appearance of cyanosis, nasal flaring, secretions, or vomitus can be seen.

HUMIDIFICATION AND HEATING

Oxygen or compressed air from a cylinder or bulk oxygen system delivered through wall outlets is dry and cold; therefore the oxygen must be warmed and humidified prior to administration to the patient. Inadequate humidification causes fluid loss from the respiratory tract and impedes tracheal ciliary activity, thereby making secretions tenacious and difficult to remove.

The oxygen must also be heated. Cold oxygen administered to a newborn may cause apnea and hypothermia, resulting in increased oxygen requirement, heightened metabolic demands, metabolic acidosis, and other deleterious effects.

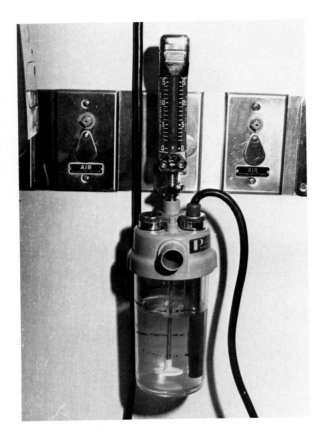

FIG. 1. Nebulizer with heating rod.

Nebulizers with heaters (Fig. 1) produce aerosols and adequately warm humidified gases. However, with the high water output, aerosol droplets may settle on the patient with the resulting evaporation causing body heat loss. Nebulizers often have venturi devices in the cap for various oxygen concentrations. Because the venturi entrains room air, and therefore any airborne organisms, it may increase the risk of infection. Despite the presence of the venturi device, an oxygen analyzer must always be used to measure the actual FiO_2 of the patient. Also, in the nebulizer pictured in Fig. 1, the heating rod is a significant distance from the infant; therefore the oxygen may become significantly cooler as it travels from the heated nebulizer to the patient. Because of these problems, we do not recommend the nebulizer for heating and humidifying oxygen. However, if this is the only device available in a hospital, it is better to use it than to administer cold, dry oxygen to the patient.

We prefer the Cascade humidifier (Fig. 2). An adjustable heater is used with the Cascade, and a high relative humidity at body temperature is easily achieved. The outlet of the humidifier is designed for large-bore tubing which is not easily obstructed by condensation. With this system, it is relatively easy to control the temperature of the oxygen delivered to the patient, in contrast to the heated nebulizers discussed above. In order to maintain oxygen temperature, a

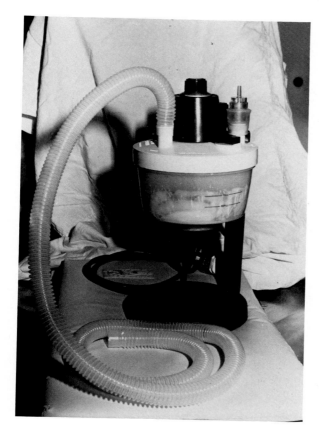

FIG. 2. Cascade humidifier.

thermometer is placed relatively close to the patient (through the lid of the hood) and the temperature of the oxygen maintained between 80° and 95°F. Another advantage of the Cascade humidifier is that it delivers water vapor rather than particles, as occurs with the nebulizer.

Because evaporative heat loss results, it is important to avoid exposing the infant to such a high humidity that water droplets precipitate on his body.

OXYGEN MASKS

Oxygen masks are usually used as a temporizing measure in emergency situations. Every delivery room and nursery should be equipped with oxygen masks designed specifically for the newborn, including the premature infant.

The most commonly used mask is the simple neonatal mask (Fig. 3), which acts as an oxygen reservoir. During inspiration the newborn inhales oxygen from the mask but may also entrain room air through the small exhalation ports on the side of the mask and areas where the mask does not fit well on the face. The exhalation holes on the side of the mask should be very small. Masks with a large exhalation port and aerosol masks should not be used. An appropriate-size mask should be available for each newborn, including the small premature

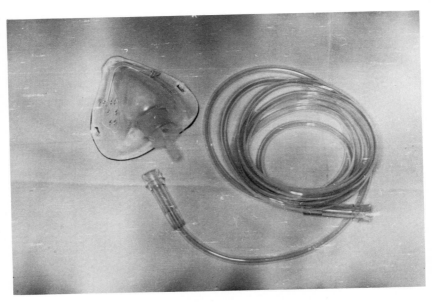

FIG. 3. Simple oxygen mask.

infant, to minimize leaks. Relatively high concentration (50 to 90%) of oxygen may be obtained with this simple mask provided it fits the infant's face tightly. When using a mask, the oxygen is administered at approximately 5 to 8 liters/min. We recommend that this simple type of mask be available in all delivery rooms and nurseries so that a cyanotic infant may be given a high concentration of oxygen in an emergency situation. Oxygen masks are not used for chronic oxygen administration, however, because it is impossible to measure adequately the inspired oxygen concentration. The primary disadvantages of oxygen masks are: (a) the difficulty in maintaining a stable oxygen concentration, and (b) adequately heating and humidifying the gases. All of the oxygen masks use small-bore tubing, which quickly fills with water condensation if the gas is adequately humidified. A mask is used only during the acute stabilization of the patient. For longer periods of oxygen administration, the oxygen hood or incubator is used.

Numerous types of oxygen masks are available. Those that deliver only a certain concentration of oxygen (venturi—see below) are not used in emergency situations in which high concentrations are required. The oxygen masks in the nursery and delivery room must be such that high concentrations of oxygen can be delivered in emergencies.

Venturi masks (Fig. 4) offer precise control of the oxygen concentration. The venturi entrains room air at a certain rate to provide a fixed amount of oxygen. Venturi masks which deliver a fixed amount (24 to 80%) of oxygen are available. With this type of mask you can achieve only the maximum FiO_2 recorded on the mask. That is, a venturi mask labeled "24%, at 4 liters/min" delivers 24% FiO_2 at that oxygen flow rate, and can achieve only a slightly greater FiO_2 at

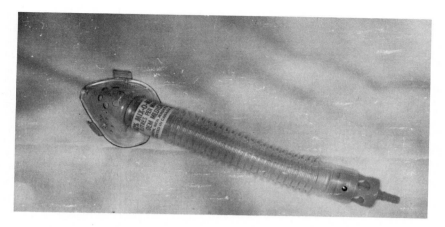

FIG. 4. Venturi oxygen mask limits concentration to a predetermined percent.

higher flow rates. Because venturi masks deliver this fixed oxygen percentage, they are generally not practical for the delivery room and the newborn nursery. In acute situations when an infant is cyanotic, an oxygen mask that can deliver 70 to 100% oxygen is usually used. There are some situations, however, in which a venturi mask may be useful, especially in stable infants on low oxygen concentrations.

The nonrebreathing oxygen masks use a reservoir bag or corrugated accumulator tubing. Since newborn infants are generally not able to generate enough pressure to open and close a nonrebreathing bag, this type of mask is not practical for the newborn.

OXYGEN HOODS

The oxygen hood (Fig. 5) provides stable oxygen concentration, visibility, and access to most of the body, thereby facilitating nursing and medical care. The large-bore tubing carries heated and humidified gas from the humidifier and is not easily obstructed by condensation.

The oxygen concentration may be regulated with an oxygen blender or with a Y connected to compressed air and oxygen source. There should always be a flow of at least 3 liters/min to maintain a stable oxygen concentration and prevent CO_2 buildup. Also, the neck opening of the hood should not be obstructed or CO_2 may accumulate in the hood.

Oxygen concentrations of 90% or higher are easily obtained with the hood. Fairly high concentrations of oxygen may be obtained without the lid on the hood, although the concentration usually remains more stable with the lid on. Whenever the concentration is altered, it is analyzed at the time of the change and 5 to 10 min later because the concentration stabilizes slowly.

The hood may be used either in an open crib or, more frequently, under a radiant warmer, depending on the patient's temperature stability. Oxygen

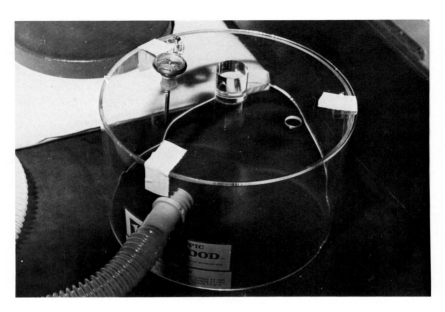

FIG. 5. Oxygen hood. Note the thermometer in the lid to measure oxygen temperature.

hoods are also used in incubators if the FiO$_2$ is greater than 0.30 to 0.40 in order to maintain a stable oxygen concentration. Otherwise, when the incubator portholes or doors are opened, the oxygen concentration within the incubator drops quickly and takes many minutes to be restored to its previous concentration.

INCUBATORS

Oxygen may be connected directly to the incubator, which warms and humidifies the oxygen. Most incubators have mechanisms to keep the FiO$_2$ below 0.40 and an alternative method to obtain higher concentrations. With the Ohio incubator (Ohio Medical Products, Madison, Wisconsin) (Fig. 6), there are two nipples on the side for oxygen administration. One nipple is labeled 40% and the other 100%, but these are gross estimates of the oxygen obtained within the incubator. With the Air Shields Isolette (Air Shields, Inc., Hatboro, Pennsylvania), the oxygen concentration usually does not go over 40% in the isolette unless the red flag in the back (Fig. 7) is raised, in which case 60 to 70% oxygen concentration *may* be obtained in the isolette. These numbers on the incubators are gross estimates and are totally inadequate for determining oxygen concentration. Rather, the oxygen in the incubator must be measured (in percent) with an oxygen analyzer.

Whenever the infant must be taken out of an incubator or an oxygen hood for a procedure (e.g., a spinal tap or blood tests), the oxygen must not be discontinued: An oxygen mask may be used so the administration of oxygen is continuous.

FIG. 6. Oxygen portholes in an Ohio incubator.

OXYGEN ANALYZERS

The oxygen analyzer is an essential piece of equipment and should be available in every nursery to measure the percent concentration of oxygen. The oxygen concentration in liters per minute is a totally inadequate measurement for regulating the patient's oxygen therapy. Different types of equipment may be using the same oxygen flow (liters per minute), but each probably is delivering a different percent concentration of oxygen. Moreover, the concentration of oxygen delivered by one device (e.g., a mask) varies from time to time (even though the flow in liters per minute remains constant) depending on such factors as how well the mask fits the patient. Oxygen analyzers may monitor the oxygen either continuously or intermittently. All oxygen analyzers should be calibrated periodically, preferably every 8 hr, against room air and 100% oxygen. Examples of oxygen analyzers are the following:

1. *Beckman D2* (Fig. 8). The sampling tube of the Beckman D2 analyzer (Beckman, Inc., Schiller Park, Illinois) is placed in the area to be analyzed (preferably close to the patient's nose). The aspirator bulb (held with the silver ball valve upright) is squeezed 8 to 12 times to draw the sample into the analyz-

FIG. 7. Red "flag" in back of an Air Shields Isolette.

ing chamber. The red button on the top is depressed, thereby turning on the light indicator on the scale and showing the oxygen concentration. The analyzer is checked at 21% and 100% O_2. If it does not calibrate correctly, it must be sent to the company or repaired by qualified personnel. A plastic tube containing blue silica gel desiccant crystals on the back of the analyzer serves to remove water vapor from the sample. These crystals should be inspected frequently and replaced when they begin to turn pink.

FIG. 8. Beckman D2 paramagnetic oxygen analyzer.

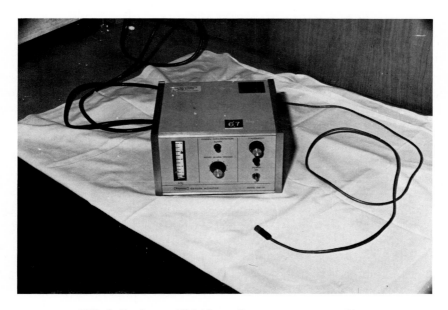

FIG. 9. Beckman OM-10 continuous oxygen analyzer.

2. *Beckman OM-10* (Fig. 9). The Beckman OM-10 is a continuous O_2 analyzer. It has a sensor and is powered from a 110-volt outlet. It should be calibrated to 21% and 100% O_2 at least every 8 hr using the adjustment knob on the front. The oxygen concentration is displayed on the meter on the front of the analyzer. There are adjustable limits on the meter for high and low oxygen concentrations. If the concentration exceeds the limit, a red light on the front of the analyzer comes on and an audible alarm is triggered. There is an adjustment on the front of the analyzer to control the volume of the audible alarm.

3. *IMI.* The IMI analyzer (Electrodyne, Sharon, Massachusetts) is also a continuous analyzer. It is powered by batteries which may be replaced by removing the bottom cover. Depressing the "test" button on the face checks the battery level. The sensor tip is covered with a disposable cap containing the membrane and is filled with electrolyte solution. A kit is supplied containing a new membrane and a package of electrolyte solution. The analyzer should be calibrated to 21% and 100% O_2 at least every 8 hr.

4. *IL.* The IL analyzer (Instrumentation Labs, Lexington, Massachusetts) is very similar to the IMI; it has a battery level check button and a sensor and electrolyte solution which must be periodically replaced. Some models have high and low concentration limits with audible and visual alarms.

5. *BMI.* The BMI (BioMarine Inc., Malvern, Pennsylvania) is a fuel cell analyzer. It produces its own electrical current from the reaction of oxygen in the sensor. No external power supply is required. It has a zero adjustment and a calibration screw. It should be calibrated to 21% and 100% O_2 at least every 8 hr. When not in use, the sensor should be disconnected from the analyzer.

MANUAL RESUSCITATORS

Manual resuscitators used for newborns should have (a) a small volume to reduce the possibility of hyperinflation, and (b) the capability of delivering high concentrations of oxygen. Adult resuscitators must not be used. *Regardless of the type of resuscitation bag used, it is mandatory that physicians, respiratory therapists, and nursing personnel be thoroughly familiar with that particular bag's characteristics.*

Anyone using a manual resuscitator on a newborn must be experienced in its use. There is little margin for error. Although excessive volume or pressure may result in a pneumothorax, volume must be adequate for gas exchange. One observes chest excursions, listens to breath sounds, and continuously monitors the heart rate. If using a mask with the bag, the mask must fit well, provide a good seal, and have a minimal amount of dead space.

1. *Hope I* (Ohio Medical Products, Madison, Wisconsin) (Fig. 10). The Hope I pediatric manual resuscitator has a volume of 730 ml. It is a self-inflating bag; i.e., it re-expands after it is compressed and does not require a gas force for inflation. During inspiration the exhalation valve rises, blocking the exhalation port, and gas goes to the patient. With exhalation, the spring pushes the exhalation valve down to allow exhaled gas to leave via the exhalation port. Also during exhalation the bag re-expands, pulling air and oxygen (if connected to an oxygen source) in through the one-way leaf valve. Oxygen tubing is connected to the oxygen inlet port. The oxygen flow rate should not exceed 10

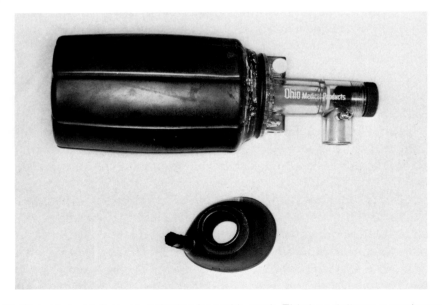

FIG. 10. Ohio Hope I infant resuscitation bag with mask. This bag delivers a maximum 40% oxygen.

FIG. 11. Blount plastic adapter with accumulator tubing enables the Hope I bag to deliver up to 80 to 95% oxygen.

liters/min or the exhalation valve may malfunction. The maximum oxygen concentration is 40 to 50%.

In order to obtain more than 40 to 50% oxygen concentration with the Hope I bag, a Blount adapter (Blount, Inc., Ashland, Virginia) and accumulator tubing (approximately 25 cm long) may be added (Fig. 11) to provide an oxygen reservoir. Concentrations may then reach 80 to 95%.

The Hope resuscitator may or may not have a 40 cm water pressure relief valve to prevent excessive pressure during inspiration. Both types are available from the company. At times, especially with severe hyaline membrane disease with poor compliance, pressures greater than 40 cm water may be required for adequate ventilation. Again, it is very important that personnel using the bag be familiar with that particular bag's characteristics.

In order to know the pressure with which the patient is being ventilated, we prefer to adapt our resuscitator bags with a pressure manometer (Fig. 12). This allows us to monitor the amount of pressure with which we are ventilating the patient.

One of the problems with the Hope I resuscitator bag is that during cleaning and sterilization the one-way flap valve may be left off or may stick because of excess heat if it is steam-autoclaved. If the valve is stuck, it is impossible to ventilate an infant because no air or oxygen is drawn into the bag. It merely collapses. If the valve is actually missing, the entire volume goes through the holes into the open air instead of being administered to the patient. To prevent this, after the bags are cleaned they are tested to ensure that they are assembled properly.

FIG. 12. Pressure manometer attached to resuscitation bag provides a means of monitoring the pressure delivered to an infant's lungs.

2. *Hope II resuscitator bag.* The Hope II pediatric manual resuscitator (Fig. 13) holds a volume of 730 ml. It is a self-inflating bag, re-expanding after it is compressed and thus not requiring a gas source for inflation. Figure 14A shows an inspiration. The exhalation valve (ball) is pushed upward, blocking the exhalation port, and gas from the bag goes to the patient. With exhalation (Fig. 14B), the spring above the ball pushes the exhalation valve (ball) down, opening

FIG. 13. Hope II resuscitation bag.

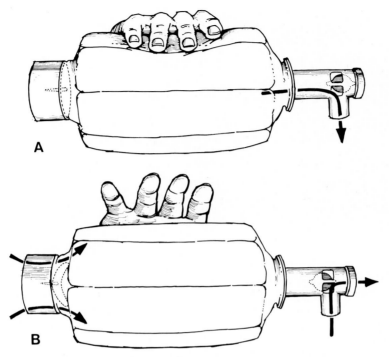

FIG. 14. Inhalation **(A)** and exhalation **(B)** with an Ohio Hope II bag.

the exhalation port through which the patient exhales. Also, during exhalation the bag re-expands, pulling air and oxygen (if connected) in through the valve in the bottom of the bag. If the accumulator hose is attached to the bottom of the bag, it fills with oxygen. Then as the bag inflates, it draws in oxygen from the accumulator instead of room air, and the patient receives higher concentrations of oxygen. Without the accumulator, the patient receives only about 50% oxygen concentration. It is important to have the accumulator on hand for infants in severe respiratory distress who would be cyanotic and hypoxic with less than 100% oxygen. The Hope II may be ordered with a pressure relief valve, which limits the peak inspiratory pressure to 40 cm water.

3. *Penlon bag.* The Penlon pediatric manual resuscitator is also a self-inflating bag. It has a detachable accumulator and can give up to 100% oxygen. The exhalation valve opens and closes in response to the pressure in the bag. When the bag is compressed during inspiration, the exhalation valve is forced upward, closing the exhalation port. When the bag is released, it re-expands during exhalation and the exhalation valve is pulled downward, opening the exhalation port to allow the exhaled gas to exit.

4. *Anesthesia bag.* Many people prefer to use an anesthesia bag when resuscitating the newborn. Its advantages are that any concentration of oxygen can be delivered if the source of oxygen is administered via an oxygen blender. In addition, a tight seal to the patient can be guaranteed because otherwise the bag

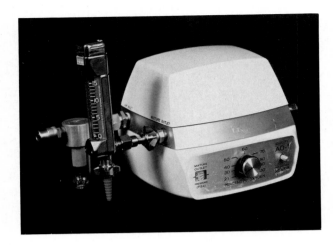

FIG. 15. Oxygen blender.

does not fill with gas. Also, continuous positive airway pressure (CPAP) can be easily administered with the bag. Its disadvantage is that many physicians, nurses, and respiratory therapists find it difficult to use.

OXYGEN BLENDERS

Whenever infants are given oxygen chronically (more than for stabilization over a few minutes to hours), oxygen blenders (Fig. 15) are used to help stabilize the oxygen concentration. In addition, when a premature infant is receiving oxygen but is having apnea and requires intermittent bagging, the resuscitation bag is connected to an oxygen blender which delivers the same concentration of oxygen the patient is receiving in the incubator or the oxygen hood. This prevents dramatic rises in the pO_2 with intermittent bagging, yet allows the physician or nurse to rapidly increase the oxygen concentration if the patient does not respond to the bagging at the same oxygen concentration he was previously breathing.

The percent oxygen dialed with the blender is not adequate for monitoring oxygen concentration. The percent oxygen concentration must still be measured with an oxygen analyzer every 1 to 4 hr.

CAVEATS

1. When an infant is receiving oxygen, the oxygen supply to the baby must *never* be interrupted.

2. Oxygen is warmed and humidified prior to administration to neonates.

3. Oxygen hoods are used for infants receiving high concentrations of oxygen in incubators to prevent the concentration from falling when the porthole or door is opened.

4. The oxygen concentration (%) is measured with an oxygen analyzer at least every 4 hr.

5. Each physician, nurse, and respiratory therapist must be familiar with the characteristics of the manual resuscitation bags used in their hospitals.

6. Some resuscitation bags deliver a maximum 40% oxygen with a maximum 40 cm water inspiratory pressure.

13

Persistent Fetal Circulation

Persistence of the fetal circulation (PFC) is a clinical process of importance to physicians, nurses, and respiratory therapists caring for newborn infants because early intervention may be preventive, whereas failure of early recognition and intervention may be catastrophic. Although much remains to be learned, the current theories regarding etiology, physiology, clinical characteristics, and therapy are reviewed.

CLINICAL PROFILE

PFC, also known as persistent pulmonary hypertension or persistence of the transitional circulation, was first recognized during the late 1960s. The general features of PFC are listed in Table 1.

Characteristically these patients are large term or near-term infants who develop respiratory distress within the first 12 hr of life. Although they may appear relatively stable during the early course, they frequently become profoundly hypoxic and cyanotic when agitated or crying. In spite of oxygen

TABLE 1. *PFC—clinical profile*

1. General
   Weight usually greater than 2 kg
   Gestational age 35 to 44 weeks
2. Respiratory
   Usually symptomatic before 12 hr of age
   Often not cyanotic in spite of pO_2 less than 50 mm Hg
   Distress and cyanosis increase with agitation or crying
   pO_2 may be less than 40 mm Hg despite 100% oxygen administration
3. Cardiac
   Frequently a systolic murmur present
   Increased right-sided forces and axis on electrocardiogram
   Occasionally congestive failure
4. Chest X-ray
   May be clear but usually some infiltrates
   Usually more benign appearing than the clinical course indicates
   Occasionally cardiomegaly

TABLE 2. *Clinical differentiation of PFC and cyanotic CHD*

Parameter	Cyanotic CHD	PFC
Time of onset of symptoms	> 24 hr	< 12 hr
Severity of distress	Minimal	Moderate to marked
pO$_2$ response to 100% O$_2$	< 40 mm Hg	> 40 mm Hg

administration and mechanical ventilation, the clinical course may continue to deteriorate with worsening cyanosis and hypoxia.

Cardiac examination in infants with PFC may be indistinguishable from that of congenital cyanotic heart disease. Right-to-left intracardiac shunting via the ductus arteriosus and foramen ovale, in addition to causing systemic oxygen desaturation, may produce murmurs. Poor contractility due to increased right ventricular load may result in atrioventricular valvular insufficiency and cardiac murmurs. Electrocardiographically, the normally increased right ventricular forces and right axis of the neonate may be accentuated. In addition to these findings, the echocardiogram may show right ventricular dilation and poor contractility. Occasionally, cardiomegaly with a gallop rhythm and hepatomegaly suggestive of congestive failure occurs.

Several clinical features make it possible to differentiate PFC from such cyanotic congenital heart defects (CHD) as transposition of the great vessels or the hypoplastic right heart complex (Table 2). First, infants with PFC usually become symptomatic within the first 12 to 24 hr of life, whereas with CHD symptoms usually do not occur until after 24 hr of age. Second, infants with PFC present with tachypnea, grunting, and retractions, whereas only tachypnea is usually present with CHD. Finally, when administered an FiO$_2$ of 1.0, infants with PFC may have a pO$_2$ greater than 40 to 50 mm Hg, whereas infants with CHD usually maintain a pO$_2$ of less than 30 to 40 mm Hg.

Virtually any X-ray pattern may be consistent with PFC including the reticulogranularity of hyaline membrane disease (HMD), the hyperinflation and diffuse infiltrates of meconium aspiration, or the bilateral stranding characteristic of transient tachypnea of the newborn (TTN). The radiograph usually appears more benign than the clinical course indicates.

To summarize the clinical presentation in PFC, these infants are usually near term, demonstrate moderately severe respiratory distress and cyanosis, and become progressively more labile and refractory to usual supportive measures. Cardiac examination may be indistinguishable from congenital heart disease, and radiographs often appear unusually benign in comparison with the infant's clinical status.

PATHOPHYSIOLOGY

Multiple physiologic adaptations occur during the immediate neonatal period, i.e., initiation of alveolar ventilation, decrease in the pulmonary vascular resistance, increase in the systemic load (resistance), and resultant closure of the ductus arteriosus and foramen ovale. Animal experimentation has shown that the muscular layer of neonatal pulmonary arterioles is thicker and more reactive than in later life. Any stress which interferes with oxygenation and transition to the infantile circulatory pattern may produce pulmonary arterial vasospasm with an increase in right heart pressure and right-to-left shunting, i.e., PFC. Shunting then causes worsening hypoxia and more stress. Once initiated, PFC results in a vicious cycle of events and a progressively worse clinical course.

Table 3 lists a number of physiologic alterations associated with PFC. It is evident that these aberrations are commonly seen in sick neonates. Clinically, these abnormalities may be initiated during the prenatal, intrapartum, or neonatal period.

Prenatally, any disturbance that causes hypoxia or distress may produce PFC (Table 4). Such factors include cord compression, fetal-maternal hemorrhage, abruptio placenta, placenta previa, and placental chorioangiosis. Maternal medication has been implicated in PFC. Indomethacin and salicylates may inhibit prostaglandin synthetase, thereby allowing closure of the ductus arteriosus *in utero* with resultant fetal hypoxia. PFC is probably more common in infants born by cesarean section.

Numerous neonatal diseases may generate enough stress and hypoxia to cause PFC (Table 4). As one might expect, most respiratory disorders, including the aspiration syndromes, pneumonia, TTN, and HMD, may be associated with pulmonary hypertension. Congenital diaphragmatic hernia (Bochdalek), frequently associated with a hypoplastic lung, is a less common disorder which is often associated with pulmonary hypertension.

A second broad group of neonatal disorders that potentially induce PFC includes those which compromise the baby's circulatory status. Naturally, congenital cardiac malformations may produce primary pulmonary hypertension as part of the altered physiology or secondary to stress and hypoxia. Other circulatory parameters include those responsible for causing either circulatory overload or intravascular depletion, e.g., shock, hypovolemia, hyperviscosity, and hydrops fetalis.

Finally, a number of miscellaneous factors deserve mention. Neonatal asphyxia and sepsis certainly may be associated with PFC. Because early-onset group B streptococcal septicemia may present in a fashion identical to PFC,

TABLE 3. *Perinatal stress factors associated with pulmonary hypertension*

Hypoxia
Hypotension
Hypothermia
Acidemia
Anemia
Hypoglycemia
Hyperviscosity

TABLE 4. *Disturbances associated with PFC*

Antenatal factors	Neonatal factors
Intrauterine distress	Respiratory disorders
Fetal hemorrhage	Aspiration syndromes
Placental chorioangiosis	HMD
Maternal medication	Diaphragmatic hernia
Indomethacin	Pneumonia
Salicylates	TTN
?Diphenylhydantoin	Pulmonary hypoplasia
Cesarean section	Circulatory disorders
	CHD
	Hyperviscosity
	Hydrops fetalis
	Volume overload
	Shock
	Hypovolemia
	Neonatal asphyxia
	Sepsis
	Metabolic disorders
	Hypoglycemia
	Metabolic acidosis
	Hypothermia

HMD, or TTN, every neonate with severe respiratory distress during the first few days of life should have cultures performed and antibiotic administration instituted. Disorders of the central and peripheral nervous systems that produce hypoventilation may induce pulmonary hypertension. Metabolic disorders, including hypoglycemia and metabolic acidosis, may be initiating disorders.

THERAPY

Management (Table 5) may be divided into clinical evaluation and immediate therapy. Clinical evaluation of an infant with PFC includes studies which should be available in any neonatal nursery. These include a thorough history, physical examination, chest X-ray (to rule out immediately correctable causes of respiratory distress such as a pneumothorax), blood pressure, temperature, hematocrit, serum glucose, calcium, arterial blood gas, and blood cultures. Therapy includes correction of any abnormalities discovered.

Early administration of a high concentration of oxygen (100%) is of utmost importance in the stabilization of an infant with PFC. This serves the following purposes: (a) It provides an optimal environment for noninvasive correction of hypoxia; and (b) it may give information concerning the possibility of the presence of cyanotic CHD as opposed to PFC. The risks of hypoxia in untreated PFC far outweigh the risks of oxygen administration. The two major adverse effects of oxygen are pulmonary parenchymal damage and retrolental fibroplasia (RLF). The risk of oxygen toxicity to the lungs is insignificant during the few hours necessary to stabilize and transfer an infant to a neonatal intensive care

TABLE 5. *PFC—management*

1. Clinical evaluation
    Review of prenatal history and physical examination
    Chest X-ray
    Blood pressure
    Hematocrit
    Serum glucose
    Serum calcium
    pO_2, pCO_2, pH
    Temperature
    Blood cultures
2. Therapy
    Avoid stress
    Correct imbalances of hematocrit, glucose, blood pressure, etc.
    Administer oxygen to relieve cyanosis
    Evaluate arterial blood gases
    Administer antibiotic
    Provide intubation and ventilatory assistance if indicated
    Make early referral to a high-risk nursery

unit. RLF is rarely produced in the mature retina of term and near-term infants who may have PFC or CHD.

Arterial blood gases are an extremely important parameter to monitor in infants at risk for PFC. There is no substitute for an arterial pO_2 determination when monitoring oxygenation. Because of the relatively high oxygen affinity of fetal hemoglobin, cyanosis occurs at a lower pO_2 (pO_2 less than 40 mm Hg) than in adults, so that skin color is not an acceptable mode of monitoring. Attempts must be made to keep the pO_2 greater than 60 mm Hg. Hypoxia (pO_2 less than 50 mm Hg) or hypercapnia (pCO_2 greater than 50 mm Hg) and acidosis (pH less than 7.25) is evidence of respiratory failure and an indication for ventilatory assistance. The therapy of respiratory acidosis (decreased pH and increased pCO_2) must be aimed at correction of the underlying disorder (hypoventilation), not at buffering the blood with sodium bicarbonate.

Further therapy in PFC includes correction of hypotension, anemia, hypothermia, or other metabolic disorders (Table 6) and early referral to a tertiary neonatal unit. Antibiotics are the only drugs indicated in the initial stabilization

TABLE 6. *Treatment of associated disorders*

1. Hypotension
    Whole blood, plasma, or colloid 10 ml/kg i.v. over 15 to 30 min
2. Anemia
    Packed red blood cells to keep hematocrit greater than 40%
3. Hypoglycemia
    Intravenous infusion of $D_{10}W$
    For acute symptoms $D_{25}W$, 1 to 2 ml/kg i.v.
4. Sepsis
    Combination of a penicillin derivative plus aminoglycoside

of an infant with PFC. Tolazoline HCl (Priscoline®), an alpha-adrenergic blocking agent which produces pulmonary arterial vasodilation, has been used in PFC, but the efficacy of this drug remains unproved. For this reason and because of its profound adverse effects (severe hypotension), tolazoline should be administered only in a prospective fashion in a high-risk center with full-time neonatologists.

CONCLUSION

PFC is a potentially fatal entity in the neonate. Relatively common stresses in the near-term infant may initiate a vicious cycle of events, including hypoxia, increased oxygen requirements, extrapulmonary right-to-left shunting, and a progressively deteriorating clinical course. Care of these neonates is supportive, with oxygen administration and early referral to a high-risk center being of utmost importance. The outlook for infants transferred early and managed in appropriate facilities is generally optimistic.

CAVEATS

1. Patients with PFC are usually large near-term or term infants.
2. Respiratory distress usually presents within the first 12 hr of age.
3. Although infants with PFC may appear relatively stable during the early course of their disease, they frequently become profoundly hypoxic and cyanotic when agitated or crying.
4. Virtually any X-ray pattern may be consistent with PFC, but the radiograph usually appears much more benign than the clinical course.
5. Early administration of a high concentration (100%) of oxygen is of utmost importance in the stabilization of an infant with PFC.

14

Apnea

Apnea is defined as the cessation of breathing for more than 20 sec, or the cessation of breathing with a concomitant decrease in heart rate, and/or the presence of cyanosis. Approximately 25% of all infants less than 2,500 g and 80% of all infants less than 1,000 g experience apnea sometime during their neonatal course when monitored using conventional techniques. When monitored with special techniques, apnea has been detected in virtually all infants less than 37 weeks' gestation, particularly those less than 1,250 g.

In contrast, periodic breathing is defined as the cessation of breathing for less than 15 or 20 sec without accompanying cyanosis or bradycardia. It is important to differentiate periodic breathing from apnea because the former is a normal phenomenon that occurs in as many as 95% of infants less than 1,500 g as well as in approximately one-third of babies over 2,500 g.

Bradycardia, which almost invariably follows soon after the occurrence of significant apnea, is thought to be mediated by a reflex mechanism. Because bradycardia ensues so quickly (usually less than 30 sec), it is the practice in many nurseries to use heart rate monitors to differentiate periodic breathing from apnea. On the rare occasion in which bradycardia is the primary event, therapy must be directed at correcting the low heart rate.

Apnea results in hypoxia if not quickly treated. Such hypoxia may result in electroencephalographic (EEG) changes, hypotonia, and permanent central nervous system (CNS) damage. Untreated apnea is thought to have been a major cause of cerebral palsy and mental retardation in premature infants in the past. Hopefully, with the utilization of sophisticated monitors and skilled nurses and physicians, permanent brain damage secondary to apnea will be much less frequent.

CAUSES OF APNEA

Understanding the potential causes of apnea is the most important aspect of the treatment (Table 1). Apnea is not a disease in itself but, rather, a symptom or sign reflecting some other condition. One of the most common causes of

TABLE 1. *Common causes of apnea*

1. Temperature instability
   Infant—increased or decreased temperature
   Environment—increased or decreased temperature
2. Sepsis
   Apnea during the first 24 hr of life is always considered secondary to sepsis until proved otherwise
3. Metabolic disorders
   Decreased calcium
   Decreased glucose
   Decreased magnesium
   Decreased sodium
   Other (inborn errors of metabolism)
4. Cardiorespiratory disorders
   Hypoxia
   Acidosis
   Patent ductus arteriosus
   Hypotension
   Anemia
   Upper airway obstruction (flexed head, phototherapy masks)
   Pneumonia
   Respiratory distress syndrome
5. Central nervous system disorders
   Congenital malformation
   Seizures
   Asphyxia
   Drugs (maternal narcotics, analgesics, "caine" drugs, anesthesia)
   Intracranial hemorrhage
   Meningitis
6. Reflexes
   Posterior pharyngeal
   Laryngeal
7. Necrotizing enterocolitis

apnea in the premature infant is temperature instability due to an inappropriate patient or environmental temperature. It is not only the hyper- or hypothermic infant who experiences apnea; the normothermic infant may also be apneic if his environmental temperature is too hot or too cold. It is important, therefore, particularly with premature infants, to maintain the infant's body temperature within normal limits as well as his environmental temperature within the "neutral thermal range" (see Chapter 5).

Sepsis is *always* considered in newborns with apnea, as this baby usually dies if untreated. The most common cause of sepsis in the newborn is group B streptococcus. *Apnea during the first 24 hr of life is always considered secondary to sepsis until proved otherwise.*

Metabolic causes of apnea include hypoglycemia, hypocalcemia, hyponatremia, and hypomagnesemia, as well as more uncommon metabolic diseases.

Any cardiorespiratory disorder may cause apnea, e.g., hyaline membrane disease, pneumonia, pulmonary hemorrhage, or pneumothorax. A patent ductus arteriosus is frequently associated with apnea in the very low birth weight infant. Severe anemia and possibly mild "anemia" (hematocrit 30 to 40%) in some very low birth weight infants may cause apnea. Upper airway obstruction, whether due to congenital anomalies, simple flexion of the infant's neck, or covering the infant's nose with an eye mask during phototherapy, may also result in apnea.

CNS disorders are frequently accompanied by apnea. Congenital infections (TORCH) and acute meningitis may be accompanied by seizures and apnea. Infants with a congenital CNS malformation such as myelomeningocele may experience apnea, and infants who suffer severe asphyxia at the time of birth may develop it. Maternal drugs, including analgesics and anesthetics such as lidocaine (from a paracervical or epidural analgesic block) and narcotic use may result in apnea in the newborn. Intracranial hemorrhage, whether subarachnoid, intracerebral, intraventricular, or subdural, is frequently accompanied by apnea.

Whether apnea is the only manifestation of seizures is uncertain. It appears that when apnea accompanies seizures there are usually other manifestations of a convulsive disorder. However, seizures are frequently difficult to diagnose in the newborn because their subtle manifestations require a high index of suspicion for detection. One should therefore always consider seizures in the differential diagnosis of the infant with apnea.

Many neurogenically mediated reflexes may precipitate apnea in the newborn. Placement of an orogastric tube into the posterior pharynx may result in a reflex fall in heart and respiratory rate. Stimulation of other areas innervated by the trigeminal nerve (face, nose) may cause apnea. Introduction of certain liquids into the laryngeal area, as can occur with nipple feeding, has been shown to cause apnea in newborn lambs and piglets.

The above discussion, as well as Table 1, notes the most common causes of apnea in the newborn, especially in the premature infant. It is important to remember that any infant who experiences apnea for the first time or who has apnea during the first 24 hr of life is always considered to have a pathologic disorder, never "physiologic" apnea of prematurity. Although apnea may be a consequence of an infant's immature physiology, it is never a benign disorder. A complete diagnostic evaluation for underlying problems is required. Therefore a systematic approach to the management of the apneic infant is essential.

THE ART OF MONITORING THE PATIENT

The first aspect of caring for the patient with apnea is detection. In general, infants with a birth weight less than 1,500 to 1,800 g are placed on an apnea and/or heart rate monitor for at least the first week of life, recognizing that the monitors never replace nursing or medical surveillance and that one treats the patient, not the monitor. When a monitor alarm sounds, one looks at the patient first, not the monitor. Obviously, if the infant is cyanotic or pale, stimulation is instituted immediately. On the other hand, if the infant is moving all extremities, looks pink, and is perfusing peripheral tissues well, it is unlikely that he is in severe distress, so a careful examination is in order before vigorous stimulation. It is also important to document the infant's appearance on his chart at the time of the alarm. His actual heart rate, the presence of cyanosis or pallor, and the type and duration of stimulation required are recorded. If one merely notes "apnea" or "bradycardia," it is very difficult for others who look at the chart later to distinguish between false positives (i.e., the alarm sounding without actual apnea or bradycardia in the patient) and true apnea and bradycardia. Many infants have a decrease in heart rate to approximately 80 to 90 beats per minute during sleep, so if the infant does not demonstrate apnea, cyanosis, or pallor, and his heart rate returns to normal without stimulation, this slowed rate simply represents a normal phenomenon that does not require intervention.

Apnea monitors are of three main types: (a) pressure-sensitive monitors activated by movement of the child's chest; (b) induction monitors, which sense movement of a magnet placed on the child's chest; and (c) impedance monitors, which detect the change in electrical impedance across the infant's thorax between inspiration and expiration.

There are several limits to the reliability of apnea monitors. They are completely unable to detect apnea due to airway obstruction until the child ceases respiratory efforts because of prolonged hypoxia. With pressure-sensitive and induction monitors, any movement registers as respirations; thus seizures or vibration of the incubator may result in alarm failure despite an absence of respiratory efforts. Impedance monitors may register cardiac activity as respiratory movement if their sensitivity is set too high. Even under the supervision of skilled intensive care unit nurses, approximately half of the episodes of apnea are missed with such monitors. For these reasons, some clinicians do not use apnea monitors but instead depend on the fall of the heart rate to less than 80 beats/min on a cardiac monitor.

APPROACH TO THE PATIENT

As always in medicine, the most important aspect of investigation is a good history and physical examination (Table 2). This is particularly important in an infant with apnea, as the likelihood of finding a pathologic cause is very high. One searches the perinatal history for maternal drugs, maternal bleeding, or fetal distress. Meconium staining, indications of a difficult delivery, and low Apgar scores indicative of perinatal asphyxia are also noted. Maternal fever, prolonged rupture of membranes (greater than 24 hr), or evidence of frank amnionitis may suggest infection. Environmental or infant temperature instability and temporal association of the apnea with feeding, stooling, or placement of a suction catheter or feeding tube are considered. On physical examination, one looks for signs of respiratory distress, heart disease [e.g., a patent ductus arteriosus (PDA)], congenital malformations, and upper airway obstruction (e.g., choanal atresia). Generalized petechiae or purpura may indicate sepsis as well as a coagulation disorder. Sucking movements, deviation of the eyes, or stereotyped movement of the extremities, if present, are usually indicative of

TABLE 2. *Approach to patient with apnea*

1. History and physical examination
   Maternal drugs
   Maternal bleeding
   Risk factors for infection (maternal fever, prolonged rupture of membranes, amnionitis)
   Fetal asphyxia
   Evidence of cardiorespiratory disease
   Temperature (patient and environment)
   Association of apnea with feeding, stooling, suctioning
2. Laboratory workup—minimal
   Hematocrit
   Glucose, calcium, sodium
   Arterial pH, pCO_2, pO_2
   Blood culture, spinal tap, suprapubic bladder aspiration
3. Laboratory workup—more extensive
   Urine for metabolic screen (amino acids, organic acids)
   Serum ammonia level
   Magnesium
   Serum, "caine" drug level
   EEG
   CAT scan, ultrasound

neonatal seizures. The abdomen is also examined for hepatomegaly (suggesting heart failure or congenital infection) and for distention (possibly indicative of necrotizing enterocolitis or bowel obstruction).

The laboratory workup (Table 2) on every infant who has a newly documented episode of apnea includes the following: hematocrit, glucose, calcium, sodium, arterial pH, pO_2 and pCO_2, blood culture, spinal tap, and urine culture (preferably by suprapubic bladder aspiration). Although this workup is obviously not indicated for every instance of apnea in any one patient, it is imperative on any infant who has apnea during the first 24 hr of life and preferably on every infant with the first episode of apnea.

When apnea persists and a diagnosis cannot be established, further laboratory evaluations which may be carried out include: urine and plasma for metabolic screening (including amino acids and organic acids), serum ammonia level, serum magnesium level, serum lidocaine or other "caine" drug level, EEG, computerized axial tomography (CAT), and ultrasound examination of the head. These assessments are reserved for infants who have apnea not responding to conventional therapy or for those in which there is a suspicion of an inborn error of metabolism, hyperammonemia, drug toxicity, or a CNS disorder, e.g., an intracranial hemorrhage.

TREATMENT OF APNEA

The first step in the management of apnea (Table 3) is to determine the cause. One first investigates and then treats accordingly such possibilities as sepsis, hypoglycemia, shock, PDA, neonatal depression from maternal drugs, seizures, and temperature instability. One then proceeds to other considerations.

TABLE 3. *Treatment of apnea*

1. Treat underlying cause (sepsis, hyaline membrane disease, decreased glucose, decreased calcium, decreased blood pressure, PDA, seizure)
2. Temperature control
   a. Maintain environmental temperature in zone of thermoneutrality or *slightly* below
   b. In a small infant, decrease heat loss: Plexiglas shield; line incubator with aluminum foil; keep incubator away from cold windows and air-conditioning; avoid drafts (O_2, air-conditioning)
3. Avoid triggering reflexes
   a. Suction catheters
   b. Tube feed instead of nipple
   c. Avoid hyperinflation during bagging
   d. Avoid cold stimulus to face
4. Maintain pO_2 slightly high (70 to 80 mm Hg)
5. Maintain hematocrit greater than 40%
6. Frequent stimulation
   a. Cutaneous
   b. Water bed
7. CPAP (2 to 4 cm water)
8. Theophylline or caffeine
9. Bag and mask ventilation. An O_2 blender should be used with the same FiO_2 as the patient is normally receiving. If not necessary, higher concentrations may result in increased pO_2 and retrolental fibroplasia.
10. Mechanical ventilation

1. Further measures are taken, if indicated, to ensure temperature stability. In small infants radiant heat loss may be decreased by using a Plexiglas shield, lining the incubator with aluminum foil, and placing the incubator away from cold windows and air-conditioners. Decreasing the environmental temperature in the incubator to the lower limit of the thermal neutral zone to provide added stimulation is occasionally successful for treating apnea in very low birth weight infants.

2. Triggering reflexes which may lead to apnea are avoided. If an infant's apnea is associated with such maneuvers as placement of an orogastric tube, nasotracheal suctioning, or flexion of the neck, these should be avoided. If the infant becomes apneic when nipple feeding, it may be helpful to change the nipple size or hole size or use gavage feeding.

3. The hematocrit is checked. Some infants have apnea if their hematocrit is less than 40%. Transfusion to a hematocrit greater than 40% may be therapeutic, particularly if the infant requires supplemental oxygen, has a very low birth weight, or has a PDA.

4. The pO_2 is checked. Although hypoxia, hyperoxia, and hypercarbia may have been ruled out in the initial evaluation, some infants have apnea with a pO_2 in the relatively normal range of 50 to 60 mm Hg but not the 70 to 80 mm Hg range. Thus increasing the environmental oxygen to allow a pO_2 in the 70 to 80 mm Hg range may be effective in reducing apnea. Avoid basing the pO_2 determination on arterial blood gases obtained while stressing the infant with a percutaneous puncture as the pO_2 may be lowered by the procedure. Transcutaneous monitoring is an ideal method to determine the pO_2 for this purpose.

5. Nasal continuous positive airway pressure (CPAP) has been shown to be very effective in the treatment of apnea. This may be due partly to improved oxygenation but is also thought to work via distention of pulmonary stretch receptors, stimulation of the nasopharyngeal area, and/or decreased work of breathing. Thus nasal CPAP is often worth a trial even in an infant with a satisfactory pO_2.

6. Such measures as oscillating water beds and apnea monitors which deliver a shock to the apneic infant have been shown to reduce apnea under strict supervision in some intensive care nurseries. These modes of treatment are still under investigation and cannot at this time be recommended for routine treatment of apnea in the newborn infant.

7. Whenever an infant is at high risk for apnea, a resuscitation bag should be at the side of the incubator or radiant warmer. Especially for very low birth weight infants, it is important that this bag be connected to an oxygen line equipped with an oxygen blender that provides approximately the same FiO_2 the infant usually receives. Otherwise, if an infant receiving 25% O_2 has a severe apneic episode and is bagged with the resuscitation bag with 100% O_2, the pO_2 may increase to 100 to 300 mm Hg (Fig. 1). Repeated episodes such as this may increase the risk of retrolental fibroplasia.

8. Theophylline and caffeine may be administered. There is considerable evidence that these methylxanthines are effective in treating apnea of prematurity. In some studies all serious apnea of prematurity disappeared in infants treated with theophylline. The most significant effect of theophylline and caffeine appears to be to an increase in the sensitivity of the respiratory center to CO_2.

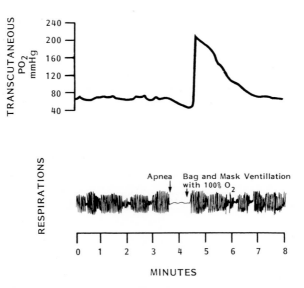

FIG. 1. An infant resuscitated with 100% O_2, when previously on 30% O_2, is shown to develop an excessively high transcutaneous pO_2. Repeated episodes of hyperoxia such as this might increase the risk of retrolental fibroplasia.

The dose requirement for theophylline and caffeine is determined by a number of considerations. The serum half-life of theophylline ranges from 12 to 57 hr. There is decreased protein binding of theophylline in prematures as compared with adults, so serum levels of 6 to 13 mg/liter in a neonate provide the same concentration of free drug as the accepted therapeutic range in adults of 10 to 20 mg/liter. Most studies have found that a serum level in the 6 to 13 mg/liter range is effective in the treatment of apnea. The beginning maintenance dose to attain such levels is 4 mg/kg/day divided into two or three doses. Aminophylline is 85% theophylline, so this dose must be multiplied by 1.2 if aminophylline is used. A minimum of four biologic half-lives must elapse before a steady-state serum level can be achieved with any drug. In the case of theophylline this may be 3 to 6 days of continuous therapy. Thus a loading dose of 5.5 to 6.0 mg/kg is often used. Serum levels are then obtained after a few doses to determine if an infant's dose requires adjustment. Blood to assay for theophylline levels can be drawn 2 hr after a dose and just prior to a dose to determine the peak and trough levels, respectively; but because of the long half-life of theophylline, a random sample is usually sufficient. Since significant amounts of theophylline are metabolized to caffeine, some authorities recommend that plasma caffeine levels be monitored as well. It is often necessary to increase the dose weekly after 3 weeks of age because of increasing clearance of the drug. The doses mentioned above are for intravenous administration. Oral theophylline is 80% absorbed, so the dose is multiplied by 1.25 if oral theophylline or aminophylline is used. The recommended caffeine dosage is determined from reasoning similar to that described for theophylline. The recommended loading dose is 10 mg/kg followed by a maintenance dose of 2.5 mg/kg/day given once daily. The suggested therapeutic range for plasma levels is 5 to 15 mg/liter. This dosage regimen is applicable for oral and intravenous administration since gastrointestinal (GI) absorption of caffeine is complete. Caffeine citrate is preferred over caffeine sodium benzoate in infants with hyperbilirubinemia because sodium benzoate displaces bilirubin from albumin binding sites.

The methylxanthines are relatively safe when used under well-monitored conditions. The major complications reported are dose-related and reversible on discontinuance of the drug. These include supraventricular tachycardia, GI toxicity (vomiting, distention), CNS stimulation (jitteriness, seizures), and possibly diuresis. There is some concern about decreased cerebral blood flow because of a documented 25 to 33% decrease in flow in adult subjects secondary to increased cerebral vascular resistance. There were no changes in mental status, cerebral oxygen consumption, or jugular venous pH in any of these subjects. A recent study showed no difference in growth or in neurologic or ophthalmologic examinations in children 18 to 40 months after being treated with caffeine as neonates. Thus decreased cerebral blood flow is probably not clinically significant but remains a question for future research.

The methylxanthines may affect neuronal growth and, via increased cAMP, may alter glucose metabolism, parathyroid function, and "brain homeostasis."

Because the multisystem effects are not fully known, the drugs cannot be considered to be without long-term risks. The only definite risks, however, involve short-term complications that are most likely to occur if the methylxanthines are used improperly. For one, toxicity is more likely to occur if serum levels are not monitored. The heart rate and urine output should be followed and signs of GI toxicity watched for. Because of the experimental nature of this drug, one is cautioned against its use outside of settings that are equipped to study its side effects and monitor serum drug levels.

CAVEATS

1. Apnea during the first 24 hr of life is almost always pathologic, not apnea of prematurity.

2. Infants with a birth weight less than 1,500 to 1,800 g are placed on an apnea and/or heart rate monitor.

3. Electronic monitoring must never replace nursing or medical surveillance, however.

4. The first step in the treatment of apnea is to determine and treat the underlying cause.

15

Treatment of Respiratory Problems

During the past 10 years there has been a remarkable reduction in the mortality and morbidity associated with neonatal respiratory disorders. These improvements have resulted, in part, from meticulous observation and management of minute-to-minute changes in the infant's condition and from a better understanding of the multitude of respiratory and nonrespiratory factors which can adversely affect outcome.

AMELIORATION OF THE PRIMARY DISORDER

Once the cause of neonatal respiratory distress is determined, specific therapeutic measures may be clearly indicated: surgical intervention for tracheo-esophageal fistula or diaphragmatic hernia, evacuation of a tension pneumothorax by chest tube drainage, antibiotics for pneumonia, and digitalis and diuretics for congestive heart failure. In the presence of acute hypovolemia or shock (e.g., with placenta previa, placenta abruptio), rapid volume expansion may be necessary. For an infant with hydrops fetalis, emergency paracentesis and/or thoracentesis to remove peritoneal or pleural fluid may be needed. Thus therapeutic measures directed at the specific underlying problem may be indicated in specific situations.

However, a favorable outcome for neonatal diseases is often jeopardized because of failure to provide other general, but nonetheless essential, adjunctive support. Following are some of the supportive measures applicable to almost all cases of neonatal respiratory distress, regardless of the underlying pulmonary, cardiac, or other pathology.

OXYGEN

Oxygen warmed to 32° to 34°C (89.6° to 93.2°F) with a 60 to 80% relative humidity is administered to maintain the arterial pO_2 at 50 to 80 mm Hg. Micro methods for periodic blood gas measurements are indispensable in the management of newborn infants who require supplemental oxygen. The method of oxygen administration must be individualized to maintain the required oxygen and yet permit reasonable access to the infant. For example, 30 to 40% oxygen can usually be maintained within an incubator equipped with portholes for patient care. When a concentration of more than 30 to 40% is necessary, it is preferable to use an oxygen hood within the incubator so that large fluctuations of ambient oxygen levels do not occur when the ports are opened. The newborn cannot tolerate even brief hypoxic episodes, so strict precautions for stabilization of the oxygen environment are mandatory. Stresses imposed by taking the child out of oxygen for X-rays, weighing, etc. can result in such serious extra- and intrapulmonary shunting that the previously stable infant may be placed in jeopardy.

See Chapters 11 and 12 for further discussion.

TEMPERATURE

There are critical nonrespiratory functions which require careful attention when managing newborn infants with respiratory distress (Table 1). One of these, sustaining body temperature, has been shown to increase the survival rate of low birth weight infants. A method commonly utilized relies on a servo-controlled heat source which maintains the abdominal skin temperature at 36° to 36.5°C (96.8° to 97.7°F). This technique generally keeps the baby's axillary temperature in the desired range of 36.5° to 37.0°C (97.7° to 98.5°F), thus providing a thermoneutral environment in which the child does not need to increase or decrease his oxygen consumption for purposes of thermoregulation.

Hypothermia has been shown to increase oxygen requirements as the skin temperature drops below 35.6°C (96°F) and may result in tachypnea, apnea, metabolic acidosis, hypoglycemia, disseminated intravascular coagulation, and peripheral vasoconstriction. Secondary complications (e.g., an increased risk of kernicterus and impaired surfactant production) may also follow inadvertent hypothermic stresses. On the other hand, hyperthermia can be equally devastating as it increases metabolic demands and oxygen consumption, and may cause episodes of apnea.

TABLE 1. *Factors influencing outcome of infants with respiratory distress*

Oxygenation
Temperature
Fluid balance
Circulation
Electrolytes
Acid-base homeostasis
Nutrition
Bilirubin
Glucose
Calcium
Hematocrit
Infection
Patent ductus arteriosus

The prevention of hypothermia must begin in the delivery room. When the birth of a premature baby is anticipated, the delivery room temperature is increased to 70°F or greater and the overhead warmer and incubator warmed in advance. The baby is dried immediately and thoroughly with absorbent towels, and all resuscitative measures are performed beneath a radiant warmer. When the infant has been stabilized, he is transferred to the nursery in a warmed incubator rather than carried in an attendant's arms. Avoiding hypothermia can significantly improve a premature infant's prognosis and prevent a mild respiratory problem from becoming a severe one.

See Chapter 5 for further discussion.

FLUID BALANCE AND CIRCULATION

Intravenous glucose and fluids are administered to all infants with significant respiratory difficulty to avoid aspiration, hypoglycemia, and dehydration. A 10% glucose solution (D_5W in infants less than 1,250 g) is normally infused at a rate of 80 to 100 ml/kg/day for the first 24 hr, and thereafter $D_{10}W$ with sodium chloride or sodium lactate (30 mEq/liter) and potassium chloride (20 mEq/liter) is administered at a rate of approximately 100 to 125 ml/kg/day. Children under radiant warmers may require 120 ml/kg/day or more from the onset. Generally, the child who weighs less than 1,250 g is *not* kept under a radiant heat device because of the difficulty of coping with enormous evaporative water losses and secondary hyperglycemia which results from the necessarily high infusion rates. One must be flexible in the use of fluids and glucose in high-risk situations, and rely on general guidelines and careful, frequent assessment of the patient.

Serum electrolytes are obtained daily (or more frequently when indicated), and the infusates are modified to compensate for abnormalities when necessary. Urine output and/or specific gravity is monitored routinely on all sick newborns. When urine flow rate falls below 2 ml/kg/hr or the specific gravity as estimated by a hand refractometer rises above 1.012, the rate of intravenous fluid administration is usually increased. The syndrome of inappropriate antidiuretic hormone secretion (i.e., hyponatremia, natriuresis, and concentrated urine) may occur in the sick newborn and must be ruled out before increasing fluid infusion rates.

Blood pressure is monitored every 1 to 4 hr or more often depending on the severity of the child's illness. The pressure of an infant with an umbilical arterial catheter can be followed continuously by means of an in-line pressure transducer. In most cases the *mean* arterial pressure is obtained by this method. If this instrumentation is not available, a sterile water manometer (such as that used for measuring spinal fluid pressures) can be filled with isotonic saline and attached intermittently to the arterial line. To convert the reading obtained to millimeters of mercury, simply divide the centimeters of water by 1.35.

At present, the most reliable noninvasive method for determining infant blood pressure is by means of Doppler technology, which provides systolic and diastolic measurements. Data on normal systolic pressures in small infants are

TABLE 2. *Average systolic, diastolic, and mean blood pressures during the first 12 hr of life in normal newborns according to weight*

Birth weight (g)	Blood pressure (mm Hg)		
	Systolic	Diastolic	Mean
1,001–2,000	49–52	26–31	35–40
2,000–3,000	57–64	32–38	41–45
Over 3,000	65–70	39–43	50–54

Adapted from Kitterman et al.: *Pediatrics,* 44:959, 1969.

limited; however, tentative guidelines for normal mean, systolic, and diastolic pressures are provided in Table 2. If the blood pressure falls below the normal range and/or the patient shows clinical signs of poor perfusion (decreased urine output, elevated specific gravity, metabolic acidosis, poor capillary filling), a careful investigation for possible causes is indicated. Potential contributing factors include sepsis, hypoxia, cardiac decompensation, or blood loss (e.g., placenta previa, fetal-maternal transfusion, twin-to-twin transfusion, or iatrogenic causes).

Decreased tissue perfusion due to hypotension frequently results in metabolic acidosis, hypoxia, and disseminated intravascular coagulation. Serious damage to vital organs such as the kidney, intestine, and brain may occur. Supportive treatment of symptomatic hypotension not caused by congestive heart failure includes the administration of plasma expanders (whole blood or 5% protein solutions) at a rate of 10 to 20 ml/kg over 30 min. One must be careful not to overload the vascular system as congestive heart failure may result.

Frequent cardiac auscultation and evaluation of the quality of peripheral pulses permit the early diagnosis of a patent ductus arteriosus. Failure of the ductus to close is relatively common in infants with respiratory difficulties, especially those born prematurely. Most close spontaneously, but it is important to identify early those patients who may require medical management or surgical ligation.

See Chapter 19 for further discussion.

ACIDOSIS

The patient's acid-base status is another parameter that requires frequent scrutiny. An elevated pCO_2 with low pH characterizes a respiratory acidosis due to a reduction in alveolar ventilation. In general, the pCO_2 should be maintained between 35 and 50 mm Hg. Whenever the pCO_2 rises above 50 mm Hg, one should be *prepared* for mechanical ventilatory support.

If the pCO_2 is not elevated and the pH and serum CO_2 content are low, a metabolic acidosis is present. Possible causes of metabolic acidosis are included in Table 3. Proper diagnosis and management of these predisposing factors are essential. A conservative approach to acidemia is considered if the cause of the

TABLE 3. *Causes of metabolic acidosis*

Tissue hypoxia (hypotension, low pO_2, severe anemia, abnormal hemoglobin-oxygen affinity)
Hypothermia
Sepsis
Necrotic tissue (necrotizing enterocolitis)
Others (diarrhea, renal defects, inborn errors of metabolism, late metabolic acidosis related to feeding)

acidosis has been determined and corrected in a patient who is not severely ill. A common example of this would be the infant with acute hypoxic stress and metabolic acidosis who, after resuscitation, appears to be in no significant distress. If there is no additional compromise, the infant will most likely correct his metabolic acidosis without a need for chemical buffering.

In the moderately or severely ill patient in whom the etiology of the metabolic acidosis cannot be determined or the primary cause is treated without a correction of the low pH, pharmacologic intervention may be appropriate. Buffers such as sodium bicarbonate and THAM (tris hydroxymethylaminomethane) are reserved for correction of uncompensated metabolic acidemia. Sodium bicarbonate has been the drug most frequently used to correct metabolic acidosis and acidemia in the newborn. As with most pharmacologic agents, the side effects observed with this drug must be recognized to avoid serious iatrogenic complications. The most commonly encountered adverse effects are summarized in Table 4. One important consideration is the increased osmolality which results from the rapid infusion of a hypertonic solution. Standard preparations of sodium bicarbonate (0.88 to 1.0 mEq/ml) have an osmolality of approximately 1,500 mOsm/liter. It is recommended that this be diluted with at least equal parts of sterile water, which still results in a concentration of almost 800 mOsm/liter—nearly three times the normal osmolality of the patient's serum. When infused over less than 5 min, the fluid shifts caused by this osmolar load may increase intravascular volume and possibly result in intracranial hemorrhage. Tissue damage may occur if this concentrated solution extravasates or is administered via a small-caliber artery. If the tip of the catheter is in a hepatic tributary, rapid infusion into the umbilical vein may cause severe hepatic necrosis. Electrolyte disturbances such as hypernatremia with its potentially adverse effects can also result from the sodium component of the bicarbonate.

TABLE 4. *Sodium bicarbonate—potential complications*

Hyperosmolality
Cellular dehydration
Intracranial hemorrhage
Tissue necrosis
Hypernatremia
Increased pCO_2
Hypocalcemia (?)

The pCO_2 of a patient may increase if the sodium bicarbonate is given rapidly and the patient has impaired pulmonary function. Since the pCO_2 level is inversely related to the pH, this elevation in the carbon dioxide tension reduces the drug's effectiveness in normalizing the acidemia. Carbon dioxide crosses biologic membranes with relative ease; therefore a rapid rise in the pCO_2 may result in cerebrospinal fluid (CSF) acidosis. This lowering of CSF pH is thought to cause central nervous system (CNS) depression and may interfere even further with the patient's ability to eliminate the accumulating CO_2. The disproportionately large rise in pCO_2 after bicarbonate infusion is observed most often in babies whose pCO_2 is greater than 50 mm Hg prior to administration.

THAM, which not only binds hydrogen ions but also reduces blood pCO_2, is an alternative to sodium bicarbonate as a buffer. Excreted by the kidney rather than the lungs, it depends less on pulmonary function for effectiveness. In the past, THAM was thought to be superior to sodium bicarbonate, but recent studies refute this assumption by demonstrating that THAM is only half as effective as bicarbonate, and therefore twice as much THAM is required. The most common potential complications associated with the administration of THAM include apnea, hypoglycemia, and an increased oxygen affinity for hemoglobin. Because THAM is excreted by the kidney, it must be used with extreme caution in patients with serious renal disease. Further, slow administration is required, as THAM is also hyperosmolar.

In summary, suggestions for treating acidosis with acidemia in the newborn are: (a) For a predominantly respiratory acidosis do not use sodium bicarbonate or THAM—the treatment is ventilation. (b) Determine and correct the underlying cause of the metabolic acidosis. (c) In general, use diluted sodium bicarbonate solutions rather than THAM. (d) Chemical correction of acidemia with either sodium bicarbonate or THAM should always be accomplished slowly, i.e., infusion rates over more than 5 min.

NUTRITION

The importance of providing adequate nutrition for infants with respiratory distress is frequently overlooked. The technique, volume, and rate of caloric administration must be individualized to the needs and limitations of each patient. A variety of methods, including intermittent gavage, continuous intragastric or transpyloric tube feeding, and peripheral hyperalimentation is available. However, the significant potential risks of each approach must be weighed against the possible adverse effects of prolonged malnutrition.

Hypoglycemia is commonly observed in any stressed infant because of limited glycogen reserves, reduced caloric intake, and an often accompanying increase in metabolic demands. Monitoring the blood sugar at frequent intervals during periods of stress is essential. In general, if the patient's blood sugar falls below 40 mg%, the amount of intravenous glucose is increased. Conversely, if the urine sugar is 0.5 g% or more on two consecutive specimens, the serum glucose, urine output, and glucose administration rates must be re-evaluated to avoid osmotic diuresis.

See Chapter 6 for further discussion.

BILIRUBIN

Hyperbilirubinemia is present in nearly all newborn babies with significant respiratory difficulties. Factors which predispose to kernicterus at lower bilirubin levels include prematurity, hypoxia, acidosis, hypothermia, hypoglycemia, and hypoproteinemia. Because many of these conditions may complicate the course of a child with respiratory distress, it is important to follow bilirubin and serum protein concentrations closely. Exchange transfusions may be required at total bilirubin levels considerably lower than those recommended for healthy infants.

See Chapter 9 for further discussion.

MISCELLANEOUS

Because of the high incidence of low total calcium values in infants with respiratory distress, it may be advantageous to add calcium gluconate to the intravenous solutions, although the efficacy of this is controversial. A 2-ml volume of 10% calcium gluconate added to each 100 ml of intravenous fluids usually corrects the serum calcium level in the asymptomatic child within 24 to 48 hr. If there is clinical evidence of hypocalcemia (i.e., seizures, irritability, apnea, or cardiac arrhythmias), a more rapid correction is indicated. Calcium gluconate 10% at a dose of 2 ml/kg body weight given intravenously over 15 to 60 min with careful monitoring of heart rate usually corrects the acute manifestations.

Iatrogenic anemia can develop rapidly, especially in the low birth weight infant who requires frequent blood sampling to monitor his progress. The hematocrit is not always a reliable index to the volume of blood removed from the newborn infant. If the baby who has had a significant fraction of blood withdrawn is suddenly stressed (e.g., sepsis, hypoxia, hypothermia), there may be a precipitous fall in the hematocrit or effective blood volume. It is important to keep precise records of the amount of blood removed. Whenever the amount withdrawn exceeds 10 to 15% of the child's blood volume, or the hematocrit falls below 45% during the acute phase of the baby's illness, a replacement transfusion is performed. The child whose cardiac status is stable can tolerate 10 ml packed cells or whole blood per kilogram if given over 30 min. Supplemental diuretics are usually not necessary. During the convalescent period blood is transfused more conservatively.

ASSISTED VENTILATION IN THE NEWBORN

Because space does not permit a thorough discussion of ventilation, only a few generalities concerning the handling of newborn infants with severe respiratory distress are reviewed. The most important factor determining the success of any ventilatory assistance program is the competence of the patient care team. Although elaborate equipment is often useful, such devices are of minor importance compared to the team of physicians, nurses, respiratory therapists, and other support personnel responsible for institution and ongoing management of ventilatory assistance. A physician experienced in assisted ventilation for the *newborn* must be available 24 hr a day. When a doctor cannot be in the hospital at all times, the nonphysician personnel must be meticulously trained to treat unexpected emergencies on an *interim* basis until the doctor arrives.

Continuous positive airway pressure (CPAP) has dramatically improved the outlook for premature infants with hyaline membrane disease. Continuous distending pressure may be administered by a number of modes, including head box, mask, endotracheal tube, nasal cannula or, negative pressure devices, and may serve as an adjunct to ventilator assisted respiration. No single mode of administration has been proved more effective than another. The main indications for CPAP at this point are disease states which respond to increased transpulmonary pressure, e.g., hyaline membrane disease, pulmonary edema, and atelectasis. Severe apnea of prematurity may also be effectively managed by the use of this technique. CPAP may have significant adverse effects, including decreased cardiac output due to impaired venous return and an increased functional residual capacity. These problems are encountered most often during the recovery phase when pulmonary compliance is improving.

It is important to remember that CPAP does not significantly improve minute ventilation. The child who is hypoventilating to the point of decompensation with an elevated pCO_2 and acidemia requires ventilator assistance and not CPAP alone.

Other complications of CPAP and ventilators include pneumothorax, pulmonary interstitial emphysema, pneumomediastinum, pneumopericardium, and pneumoperitoneum. When administered by head box, there may be lacerations of the neck, elevated noise levels, and possibly an increased incidence of intracranial hemorrhage. Nasal prongs and endotracheal tubes predispose to infection, may cause nasal necrosis, or may become inadvertently occluded. Gastric distention, which can result from all methods of delivery, may require an intragastric tube for decompression.

CONCLUSION

The remarkable improvement in the outlook of preterm infants, especially those with respiratory distress, is due to a number of developments in neonatal care. Ventilators have been designed for the smallest critical patients. Their place in the management of respiratory problems is no longer that of a desperate measure used for a dying infant but as a judicious intervention in the course of a serious illness. The use of constant distending airway pressure has been a major advancement in the supportive management of hyaline membrane disease and has allowed many infants to recover without the necessity of intubation and the attendant risks of mechanical ventilation. The development of referral centers for newborns has made available around the clock the special skills and services necessary for seriously ill babies.

The most important contributions have been in prevention, appropriate early management, recognition of the baby who is developing serious problems, and transport of that patient while he remains in stable condition. With the continuing improvements in the total care of the baby during fetal life and the intrapartum and immediate postpartum periods, the trend toward lower mortality and morbidity should be sustained.

CAVEATS

1. In addition to treatment of the primary disorder, general supportive measures in the infant with respiratory distress are essential for a favorable outcome.

2. The newborn, especially when sick, cannot tolerate even brief hypoxic episodes.

3. Avoiding hypothermia can significantly improve a premature infant's prognosis and prevent a mild respiratory problem from developing into a severe one.

4. The circulatory status of a neonate with respiratory distress is evaluated by measuring blood pressure, urine output, and specific gravity, and by detecting the presence of metabolic acidosis and poor capillary filling.

5. Respiratory acidemia (decreased pH, increased pCO_2) is treated with ventilation, not drugs.

6. Metabolic acidemia (decreased pH, normal or decreased pCO_2) is most often caused by hypotension and/or hypoxemia. Initial treatment of metabolic acidemia includes correction of these factors.

7. Sodium bicarbonate is infused slowly, over at least 5 min.

8. In neonates with acute respiratory distress, the hematocrit should be maintained at greater than or equal to 40 to 45%.

9. If possible, assisted ventilation is judiciously instituted before hypoxia and severe hypercapnia ensue; its use is not restricted to that of a desperate measure in a dying infant.

10. The most important contributions to the treatment of neonatal respiratory distress have been in prevention, appropriate early management, recognition of the baby who is developing severe problems, and transport of the patient while he is still in a stable condition.

16

Neonatal Bacterial Sepsis

Although only bacterial sepsis is considered in this chapter, it is reasonable to assume that viral infections are as common as, or possibly more common than, bacterial infections.

During the past 30 years, a dramatic change has occurred in the bacterial etiology of neonatal sepsis. Group A β-hemolytic streptococcus was a common cause of sepsis during the 1940s, *Staphylococcus aureus* during the 1950s, the coliforms during the 1960s, and now group B β-hemolytic streptococcus (GBBS). The most common agents currently responsible for neonatal bacterial sepsis are listed in Table 1. Other bacteria observed with increased frequency during recent years include group D streptococcus, *Hemophilus,* and *Bacteroides.*

PREDISPOSING FACTORS

A number of perinatal events cause one to suspect sepsis. These include maternal fever, pyuria, prolonged rupture of the membranes, prolonged difficult labor, low birth weight, prematurity, meconium staining, neonatal depression or asphyxia (low Apgar score), congenital anomalies, and surgical procedures.

When membranes are ruptured for more than 24 hr, the incidence of neonatal bacteremia is increased. Although we do not believe that *every* infant of a

TABLE 1. *Bacterial etiology of neonatal sepsis*

Group B streptococcus
E. coli
Group D streptococcus (enterococcus and nonenterococcus)
Klebsiella
Enterobacter
Proteus
Pseudomonas
Staphylococcus (coagulase negative and positive)
Hemophilus influenzae
Bacteroides

mother whose membranes have been ruptured for 24 hr or more should have a spinal tap, blood culture, and urine culture, we do recommend that every such infant who also demonstrates some other problem (e.g., prematurity, low Apgar score, respiratory distress, meconium staining, or any other predisposing factor, symptom, or sign of sepsis) have a complete set of cultures and receive antibiotics. However, the full term, perfectly normal infant whose mother had ruptured membranes for slightly more than 24 hr but who has no fever or other evidence of amnionitis probably does not require a complete septic workup and institution of antibiotics. We prefer simply to obtain a blood culture on these infants and observe them closely.

In any discussion of predisposing factors, it is important to emphasize the role of cross contamination by nursery personnel. A recent study showed that 24.6% of infants admitted to a newborn intensive care unit suffered nosocomial infections. Of the infants, 7.2% exhibited pneumonia or bacteremia with such organisms as *Pseudomonas, Staph. aureus, Escherichia coli,* and *Klebsiella,* and 3.4% developed septicemia. *Thorough washing of the hands before touching any infant is absolutely mandatory in the nursery.*

CLINICAL SIGNS OF SEPSIS

Table 2 lists the clinical symptoms and signs of sepsis. Essentially, whenever an infant is not normal, sepsis must be considered. Some of the most common presenting symptoms are change in feeding habits, lethargy or irritability, low or high temperature, apnea, and respiratory distress. All symptoms and signs must be regarded with extreme suspicion. Sepsis, like hypoglycemia, must be diagnosed and treated as soon as possible to obviate long-term sequelae or death. Low or high temperature specifically demands cultures and therapy until neonatal sepsis is ruled out. A normal temperature never excludes the possibility of sepsis in the newborn as one-third of infants with bacteremia have a normal temperature.

TABLE 2. *Clinical signs of neonatal sepsis*

Not doing well
Lethargy, irritability, seizures
Poor feeding, vomiting, diarrhea
Temperature instability (high or low)
Abdominal distention, ileus
Apnea, tachypnea, cyanosis, respiratory distress
Hypoglycemia, hyperglycemia
Jaundice, pallor, petechiae
Tachycardia, bradycardia
Low blood pressure, poor perfusion
Hepatosplenomegaly
Congestive heart failure

LABORATORY TESTS

Table 3 lists the laboratory tests that various investigators have suggested for evaluating infants for neonatal sepsis. The most important are the cultures—blood, cerebrospinal fluid (CSF), and urine. Blood cultures from umbilical catheters are not reliable unless they are performed at the time of sterile insertion of a catheter, and even then the data are controversial. Cultures obtained after a catheter has been in place for a few hours are probably not reliable. A chest X-ray is also obtained to rule out pneumonia.

The necessity of a spinal tap depends on the physician's index of suspicion. Some physicians obtain blood cultures more often than others because they have a much higher index of suspicion of sepsis. In some cases, it is reasonable to obtain a blood culture without a spinal tap. For example, the patient who presents at 2 hr of age with mild respiratory distress should always have a blood culture performed, but it is not absolutely mandatory that he have a spinal tap. As a general rule, though, spinal taps are performed whenever there is a possibility of sepsis.

Urine cultures are also very important when evaluating the infant with possible sepsis. It is very difficult, if not impossible, to get a clean urine specimen in

TABLE 3. *Laboratory tests in neonatal bacterial sepsis*

1. Cultures
   *Blood (not from umbilical catheters)
   *CSF (including cell count, glucose, protein, Gram stain)
   *Urine (preferably suprapubic)
   Stool ⎫
   Skin ⎪
   External ear ⎬ Generally not helpful
   Umbilical stump ⎪
   Gastric aspirate ⎭
   Maternal cultures (vaginal, amniotic fluid, urine, blood)
2. Hematology
   Neutrophil count: after 4 days, normal is approximately 1,500 to 15,000/mm³. May be high in hemolytic disease and asphyxia. May be high, normal, or low in sepsis.
   Bands: after 4 days, maximum normal is approximately 1,500/mm³.
   Platelets (decreased).
3. Other tests
   *Chest X-rays
   IgM
   Serum orosomucoid level
   Gastric smear for polymorphonuclear neutrophils (PMNs) and bacteria within PMNs
   Eosinophils: toxic granulations may appear with infection
   Nitroblue tetrazolium
   Pathologic section of umbilical cord for inflammation
   C-reactive protein
   Counterimmunoelectrophoresis

Blood, CSF, and urine cultures are most important, and no septic workup is complete without them. The value of all of the above tests except these cultures and the chest X-ray is controversial.

the newborn by awaiting spontaneous voiding. For this reason, suprapubic taps are usually performed. It must be remembered that these procedures are not benign; occasionally they result in significant bleeding with hematuria, and in rare instances rectal perforation occurs (see Chapter 26).

Surface cultures (e.g., skin, rectum, ear canal, throat, and gastric aspirate) are usually not helpful; they may be done in addition to the blood, urine, and CSF cultures, but they must never replace them. If these surface cultures are done *instead* of the urine, CSF, and blood cultures, they may contribute to a false sense of security.

Blood counts are also frequently used in the evaluation of infants for sepsis. After 4 days, the normal neutrophil count is approximately 1,500 to 15,000/mm^3. In the presence of sepsis, it may be high, normal, or low. The count may also be high in hemolytic disease and asphyxia. After 4 days, a normal band count is usually less than 1,500/mm^3. Other tests, listed in Table 3, have been advocated to evaluate infants with sepsis. All of these tests (except the blood, urine, and CSF cultures and the chest X-ray) may be helpful if used for screening purposes only. Our preference is to use the white blood cell count and differential for screening. If an infant has predisposing factors and symptoms or signs suggestive of sepsis, the latter tests must never be used to negate the need for appropriate cultures and treatment. All of these tests give a very high percentage of false-negative results. When dealing with a disease as devastating as neonatal sepsis, there is no room for false negatives.

TREATMENT OF SEPSIS

The antibiotic treatment of sepsis is outlined in Table 4. In general, there is no place for the use of oral antibiotics in the care of newborns. Intravenous antibiotics are necessary in infants with meningitis, in very low birth weight infants who have little muscle, and in infants with poor circulation (poor skin perfusion and low blood pressure). However, intramuscular antibiotics are usually adequate in larger infants who are not critically ill, who have a good blood pressure, and who do not have meningitis.

Antibiotics are not the only aspect of treatment of infants with sepsis. The general supportive care of the infant is just as important as the antibiotics. This includes monitoring the circulatory status, oxygenation, acid-base balance, electrolytes, glucose, bilirubin, platelet count, and other clotting tests. Complications such as ileus, meningitis, osteomyelitis, septic arthritis, and abscesses must be considered.

GBBS INFECTIONS

Streptococci are divided into groups on the basis of the polysaccharide coating of the organisms. The group B polysaccharide, of course, is common to all group B streptococci. In addition, the GBBS are typed according to another polysaccharide on the bacterial wall: types Ia, Ib, Ic, II, and III. Between 3 and

TABLE 4. *Initial therapy for suspected neonatal bacterial sepsis*

Therapy	Mode of administration	< 1 Week old	> 1 Week old
Ampicillin			
Sepsis	i.v./i.m.	100–150 mg/kg/day (q 12 hr)	100–150 mg/kg/day (q 8 hr)
Meningitis	i.v.	200–300 mg/kg/day (q 8 hr)	200–300 mg/kg/day (q 8 hr)
or			
Aqueous Pen G			
Sepsis	i.v./i.m.	50,000–100,000 U/kg/day (q 12 hr)	50,000–100,000 U/kg/day (q 8 hr)
Meningitis	i.v.	200,000–250,000 U/kg/day (q 8 hr)	200,000–250,000 U/kg/day (q 8 hr)
plus			
Kanamycin	i.m.	< 2,000 g: 15 mg/kg/day (q 12 hr)	< 2,000 g: 20 mg/kg/day (q 12 hr)
	or		
	i.v. (over 20–30 min)	> 2,000 g: 20 mg/kg/day (q 12 hr)	> 2,000 g: 30 mg/kg/day (q 8 hr)
or			
Gentamicin	i.m.	5 mg/kg/day (q 12 hr)	7.5 mg/kg/day (q 8 hr)
	or		
	i.v. (over 20–30 min)		

Any neonate with suspected sepsis has appropriate cultures (at least blood, urine, and CSF) and is started on the above antibiotic schedule. If cultures are negative after 3 days, antibiotics are usually discontinued. If cultures are positive, the antibiotic regimen is adjusted appropriately. If the blood culture is positive, antibiotics are continued for a *minimum* of 10 days.

TABLE 5. *Early-onset group B streptococcal infection*

1. Symptoms (respiratory distress, apnea, hypotension) within 48 hr of birth
2. Subtypes usually similar to those in maternal vagina
3. Occasionally associated with obstetric complications (prolonged ruptured membranes, maternal fever)
4. May be confused with respiratory distress syndrome (HMD) or TTN
5. High mortality
6. All GBBS serotypes involved, but when meningitis is present it is usually type III

40% of all pregnant females in their third trimester have GBBS in their vagina; 1 to 20% of all newborns are colonized with GBBS. The frequency of neonatal GBBS sepsis and meningitis is somewhere between 2/1,000 and 3/1,000 live births; the incidence is increased in low birth weight infants. The mortality of GBBS is between 30 and 80%. Additionally, as many as 45% of people who work in obstetric or nursery areas are colonized with GBBS. It is important to keep these large numbers in mind when considering routine prophylactic therapy of antibiotics for mothers and infants colonized with GBBS.

Clinical GBBS is usually categorized into early-onset and late-onset disease. In early onset infection (Table 5), symptoms usually occur within 24 to 48 hr after birth. The most common symptoms are respiratory distress, apnea, and hypotension. The subtype of GBBS is usually similar to that in the maternal vagina. Obstetric complications such as prolonged membrane rupture and fever are more common than in the normal population. The disease may very easily be confused with respiratory distress syndrome or transient tachypnea of the newborn (TTN); therefore *every infant who presents with significant respiratory distress, apnea, or hypotension should have a septic workup and be started on antibiotics.* The mortality of early-onset disease is very high, i.e., 30 to 90%. All GBBS serotypes are involved, but when meningitis is present, 90% of the time it is type III.

The chest X-ray may be normal or may show a picture indistinguishable from that of TTN or hyaline membrane disease (HMD). There is a higher incidence of pleural effusions in infants with GBBS. Because of this similarity, any neonate with respiratory distress, with or without a history of obstetric complications in the mother, should be cultured and given antibiotics.

Late-onset GBBS usually occurs after 7 days of age. In general, the GBBS serotypes are not related to the maternal vaginal flora. Therefore it is thought that this disease, unlike early-onset GBBS, is not acquired during delivery. Most of the cases of late-onset GBBS are associated with meningitis and usually are due to GBBS serotype III. The mortality is much lower than with early-onset disease, but neurologic sequelae may occur in survivors. There is also an increased incidence of infection at other sites, e.g., otitis media, septic arthritis, osteomyelitis, ethmoiditis, facial cellulitis, and conjunctivitis.

During recent years there has been an increased incidence of relapse in infants with GBBS meningitis who had been treated with ampicillin or penicillin. This may be due to a number of factors. The current recommendations for

152

TABLE 6. *Treatment recommendations for group B streptococcus meningitis*

1. Use penicillin 200,000 to 250,000 U/kg/day or ampicillin 200 to 300 mg/kg/day, intravenously.
2. Consider continuing penicillin-aminoglycoside combination because of possible enhanced killing of group B organisms.
3. After sterilization of the spinal fluid, continue intravenous antibiotics for at least 10 to 14 days.
4. Repeat spinal tap, blood culture, and urine culture 72 hr after cessation of treatment.

treatment of GBBS meningitis are listed in Table 6. Intravenous antibiotics are given for at least 10 to 14 days after the CSF is sterile. Seventy-two hours after treatment, a spinal tap, blood culture, and urine culture are obtained.

A significant problem in evaluating GBBS infections is the marked variation in colonization rates that have been reported. Why do researchers in one area find 40% of the women colonized with GBBS, whereas those in another area find only 3%? Probably the most important contributing factors are the number of specimens collected from each individual, the sites cultured, and the culture technique. It has been shown that culturing more frequently; culturing the cervix, vagina, and perianal area; and using a special culture medium dramatically increase the frequency of positive cultures for GBBS.

Most laboratories screen for group B streptococci by observing for β-hemolysis. However, a significant percent of group B streptococcal infections are not β-hemolytic; rather, they are gamma or nonhemolytic. This is true even if the cultures are performed under anaerobic conditions. Therefore laboratories should evaluate every streptococcus obtained from the blood, CSF, or urine of any infant, regardless of whether the streptococcus is β-hemolytic. These should be evaluated by biochemical or immunological methods more specific for GBBS, including hippurate hydrolysis, CAMP reaction, and immunofluorescence.

Many questions regarding GBBS remain unanswered. For example, is antibiotic prophylaxis in pregnant female carriers an appropriate means of eradicating the carrier state? The few data available, inadequate as they are, suggest that antibiotics may not be effective in eliminating the carrier state of GBBS. Also, there is good evidence that GBBS occurs in males and is transmitted venereally. Therefore if one treats all mothers with positive GBBS cultures, approximately 10 to 30% of all women and their husbands will be treated. More importantly, there is no evidence that the antibiotics rid the woman of the colonization state, or that they decrease the incidence of disease in the neonate.

Should a physician treat all infants born to mothers who have positive vaginal cultures for GBBS at term? This might include 20 to 30% of all newborns. Although many infants are colonized with GBBS, the incidence of symptomatic infection in the newborn is very low (1/1,000 to 2/1,000 births) in comparison. In addition, treating the infants or mothers who are colonized with GBBS does not eradicate late-onset GBBS as this disease does not seem to be acquired from the maternal vagina. Further, if one treats 20 to 30% of all newborns, what will be the effect of sensitizing them to penicillin allergy later in life?

Because of the above problems, we do not think it reasonable to treat every mother or every baby whose mother is colonized with GBBS. However, it may be prudent to treat the mother during labor or the baby whose mother is colonized with GBBS if the infant has any predisposing factors, signs, or symptoms.

CAVEATS

1. The most common bacterial causes of neonatal sepsis are group B streptococcus and *E. coli.*

2. Thorough hand washing before touching an infant is absolutely mandatory to prevent nosocomial infection.

3. Sepsis must be considered in any ill neonate.

4. The signs of neonatal sepsis are frequently vague; they include a change in feeding habits, lethargy, irritability, apnea, and respiratory distress.

5. Sepsis must be considered in every neonate with respiratory distress, apnea, or hypotension.

6. A low or high temperature always suggests sepsis; a normal temperature is never used as evidence against sepsis.

7. The most important laboratory tests for the evaluation of infants with possible sepsis are cultures of the blood, urine, and CSF.

8. Urine for culture is obtained by suprapubic bladder tap.

17

Newborn Transport—Stabilization of the Infant Before Arrival of the Transport Team

Transport of the critically ill newborn is a complex procedure requiring an organized system of communication, experienced personnel, equipment, and ambulance vehicles. The transport of critically ill neonates (but not necessarily mildly ill infants) should be performed by tertiary neonatal intensive care units. However, there is always a significant time lapse, frequently 1 to 2 hr, between the recognition of the acute illness in the infant and the arrival of the transport team. Therefore a great deal of responsibility lies with the physicians and nurses at the referring hospital to provide continuing care to the acutely ill infant. If this care is not provided before the arrival of the transport team, the mortality and morbidity increase. The best intensive care cannot undo hypoxic brain damage that has already occurred. It is necessary, therefore, that personnel in every hospital with an obstetric service be trained to recognize illness in the neonate and to initiate stabilizing measures. The role of the physicians and nurses in the referring hospital in stabilizing the infant is of equal importance to the actual transport of the infant by the level III tertiary center.

It would be ideal for every mother who delivers an infant who will become seriously ill to be delivered in a level III tertiary center with a newborn intensive care unit. However, 25 to 50% of infants who become sick do so unpredictably, a compelling reason for all hospitals to have personnel capable of stabilizing the acutely ill newborn infant. However, in 50 to 75% of cases, the need for intensive care can be predicted during the prepartum and intrapartum period. The mortality and morbidity of these infants could be decreased if they were delivered at tertiary medical centers staffed by perinatal obstetricians and neonatologists. Experience at numerous centers across the country shows that the mortality of infants born in level III centers is significantly less than similar infants born in level I and II centers and later transferred to level III centers. Therefore when high-risk prenatal conditions are known to be present, serious consideration should be given to referring the mother to a level III tertiary center.

CRITERIA FOR TRANSPORT

Personnel at each hospital must decide their capabilities for handling sick newborns. Preferably the decision to refer a sick infant is made in consultation with the tertiary level III neonatal intensive care unit. Caring for the sick newborn is a complex challenge which cannot be properly done without extensive experience and constant practice.

Table 1 lists the criteria for consultation, evaluation, and consideration of transport of infants from a level I to a level II hospital as well as criteria which necessitate transport to a level III center. These guidelines—not rules—are published in the American Academy of Pediatrics publication *Hospital Care of the Newborn.* Whenever there is doubt as to whether a newborn should be referred, consultation with a physician at the consulting hospital should be initiated.

PREPARATION OF THE INFANT FOR TRANSPORT

For all infants who require transport, certain information is documented and a number of procedures performed. Vitamin K_1 1 mg i.m. is given to each infant unless he previously received vitamin K. Eye prophylaxis is also provided to each infant. Consent for transfer from the referring hospital and for treatment at the referral center is obtained on standardized forms. Photocopies of the mother's and infant's charts accompany the infant. A detailed perinatal history sheet (see *Appendix*) is also completed by nurses or physicians caring for the infant. Maternal blood, 5 to 10 ml in a red stoppered tube and 5 to 10 ml in a

TABLE 1. *Criteria for consultation, evaluation, and possible transport of infants*

---

1. Criteria to be considered for infants who might require transfer to a level II or III hospital
    Gestation less than 35 weeks or weight less than 2,500 g
    Neonatal sepsis or infection
    Respiratory distress and metabolic acidosis persisting after 2 hr of age
    Neonatal blood loss
    Hypoglycemia
    Hemolytic disease of the newborn
    Infants of mothers taking hazardous drugs
    Infants needing more than routine observation
2. Criteria to be considered for infants who might require transfer to a level III hospital
    Any of the foregoing conditions
    Infants of diabetic mothers
    Neonatal seizures
    Sepsis and/or meningitis
    Congenital malformation requiring surgical care or observation
    Shock or asphyxia persisting beyond 2 hr
    Neonatal cardiac disorders with persisting cyanosis
    Persistent or recurring hypoglycemia
    Progressive, increasing respiratory distress
    Any neonatal condition requiring ventilatory support for more than 1 hr

---

From *Standards and Recommendations for Hospital Care of Newborn Infants.* American Academy of Pediatrics, 1977.

lavendar stoppered tube, and if available cord blood and placenta, are sent. All X-ray films (not reports) are transferred with the patient.

The hematocrit and blood glucose level are determined on every acutely sick infant. Arterial pH, pO_2, and pCO_2 values are obtained for every infant with cyanosis, apnea, or respiratory distress. Ideally, these are done on blood from a peripheral arterial stick, but a properly performed heelstick (capillary blood gas) may be adequate. For every infant with cyanosis or respiratory distress, X-rays are obtained in the newborn nursery using a portable machine. If the infant is being given oxygen, the X-ray is obtained with the infant still in the incubator or under a radiant warmer.

Temperature

One of the most important aspects of neonatal care is maintenance of an optimal thermal environment. Despite numerous articles, books, and lectures on thermoregulation, many infants, especially premature infants, are still not provided proper thermoregulation.

First, the infant's axillary temperature is measured. He is then dried and placed under a radiant warmer or in an incubator. The neutral environmental temperature is determined (see Chapter 5) and the incubator adjusted accordingly. If the infant is hypothermic, rewarming measures are initiated. The axillary temperature is maintained at 36.5° to 37.0°C (97.7° to 98.5°F). Whenever oxygen is administered, it is heated as well as humidified. Neonates are never placed directly on X-ray cassettes, scales, or other cold surfaces.

Hypoglycemia

Blood glucose is determined on all sick infants by a screening method (Dextrostix) or by means of a heelstick specimen sent to the laboratory. If the value is under 40 mg%, an infusion of $D_{10}W$ is started in a peripheral vein. If the infant has symptomatic hypoglycemia and the physician or nurse is unable to start a peripheral intravenous infusion (IV), umbilical venous catheterization is indicated.

See Chapter 8 for further discussion.

Intravenous Fluids

If an infant is in respiratory distress or has a distended abdomen, he should not be fed. An IV needle is placed in a peripheral vein. Usually $D_{10}W$ is given at a rate of 100 ml/kg/24 hr. If hypoglycemia, hypotension, metabolic acidosis, or gastrointestinal obstruction is present, further fluid adjustments are indicated after consultation with the referral center.

See Chapter 19 for further discussion.

Oxygenation/Ventilation

Oxygen is always provided at whatever concentration and by whatever method is necessary to relieve cyanosis, even if 100% O_2 is required. If possible, the ambient oxygen requirements are adjusted according to arterial blood gas analysis. Adequate oxygen is administered to maintain the arterial pO_2 at 50 to 80 mm Hg. It is important to be familiar with the characteristics of the resuscitation equipment being used; for example, some resuscitation bags deliver a maximum of 40% oxygen unless appropriately modified. Some incubators deliver only 40% oxygen unless the red flag in the back is turned in the vertical position; then it may reach 60%. If the infant is still cyanotic, warm humidified oxygen is administered by an oxygen mask or with an oxygen hood. Endotracheal intubation should be performed if: (a) the pO_2 is less than 50 mm Hg and the infant is in 100% oxygen; (b) the pCO_2 is greater than 60 mm Hg; or (c) the patient has persistent and intractable apnea not responding to stimulation. If someone with expertise in intubating infants is not available, a bag and mask with 100% oxygen can be used for ventilation. An oral gastric tube is placed to prevent gastric distention. The infant is ventilated continuously at a rate of 40 to 60 breaths/min.

Preventing Aspiration

All acutely ill infants should have an oral gastric tube placed via the mouth into the stomach and the stomach aspirated. In nonsurgical conditions the tube may be left in place to open gravity drainage. If a surgical lesion is present, a larger tube (10 to 12 Fr.) is used and intermittent suction applied to the gastric tube.

Shock

Hypotension in infants may be recognized by pallor, cyanosis, metabolic acidosis, mottling of the skin, poor capillary filling, and/or a low blood pressure. If acute blood loss is suspected (placenta previa, abruption), noncrossmatched O Rh^- whole blood or mother's blood may be given to the infant. In most infants the appropriate treatment includes volume expansion. This can be achieved most effectively by administering intravenously whole blood 20 ml/kg or a 5% protein solution (Plasmanate, Plasmatein, plasma, 5 ml of 25% salt-poor albumin diluted with 20 ml sterile water or D_5W). It is important to remember, however, that hypotension may also be secondary to such disorders as hypoxia, hypoglycemia, sepsis, congestive heart failure, and metabolic acidosis, in which case appropriate measures to treat these disorders should be instituted. Volume expansion is performed cautiously, as overzealous treatment may result in vascular overload with congestive heart failure and possibly intracranial hemorrhage.

Acidosis

The maintenance of adequate ventilation, oxygenation, and perfusion—not the liberal use of sodium bicarbonate—is the cornerstone of successful resuscitation. It is important to distinguish between metabolic and respiratory acidosis. If the pCO_2 is greater than 60 mm Hg, endotracheal intubation or ventilation with a bag and mask is performed. If a metabolic acidemia is present (low pH with normal or low pCO_2), one must consider the causes of metabolic acidosis (hypotension, hypoxia, sepsis, hypothermia, and necrotizing enterocolitis). Attempts to correct these abnormalities should be implemented promptly. In cases of severe metabolic acidemia (pH lower than 7.20 with normal or low pCO_2) which do not respond to the above therapy, sodium bicarbonate (2 to 3 mEq/kg) is administered intravenously by slow infusion over at least 5 min. The solution is first diluted 1:2 with sterile water. As infusion over 5 min is sometimes difficult, it may be helpful to stop the infusion part way and perform another procedure (e.g., blood pressure) before continuing.

Pneumothorax

Most infants with moderate or severe respiratory distress and a pneumothorax can be managed by placing a chest tube prior to transport. In infants without significant respiratory distress, placement of the chest tube may be delayed until arrival of the transport team.

In term infants who are in only mild or no respiratory distress, 100% inspired oxygen concentration may be used for a brief period to treat a pneumothorax. The pneumothorax is resolved by the principle of nitrogen washout. This treatment must *never* be used in premature infants, and never as the only therapy in infants with moderate to severe distress.

In emergencies, a No. 23 scalp vein needle may be used to aspirate the pneumothorax. The needle, connected to a stopcock and a 20-ml syringe, is inserted into the chest in the anterior axillary line with the needle passing over the superior edge of the third or fourth rib. While the needle is being advanced into the chest, negative pressure is applied with the plunger of the syringe. This technique may be used to relieve a pneumothorax temporarily until support personnel arrive.

A medium-sized intracath may be used as a temporary chest tube by inserting the catheter in the same position described above. After removal of the needle, the catheter may be connected to either a stopcock and syringe for aspiration of the pneumothorax or connected to an IV tubing with an underwater seal drainage.

See Chapter 33 for further discussion.

Ruptured Omphalocele or Gastroschisis

An omphalocele is a defect in the umbilicus accompanied by protrusion of intestine from the umbilicus. If the peritoneal covering is still intact, the infant may be managed with a sterile dry dressing applied to the defect; if the peritoneal covering has ruptured *in utero* and the intestines are exposed to the environment, the treatment is the same as that for an infant with gastroschisis.

A gastroschisis is a defect in the abdominal wall, usually at the base or lateral and inferior to the umbilicus. There is never a peritoneal covering, and peritonitis is always present. Infants with a ruptured omphalocele or gastroschisis have significant fluid losses and are often hypovolemic.

An intravenous line is placed and a 5% protein solution 10 to 20 ml/kg administered over 30 min. The entire lower half of the baby is wrapped in an intestinal bag (clear sterile plastic bag), an item available in most hospital central supply departments, and the drawstring of the bag tightened at the level of the axillae; this dramatically prevents fluid loss. To aid in the preservation of temperature, the child may be doubly covered with two such intestinal bags. A 10 Fr. oral gastric tube is inserted and intermittent suction applied to prevent distention of the intestines.

See Chapter 21 for further discussion.

Diaphragmatic Hernia

A diaphragmatic hernia occurs in about 1/2,200 live births. Ninety percent are on the left side. Infants with diaphragmatic hernia present with tachypnea, retractions, cyanosis, a flat or scaphoid abdomen, and an increased anterior/posterior (AP) diameter of the chest. If the hernia is on the left side, the heart sounds may be displaced to the right. The diagnosis is made by clinical suspicion and a chest X-ray. As soon as the diagnosis of diaphragmatic hernia is suspected or confirmed, 100% oxygen is administered to the infant if he is in respiratory distress. The mortality of neonates with diaphragmatic hernia who present with severe distress during the first few hours of life is extremely high. All such infants should receive 100% oxygen. A large 10 or 12 Fr. oral gastric tube is inserted into the stomach and low intermittent suction applied. If the infant is symptomatic with respiratory distress, endotracheal intubation is performed immediately to administer positive-pressure ventilation. Bag-to-mouth resuscitation without an endotracheal tube is avoided as this increases intestinal distention and further compromises pulmonary function.

See Chapter 21 for further discussion.

Esophageal Atresia and Tracheo-esophageal Fistula

Eighty-five percent of infants with tracheo-esophageal fistula have a proximal blind esophageal pouch with a fistula from the trachea to the distal esophagus and stomach. The clinical signs include respiratory distress with pneumonia, excessive oral secretions, coughing, choking, vomiting, and abdominal distention. The diagnosis is suspected when there is maternal polyhydramnios and can be confirmed by inability to pass a nasogastric tube into the stomach. An X-ray is always obtained with a nasogastric tube in place to document the proximal esophageal pouch.

The infant is treated with intravenous fluid therapy. A 10 or 12 Fr. oral gastric feeding tube is placed in the esophageal pouch and intermittent low suction provided to prevent accumulation of secretions. Because of the frequent occurrence of pneumonia, antibiotics are administered after blood cultures are obtained. The infant is kept in a head-up (30°) prone position to avoid gravity drainage of gastric secretions into the lungs via the distal tracheo-esophageal fistula. Oxygen is administered as needed to relieve cyanosis and maintain normal blood gases. The acid-base status is monitored and corrected.

See Chapter 21 for further discussion.

Bowel Obstruction

The cardinal signs of bowel obstruction in the newborn include: (a) a history of maternal polyhydramnios or aspiration of more than 20 ml gastric fluid from the infant at delivery; (b) failure to pass meconium during the first 24 hr of life; (c) persistent vomiting, especially bilious vomiting; and (d) abdominal distention. Any of these signs strongly suggest the possibility of intestinal obstruction and constitute a presumptive diagnosis until proved otherwise. A flat plate and upright (or lateral decubitus) X-ray of the abdomen is obtained. A large 10 or 12 Fr. oral gastric tube is placed with intermittent low suction. Usually a 5% protein solution 20 ml/kg is administered intravenously over 30 to 60 min because of the high incidence of hypovolemia in these infants.

See Chapter 21 for further discussion.

Suspected Sepsis

Any infant with suspected neonatal sepsis should have a blood culture, urine culture (preferably by suprapubic puncture), and a spinal tap, followed by the administration of antibiotics.

CARE OF THE FAMILY

The birth of an infant who is premature, critically ill, or has a serious congenital malformation is an unexpected event and usually results in an acute emotional crisis within the family. Regionalization of neonatal care has resulted in the transfer of these critically ill infants long distances to secondary or tertiary newborn intensive care units. As a result, parents are frequently long distances from their newly born child. Most neonatal intensive care units have a liberal policy for family visiting, but for medical, economic, or other reasons it may be several days or even weeks before the parents are able to visit the regional center.

Therefore, whenever possible, the parents are encouraged to see and touch their infant before the infant is transferred. A packet of information concerning the referral center, including a parent booklet, is given to the parents so they may familiarize themselves with the newborn intensive care unit to which their infant will be admitted. The parents are encouraged to call the referral center at least daily or, preferably, more often. The physicians and nurses at the referring community hospital should also call the newborn intensive care unit daily to check on the progress of their patient. They can then share this information with the parents and thus provide emotional support for the mother, who will probably not see her new infant again for many days.

RETURN TO THE NURSERY OF ORIGIN

For a number of reasons, it is preferable that infants be transferred back to the hospital of origin as soon as the services of the newborn intensive care unit are no longer required. According to the *Hospital Care of the Newborn*, the following criteria for adequate care in the primary hospital must be met: There must be (a) qualified medical care with a physician who will assume the direct care of the infant; (b) adequate staffing with qualified nursing personnel; (c) an infection surveillance program to ensure against cross contamination between institutions; and (d) a program to allow parents to care for their infant in the nursery with support, education, and appropriate instruction in hand washing techniques.

CAVEATS

1. Personnel in each hospital with an obstetric service must be trained to recognize illness in the neonate and to initiate stabilizing measures.
2. In high-risk prenatal cases, serious consideration should be given to the referral of the pregnant woman to a level III tertiary center.
3. In each infant with respiratory distress, a hematocrit, serum glucose, arterial pH, pCO_2, and pO_2, as well as a chest X-ray by portable instrumentation are obtained.
4. Oxygen is always provided at whatever concentration is necessary to relieve cyanosis.
5. In infants with gastroschisis or ruptured omphalocele, the lower half of the body is wrapped in an intestinal bag.
6. In infants with gastrointestinal diseases, an orogastric tube is placed and intermittent suction applied.
7. Parents are encouraged to see and touch their infant before the baby is transported.

18

Problems of the Very Low Birth Weight Infant

Currently, babies weighing less than 1,500 g comprise almost 50% of all admissions of infants below 2.5 kg to intensive care nurseries, and a similar increase in the number of very low birth weight (VLBW) babies weighing less than 1,000 g is being encountered (Fig. 1). Hence a working knowledge of the perinatal and postnatal problems of such infants is important to those involved in the delivery or early care of these infants.

The survival rate of such infants (500 to 1,000 g) is improving. Furthermore, the results of relatively short-term follow-up studies are encouraging in that the majority of these infants appear to be developing normally. With this background and the realization that the management of infants weighing less than 1,000 g at birth will undoubtedly change as our knowledge and skills increase, certain guidelines may be helpful when approaching the tiny baby.

PRENATAL AND INTRAPARTUM MANAGEMENT

Very few fixed rules can be given regarding intrapartum management of the VLBW infant. As the fetal weight and actual gestational age of such infants are often imprecisely known (e.g., 24 weeks versus 28 weeks), several conservative measures are warranted to optimize the intrauterine environment of the fetus.

1. Fetal size and gestational age are documented as accurately as possible when time permits (careful history, physical examination, ultrasound, etc.).

2. Potentially depressant drugs are avoided (e.g., anesthetics, narcotics, analgesics) as much as possible.

3. Maternal hypotension or uterine hypoperfusion is treated as indicated by volume expansion and positioning the mother on her side.

4. The fetus is monitored for evidence of fetal distress or compromise. Appropriate treatment of fetal distress may include maternal oxygen therapy, maternal positioning, or delivery of the baby.

5. If time permits, delivery of the infant in an appropriate facility capable of maternal and neonatal intensive care is ensured.

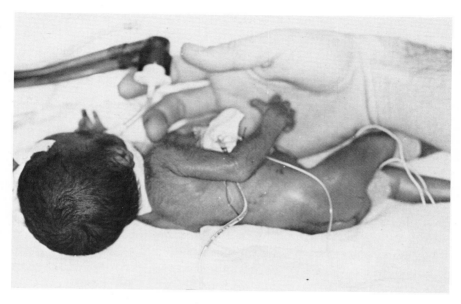

FIG. 1. A typical VLBW infant weighing less than 1,000 g (compare to the size of the hand) and requiring ventilator support.

The appropriate mode of delivery of such infants (cesarean versus vaginal) has not been established. For example, whether to perform cesarean section for a possible 26-week gestation infant weighing approximately 700 g is a decision with an unknown risk/benefit ratio. However, at some point between 26 and 30 weeks' gestation, cesarean section would be warranted for classical indications (e.g., unremitting signs of fetal distress, abnormal presentation).

RESUSCITATION/STABILIZATION

There is very little correlation between the degree of asphyxia and the Apgar score of the very small infant. As most babies less than 30 weeks' gestation demonstrate classic findings of immaturity with decreased muscle tone, impaired respiratory effort, etc., the Apgar score is low. Furthermore, there is a poor correlation between umbilical artery pH at the time of birth and the Apgar score in the low birth weight baby. Therefore, it is often impossible to make a reliable decision concerning potential survival while in the delivery room setting (unless lethal anomalies are apparent). Usually it is prudent to vigorously resuscitate and initially stabilize the very small infant. After a period of time (often 12 to 72 hr), it will become apparent whether the baby has a reasonable chance for survival. Prompt stabilization and transfer to a tertiary care facility are of primary importance in maximizing the chances for long-term intact survival.

Resuscitation and stabilization of these babies entail prompt and meticulous attention to the basic aspects of newborn care. These include: (a) Adequate ventilation and oxygenation. This often necessitates positive-pressure ventilation by either mask or endotracheal intubation. (b) Cardiovascular support. As the tiny infant is predisposed to hypovolemia at the time of birth, volume expansion may be beneficial if clinical signs of hypovolemia are present. For example, in the face of marked pallor, decreased blood pressure, or persistent metabolic acidosis, volume expansion with warmed blood, 5% protein, or a crystalloid solution (approximately 10 ml/kg over 5 to 30 min) may be indicated. (c) Temperature control is absolutely imperative but frequently difficult to achieve and maintain in the VLBW baby. Appropriate use of a preheated warmer, immediate drying, the use of Saran Wrap or other plastic wrapping, an increase in the delivery room temperature to 75° to 80°F, and heated mattresses may be useful.

After initial resuscitation, stabilization efforts include: (a) Documentation of adequate ventilation and oxygenation by either peripheral arterial blood gas sampling or the placement of an umbilical artery catheter for central arterial blood gas sampling. Usually it is best initially to supply a high, rather than a low, ambient oxygen environment to an infant who may be critically ill and then rapidly decrease the oxygen to a level which maintains an adequate arterial oxygen tension between 50 and 80 mm Hg. Such an approach is recommended for two reasons: First, clinical assessment of adequate oxygenation may be very misleading; and second, once hypoxemia is present, it may be more difficult to achieve adequate oxygenation. (b) Fluid replacement: the VLBW infant beneath a radiant warmer may lose inordinate quantities of water through the skin and respiratory tree. Because dramatic changes in water balance can occur within hours, the placement of a peripheral intravenous needle (IV) or central catheter to begin appropriate fluid replacement at approximately 100 to 150 ml/kg/day is imperative. The fluid normally consists of 5 to 10% dextrose and is given by constant infusion via a mechanical pump. (c) Glucose maintenance: although hypoglycemia (a blood sugar less than 40 mg%) does occur in the VLBW infant, it is relatively uncommon, as most of these infants acquire an intravenous line for parenteral glucose administration within the first minutes of life. Hyperglycemia is much more prevalent, occurring in 20 to 80% of the VLBW babies, with blood sugars occasionally reaching 700 to 800 mg%. For this reason it is often recommended that 5% dextrose be used initially in the VLBW infant for maintenance fluid and glucose administration when the baby is appropriately grown for his gestational age. If a baby is obviously small for gestational age, having suffered from intrauterine growth retardation, then 10% dextrose is recommended for his initial fluid and glucose replacement.

Many other problems encountered with increased frequency in the VLBW baby often require the attention of a neonatologist within the tertiary care center. Some of these additional problems include: (a) severe respiratory distress with pulmonary immaturity and hyaline membrane disease; (b) significant apnea and bradycardia, often lasting several days to several weeks; (c) serious fluid and electrolyte aberrations; (d) patent ductus arteriosus; (e) intracranial hemorrhage (intracerebral and intraventricular); (f) a high incidence of associated anomalies; (g) difficult nutritional management problems; (h) necrotizing enterocolitis; (i) retrolental fibroplasia; (j) increased risk of kernicterus from hyperbilirubinemia; and (k) an apparent increased risk of sudden infant death.

In spite of the sometimes monumental difficulties which may confront the family and physicians caring for the very small baby, the trend for intact survival of these infants is continually improving. Certainly the efforts of the primary physician responsible for the initial resuscitation and stabilization may dramatically affect their clinical course and ultimate outcome.

CAVEATS

1. The Apgar score does not correlate well with the degree of asphyxia in the VLBW infant.

2. Thermoregulation is especially important and difficult in the VLBW infant.

3. Hyperglycemia is a frequent problem in VLBW infants. D_5W is probably preferable to $D_{10}W$ as the initial intravenous fluid.

4. The survival rate and quality of survival of VLBW infants has improved dramatically during the past 10 years.

5. The care of the fetus and the initial resuscitation and stabilization of the VLBW infant dramatically affect the ultimate outcome.

19

Fluid and Electrolyte Management

Although the approach to the management of fluid and electrolyte problems in the newborn is similar to that in the older infant and child, several qualitative and quantitative differences exist. These relate primarily to the state of maturation of renal function, neonatal body composition, and endocrine control of fluid and electrolyte balance. Fluid requirements of newborns, particularly the immature, may vary tremendously in the same infant over time, as well as between infants. Familiarity with the usual water and electrolyte requirements of the newborn, the factors which may alter these requirements, and practical means for monitoring the newborn's fluid/electrolyte status permits most fluid and electrolyte problems in the newborn to be effectively anticipated and prevented.

WATER REQUIREMENT

Total body water is customarily divided into the intra- and extracellular compartments. In the adult the intracellular compartment normally comprises approximately two-thirds of the total body water space, which in turn comprises approximately 70% of total body weight. In the fetus and newborn, however, the total body water compartment is relatively larger, ranging from approximately 94% during fetal development to approximately 80% of body weight at term. This large total body water space is primarily due to a large extracellular water component. Indeed, at term the extracellular water comprises almost two-thirds of the total body water space, the reverse of the situation in the adult. The weight loss normally observed in the newborn during the first days of life is thought to reflect, in part, a physiologic loss of some of the extracellular fluid. This normal phenomenon may be anticipated in the normal newborn infant during the first days of life.

After birth, several potential routes of water loss may be identified in the newborn. The total water requirement of an infant, which represents the sum of these losses, is the summation of insensible water loss (IWL), urinary loss, stool loss, and abnormal losses (if any).

IWL is that water lost from the skin and respiratory tract. In the normal term infant, this comprises approximately 35 ml/kg/day. Although the respiratory component is generally very small, in low-humidity environments it can increase from approximately 5 ml/kg/day to 10 to 15 ml/kg/day. Evaporative water loss through the skin is certainly one of the principal components of fluid loss in the newborn infant. A major factor in determining the amount of this loss is the size of the infant. As body weight decreases, the proportional surface area from which evaporative loss can occur increases. For example, given the same environmental conditions, the water loss through the skin of a 1-kg infant is approximately 50% greater than that of a 3-kg baby (per kilogram infant weight). Environmental factors are other important determinants of the IWL. Factors which increase the IWL include the use of a radiant warmer (which may increase the obligatory IWL from the skin by 100 to 200%), the use of phototherapy (which may double evaporative water loss), increased body temperature, and low relative humidity.

Stool losses are normally low (5 ml/day) and are usually not considered a significant variable in the fluid management of a newborn infant; however, such losses may become considerable with phototherapy (which reduces transit time and increases stooling) or diarrhea.

Approximately 95% of normal newborn infants void within the first 24 hr of life. The usual flow rates of urine are approximately 1 to 3 ml/kg/hr (25 to 75 ml/kg/day). Spontaneous voiding occurs every 1 to 4 hr. The normal urine output of newborn infants is extremely variable. In some cases this variability may reflect the underlying state of hydration of a particular infant, assuming there are no other complicating factors. For example, in an infant who is dehydrated, the urine may be concentrated in an attempt to reduce urine output.

The ability of the newborn to adapt to fluid restriction or excess is limited. Because the glomerular filtration rate is reduced in the term infant, and even more so in the premature baby, the newborn baby has a limited, although appropriate, response to either under- or overhydration. In other words, a baby's limits of tolerance are much narrower than those for an older infant or child. Other factors that contribute to the newborn's inability to finely regulate his fluid balance include an incompletely developed endocrine system for controlling water homeostasis (antidiuretic hormone secretion, adrenal function), and renal tubular function.

Methods for limiting excessive fluid losses, and thereby decreasing fluid replacement needs, include: (a) judicious use of radiant warmers and phototherapy; (b) use of Perspex plastic shields (Fig. 1), Saran Wrap, or plastic coverings (Fig. 2); (c) humidification; and (d) maintenance of the neutral thermal environment.

In summary, the water requirements for a normal term infant during the first days of life approximate 90 ml/kg/day (IWL 35 ml/kg/day, urine loss 50 ml/kg/day, stool loss 5 ml/kg/day). The premature infant normally has a water

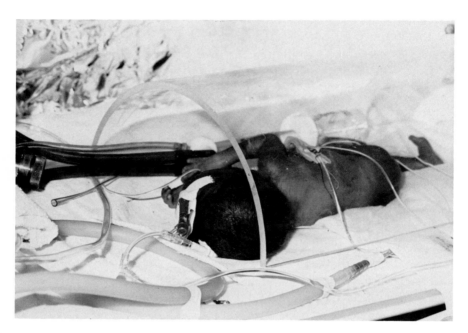

FIG. 1. A Perspex plastic shield is shown covering a small premature infant within an incubator. This device acts as a double-walled incubator, permitting better temperature and fluid management when frequent access to the patient is necessary.

FIG. 2. A plastic "bubble" covering is shown with properties similar to those of the Perspex plastic shield.

requirement of 100 to 140 ml/kg/day during the first days of life (IWL 45 to 60 ml/kg/day, urine 50 to 75 ml/kg/day, and stool loss 5 ml/kg/day). These values are only approximate, so each baby must be assessed frequently for evidence of normal water balance.

ASSESSMENT OF FLUID BALANCE

From the above, it is apparent that the water requirements for newborns may be affected by a variety of factors which may vary from hour to hour or day to day. Close supervision of fluid balance in the newborn is imperative as inadequate fluid replacement may result in acute dehydration and poor tissue perfusion; excessive water replacement may cause congestive heart failure, cerebral or other tissue edema, as well as the possible development of a patent ductus arteriosus. The following parameters may be utilized to monitor the fluid balance of an infant.

Body Weight

Body weight is the most reliable method of monitoring fluid status. Normal weight loss during the first week of life is 5 to 10% of birth weight, usually reaching a nadir between 3 and 7 days postnatal age. In very low birth weight infants (less than 1,200 g), weight losses of up to 15% have been observed in relatively "normal" circumstances. Serial body weights are determined on a routine daily basis or more often as clinically indicated. Serial weights which change by more than 30 g (1 ounce) between consecutive measurements should be checked. It is imperative that an accurate scale and consistent routine be utilized for determining an infant's weight. For example, any equipment (e.g., an armboard) added to an infant between weighings is separately weighed and noted on the chart.

Tissue Turgor

Turgor is often difficult to assess reliably in babies. Gross dehydration is normally evident by classic signs, e.g., dry skin, dry mucous membranes, sunken eyes, and perhaps tenting of the skin. Conversely, generalized edema indicates total body water excess. Edema is not a disease in itself, but it represents a symptom of underlying pathology which needs to be identified and treated when possible (e.g., congestive heart failure, iatrogenic fluid overload, etc.). Edema does not necessarily mean intravascular fluid overload. In fact, most infants with severe hydrops fetalis (anasarca) during the immediate newborn period have normal or reduced blood volumes. Therefore vigorous treatment with diuretics may jeopardize vascular perfusion in such an infant. It is important to evaluate thoroughly an infant's total status before treating edema aggressively.

Blood Studies

Hematocrit

Hematocrit is too variable during the newborn period to be helpful in assessing hydration.

Blood Urea Nitrogen

Blood urea nitrogen (BUN) is also variable, depending on renal function, tissue catabolism, and dietary protein intake. A BUN of greater than 15 to 20 mg%, however, is relatively unusual in the newborn and may reflect some degree of dehydration if renal disease is not present.

Serum Osmolality and Serum Sodium

Osmolality may be determined in the laboratory by direct measurement (usually freezing point depression) or calculation. The most reliable formula for calculating osmolality is:

$$\text{Osmolality (mOsm/liter)} = 1.86 \text{ sodium (mEq/liter)} + \frac{\text{BUN (mg\%)}}{2.8} + \frac{\text{glucose (mg\%)}}{18} + 9$$

The normal serum osmolality is approximately 285 mOsm/liter. However, the serum sodium level is the most readily available parameter that can accurately reflect osmolality. (The approximate serum osmolality is obtained by doubling the serum sodium value.) *A combination of body weight measurements, urine output and specific gravity, and serum sodium level provides the best assessment of overall hydration and electrolyte balance.* Serum sodium measurements may be required daily or more often depending on the clinical situation.

Usually a low serum sodium level reflects overhydration (evidenced by an increase in weight). This is usually the result of excessive fluid administration, perhaps in the presence of compromised renal function, or secondary to more unusual problems (e.g., inappropriate antidiuretic hormone secretion). In addition, excessive sodium loss from the urine, intestinal drainage, thoracic drainage, or other sites must be considered. The determination of serial body weights aids in the diagnosis. Increased serum sodium may reflect dehydration with a disproportionate loss of free water (e.g., an infant under a radiant warmer) or excess replacement of solutes (i.e., excessive administration of sodium chloride or sodium bicarbonate).

Urine Studies

Specific Gravity

Specific gravity, as determined by hand refractometer, is directly proportional to urine osmolality. The normal specific gravity in the newborn is 1.005

to 1.012, reflecting a urine osmolality of 150 to 300 mOsm/liter. The newborn kidney is capable of concentrating urine to within this range; however, maximal concentrating and diluting capacities in the newborn are limited as compared to those in the adult. Some newborn infants can concentrate their urine to a maximum of approximately 700 mOsm/liter, or a specific gravity of 1.019 to 1.020. An infant who is excreting urine with a specific gravity of 1.015 without other evident problems may therefore be more than normally concentrating his urine and thus relatively dehydrated.

It is important to remember that glucose and protein in the urine artifactually raise the specific gravity by a small factor. For example, 3+ glucose in the urine may raise the specific gravity approximately 0.006. Albumin increases the specific gravity by a smaller degree.

Quantitative Urine Output

In critically ill neonates, careful input/output records should be maintained on an hourly basis. Although factors such as congestive heart failure and renal failure may affect urine output, the flow rate of urine may be a useful guide to hydration status. A normal urine flow rate is 1 to 3 ml/kg/hr. The most difficult problem is finding a reliable means of urine collection and quantitation. In a large infant, standard urine collection bags may be suitable, particularly in the female (Fig. 3). In the male infant, a test tube or syringe barrel may be taped to the penis (Fig. 4). Another alternative for collecting urine from a female is the

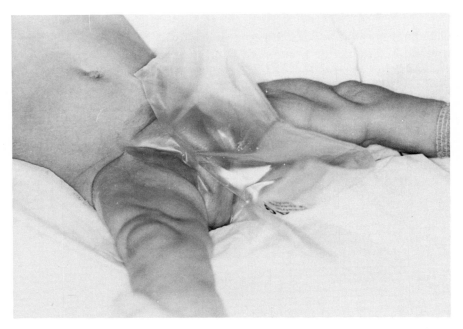

FIG. 3. A urine collection bag is attached over the perineum of a female infant. This is useful for urine collection but is not suitable for obtaining "sterile" urine specimens for culture.

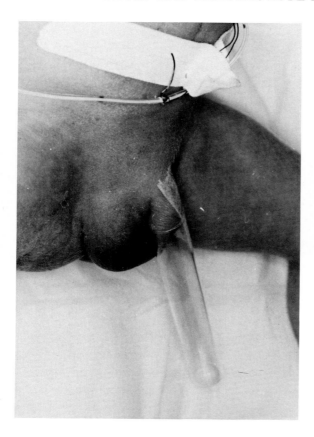

FIG. 4. A test tube is attached to the penis of a male infant for urine collection. A feeding tube and syringe may be used to aspirate urine from the tube at regular intervals, without retaping the tube in place.

use of a diaper or cotton balls over the perineum. Urine may be aspirated with a syringe from a diaper or a cotton ball and used reliably for measuring specific gravity and other parameters (glucose, protein, blood, etc.). Figure 5 depicts an infant with cotton balls placed over the genitalia and maintained in place by an improvised Saran Wrap diaper. Because of its transparency, this diaper permits immediate recognition of freshly voided urine, which may be quantitated by either weighing the cotton balls or expressing the urine into a volumetric container. Bladder catheterization is rarely (if ever) indicated in the newborn.

ELECTROLYTE BALANCE IN THE NEWBORN

Electrolyte requirements are somewhat variable in the newborn infant, particularly in the very small baby.

Sodium

The sodium requirement varies inversely with gestational age. The very small infant at 28 weeks' gestation weighing 1,000 g may require sodium up to 5 to 6 mEq/kg/day, during the first days of life. The normal term infant requires 2 to

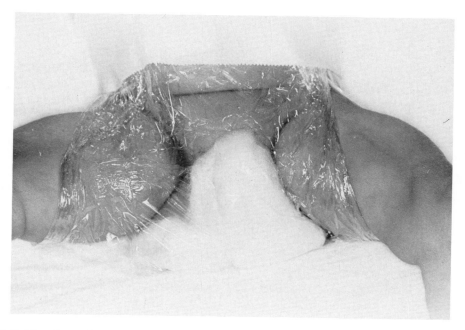

FIG. 5. The Saran Wrap "diaper" with cotton balls is properly placed for urine collection from a female infant.

3 mEq/kg/day. The sodium requirement is determined primarily by urine losses and any other ongoing abnormal losses. If precise quantitation of sodium output is required, 24-hr quantitation of the urine output (or other losses) may be performed and a spot specimen sent to the laboratory for sodium determination. In this way, the 24-hr output of sodium may be calculated more precisely and the sodium replaced appropriately over the 24-hr period. Requirements for the low birth weight infant may change dramatically over the first days or weeks.

Potassium

The potassium requirement is approximately 2 to 3 mEq/kg/day. Exaggerated losses may occur through the intestinal tract, particularly during episodes of diarrhea.

Chloride

Although the requirement for chloride in the newborn is not precisely known, sodium replacement is frequently provided as sodium chloride. Therefore the baby usually receives chloride at approximately 2 to 3 mEq/kg/day.

SUMMARY

Fluid and electrolyte problems are some of the most commonly encountered difficulties during the newborn period. Familiarity with the basic factors that may alter fluid balance, as well as the parameters to monitor changes in fluid status, normally provide the tools to prevent serious complications. In most cases fluid and electrolyte disorders in the newborn may be anticipated and serious aberrations effectively prevented by appropriate intervention.

CAVEATS

1. Approximately 95% of normal newborn infants void within the first 24 hr.
2. The ability of the newborn to adapt to fluid restriction or excess is impaired.
3. Factors which increase fluid requirements include radiant warmers, phototherapy, increased body temperature, and low environmental humidity.
4. The most helpful parameters for monitoring fluid balance are body weight, urine output and specific gravity, and the serum sodium level.

20

Necrotizing Enterocolitis

Necrotizing enterocolitis (NEC) of the newborn has been reported with increasing frequency over the past 10 to 15 years. Indeed, in recent years NEC has become the single most common surgical emergency in many newborn intensive care units. NEC, which varies greatly in incidence from hospital to hospital, occurs in 1 to 20% of premature infants admitted to intensive care centers. This chapter provides information concerning the pathophysiology, possible etiologies, clinical diagnosis, and management of infants with NEC.

CLINICAL PICTURE AND DIAGNOSIS

NEC is almost exclusively a disease of the premature infant, especially those who weigh less than 1,500 g. It is more common in infants who sustain significant intra- and extrauterine stress (Table 1). Exactly how these factors are involved in the pathogenesis of NEC is not known. The basic underlying mechanism of NEC is mucosal damage (Fig. 1), which may result from bowel ischemia secondary to hypotension, thrombosis, shunting of blood away from the gut ("diving reflex"), or hypoxia. The role of infection in the pathophysiology of NEC is uncertain. At present, it seems likely that the septicemia may be

TABLE 1. *NEC—predisposing factors*

Prematurity
Asphyxia
Shock
Hypoxia
Respiratory distress
Formula feeding (age of initiation, volume and rate of feeding, concentration and osmolality of formula)
Sepsis
Umbilical catheters
Exchange transfusion
Patent ductus arteriosus

secondary to the damage to the gut mucosa. Immunologic deficiencies associated with lack of breast feeding may predispose the gut mucosa to infection.

Finally, early enteral feedings, rapid increases in the volume of feedings, and the use of hypertonic formulas may predispose to NEC by directly damaging or "stressing" the mucosa.

The signs and symptoms of NEC are shown in Table 2. The number and severity of symptoms are highly variable, ranging from mild abdominal distention to peritonitis.

The most important point in the diagnosis of NEC is to suspect the disease in a baby with suggestive clinical signs and to confirm it radiographically and with appropriate laboratory tests (Table 3). At the first sign of possible NEC, a supine and either upright or lateral decubitus X-ray of the abdomen is obtained. Findings which may be seen on X-ray are listed in Table 4.

MANAGEMENT OF INFANT WITH NEC

Prompt recognition and treatment are critically important (Table 5). All infants are given nothing orally, and a nasal or oral gastric tube is placed to low intermittent suction. All infants are given intravenous fluids as well as parenteral antibiotics for gram positive and gram negative microbial coverage. The role of oral antibiotic therapy (kanamycin, gentamicin, and neomycin) is controversial at this time, but not generally recommended.

The baby's circulatory status must be evaluated frequently by monitoring the blood pressure, urine output, and urine specific gravity. Infants with NEC are frequently hypovolemic because of pooling or "third spacing" of fluid in the damaged intestine. Therefore, with evidence of hypovolemia (low blood pressure, decreased urine output, high specific gravity), plasma expanders such as 5% protein solution or whole blood are administered at 10 to 20 ml/kg. The oxygen and acid-base status of the patient must also be monitored closely. Environmental oxygen is administered to maintain the arterial pO_2 at 60 to 80

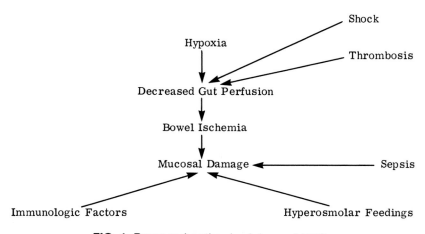

FIG. 1. Proposed pathophysiology of NEC.

TABLE 2. *NEC—clinical signs*

Temperature instability
Apnea
Abdominal distention
"Looking poor," lethargy
"Feeding poorly," increased gastric residual (greater than 3 to 5 ml)
Vomiting (bilious)
Bloody stools
Peritonitis (tender, erythematous abdomen; mass)
Impaired circulation (decreased blood pressure, decreased urine output, increased specific gravity, poor perfusion)

TABLE 3. *NEC—laboratory work-up*

X-rays (including upright or lateral decubitus)
Cultures (stool, blood, urine, CSF)
pH, pCO_2, pO_2
Serum electrolytes, calcium, bilirubin
Urine specific gravity
Hematocrit, white blood count
Platelet count
Stool guaiac/Hematest
?Clotting studies (PT, PTT, FSP, fibrinogen)

TABLE 4. *NEC—x-ray findings*

Nonspecific bowel gas pattern (Fig. 2)
Ileus
Decreased bowel gas
Dilated loop(s) of bowel (Fig. 3)
Thick (edematous) bowel wall
Pneumatosis (intramural air) (Fig. 4)
   Linear streaks
   Bubbly appearance
Peritoneal fluid (bulging flanks, centrally positioned bowel)
Portal venous air
Free peritoneal air

mm Hg. Respiratory support is provided if persistent apnea or hypercapnia ensues. Metabolic acidosis is treated appropriately with sodium bicarbonate, and with plasma expanders if hypovolemia is present.

The serum sodium level is determined at least daily. Blood transfusions are provided to maintain a hematocrit above 40 to 45%. Infants with NEC frequently develop thrombocytopenia as a result of localized or disseminated intravascular coagulation. Appropriate coagulation studies [platelet count, prothrombin time (PT), partial thromboplastin time (PTT), fibrinogen level, fibrin split products (FSP) assay] may be indicated in the presence of thrombocytopenia or clinical evidence of bleeding problems (e.g., oozing from heelsticks). Platelets are administered if the platelet count drops below 20,000 to 50,000/mm³. All stools are checked routinely for blood, grossly and by Hema-

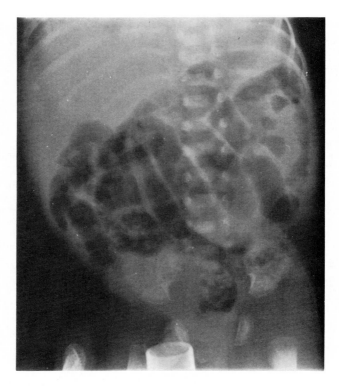

FIG. 2. Nonspecific bowel gas pattern with possible pneumatosis in right lower and left lower quadrants.

test® or guaiac test. Infants with a definite diagnosis of NEC but who do not meet criteria for surgery are treated for a minimum of 10 days. Because of the inability to feed the patient during this time, parenteral alimentation (glucose, amino acids) by peripheral vein is instituted.

The indications for surgical treatment of infants with NEC (Table 6) remain somewhat controversial. However, the following guidelines are generally acceptable: (a) bowel perforation; (b) a deteriorating clinical course—either persistent apnea, metabolic acidosis, or hypotension in spite of appropriate medical support; and (c) evidence of peritonitis, e.g., a tender abdomen with edema or inflammation of the abdominal wall, or an abdominal mass. A persistently dilated intestinal loop associated with pneumatosis may be an additional radiographic indication for operation.

The management outlined above for definite cases of NEC is relatively straightforward. A more frequent problem for the clinician is what to do with the baby with questionable NEC, i.e., the infant with mild abdominal distention or increased gastric residual but *no other abnormality suggestive of NEC*. Table

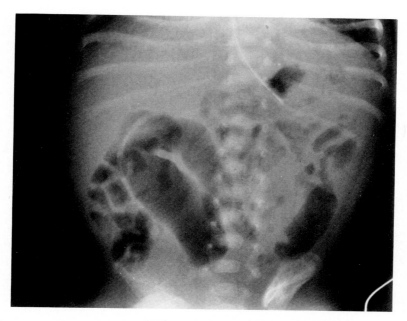

FIG. 3. Single dilated loop of bowel with decreased bowel gas in the remaining part of the bowel.

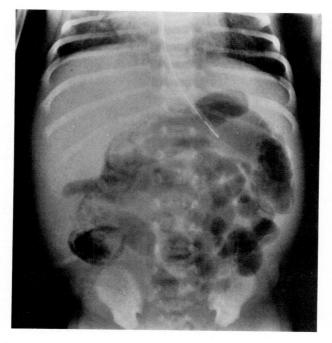

FIG. 4. Classical pneumatosis in right lower and left upper quadrants.

TABLE 5. *NEC—treatment, medical*

General
  Frequent physical examination (q 2-4 hr), X-rays
  Nothing orally for at least 10 days
  Nasogastric suction
Infection
  Antibiotics
    Systemic
    ??Oral
Circulation monitoring
  Blood pressure (B.P.)
  Urine output, specific gravity
  If evidence of poor perfusion (decreased B.P., decreased urine output, increased specific gravity), give colloid or blood 10-20 ml/kg
Respiratory monitoring
  Maintain pO_2 at 60-80 mm Hg
  Maintain hematocrit greater than 45%
  Acid-base monitoring
Coagulation monitoring
  Platelets, ?PT, ?PTT, ?FSP, ?fibrinogen
Treatment of patent ductus arteriosus
Hyperalimentation

TABLE 6. *NEC—indications for surgery*

Perforation
Deterioration of clinical course (decreased platelets, decreased pH, apnea, decreased blood pressure)
Peritonitis (tender, erythematous abdomen)
?Persistently dilated loop of bowel

7 lists our approach to these infants. Obviously clinical judgment and expertise are needed in these situations. In general, we advocate treating the infant when there is any doubt.

A number of reports in the literature have suggested new "discoveries" concerning the etiology and treatment of NEC. Some of these are listed in Table 8. The answer to these questions must await further research.

PROGNOSIS

Most studies have shown a consistently improved mortality rate in the medical and surgical management of NEC. This probably reflects early recognition of the disease, improved supportive medical care, better operative preparation,

TABLE 7. *Management of "questionable NEC"*

1. Definition: minimal signs.
2. Initially the same as treatment of definite NEC.
3. If clinical and laboratory signs do not progress and, in fact, resolve quickly (i.e., patient did not have NEC):
   a. Treat for 24 to 48 hr.
   b. Remove nasogastric suction and observe for 24 hr.
   c. Begin feeding *slowly* with dilute formula.
4. If clinical or laboratory signs are significant or persist, and there is serious question about the diagnosis, treat for 7 to 10 days.

TABLE 8. *Current unanswered questions*

1. What is the role of the gastrointestinal microflora (*Klebsiella, E. coli, Clostridium*) in the pathogenesis of NEC?
2. Does fresh breast milk provide protection?
3. Do early feeding and the rate of advancement of feedings increase the risk of NEC?
4. Is the formula concentration (10 cal/ounce vs. 24 cal/ounce) related to the risk of NEC?
5. Do oral aminoglycosides decrease the risk of NEC?
6. Are oral aminoglycosides helpful in the treatment of NEC?

and more vigorous supportive postoperative care, including the use of parenteral nutrition. In some infants, especially those treated medically, bowel obstruction secondary to stricture formation may develop later (within several weeks or months of the initial episode).

CAVEATS

1. The most important point in the diagnosis of NEC is to maintain a high index of suspicion in susceptible infants.

2. The most common presenting signs of NEC are abdominal distention, increased gastric residual, bilious gastric residual, and the varied signs of sepsis.

3. Overaggressive feeding of the very low birth weight infant may predispose to NEC.

21

Surgical Emergencies in the Newborn

Neonates are not infrequently born with life-threatening congenital anomalies that require immediate surgical correction if the infant is to survive. This chapter deals with the recognition and stabilization of common surgical emergencies in the newborn, including esophageal atresia with tracheo-esophageal fistula (TEF), alimentary tract obstructions, abdominal wall defects, and congenital diaphragmatic hernia. Prompt recognition, stabilization, and transfer to an appropriate tertiary care facility may be life-saving in many instances. Contrast radiographic studies to confirm the diagnosis, as well as surgical treatment, may be fraught with significant complication and require extensive expertise and experience.

ESOPHAGEAL ATRESIA AND TEF

Infants with esophageal atresia frequently present with respiratory distress and excess salivation (Fig. 1). Choking, coughing, and cyanosis are often encountered during the first feeding. Infants with an associated TEF often develop acute gastric dilation caused by air entering the distal esophagus and stomach with each inspired breath. Because most neonates have an incompetent lower esophageal sphincter, the gastric dilation ultimately leads to reflux of gastric acid through the fistula into the lungs, resulting in aspiration and chemical pneumonitis.

The five recognized anatomic variants of TEF are seen in Fig. 2, the most common (approximately 90%) being proximal atresia with a distal TEF. The incidence of this anomaly is approximately 1/1,500 births, with boys and girls equally affected. The ultimate survival of these infants usually depends on prompt recognition and expeditious transfer to institutions fully equipped and staffed with experienced personnel familiar with the complicated care required. Approximately one-third of the infants are of low birth weight. Associated

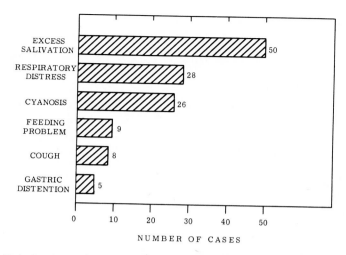

FIG. 1. Relative frequency of presenting symptoms among 84 cases of TEF.

anomalies are common (70%), particularly of the cardiovascular system, gastro-intestinal tract (imperforate anus and duodenal atresia), genitourinary tract, and musculoskeletal system. TEF has also been observed in patients with Down's syndrome and trisomy-18. In addition, many may have the VATER association (V, vertebral or vascular defects; A, anal anomalies; T, TEF; E, esophageal atresia; and R, radial limb or renal anomalies).

The defect may be anticipated if maternal polyhydramnios is noted prior to the baby's delivery. The diagnosis of esophageal atresia is not difficult to confirm: attempted passage of a firm red rubber or synthetic catheter through the nose into the esophagus demonstrates obstruction at the level of atresia. Frontal and lateral X-rays of the chest and abdomen are obtained with the catheter in place, showing the tip of the catheter at the end of the atretic proximal esopha-

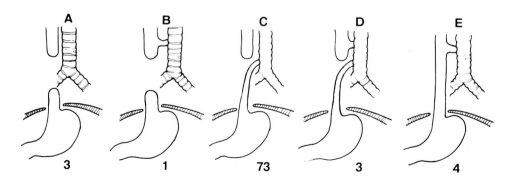

FIG. 2. Relative frequency of anatomic variants of TEF among 84 neonates with esophageal atresia admitted to Indiana University Medical Center. The numbers at the bottom indicate the number of cases.

geal pouch. If gas is present in the gastrointestinal tract, a TEF must therefore also be present. If no gas pattern is observed below the diaphragm, a fistula is unlikely. These simple observations allow a diagnosis in at least 95% of cases of esophageal atresia. Occasionally, contrast studies are required for diagnosis of the rarer forms of proximal esophageal fistula, a double fistula from the proximal and distal esophageal segments, and the H-type fistula without atresia.

Emergency care of the infant involves aspiration of the oral pharynx to clear secretions. This may be accomplished by insertion of a double-lumen Replogle sump catheter into the blind pouch. The catheter is maintained on continuous suction to keep the pouch dry, and the infant is started on antibiotic therapy. The truly emergent aspect in the care of this anomaly concerns the occurrence of potentially lethal aspiration pneumonia due to reflux of gastric juice from the dilated stomach through the TEF. The infant is maintained with the head slightly elevated and on the right side to keep the gastric fluid meniscus low in the stomach, reducing reflux. After ensuring adequate hydration, glucose intake by peripheral intravenous infusion (IV), temperature control, and management of other concurrent problems, the infant is transferred promptly to an appropriate facility for further treatment.

ALIMENTARY TRACT OBSTRUCTION

The four cardinal signs of alimentary tract obstruction in the newborn include maternal polyhydramnios, bilious vomiting, abdominal distention, and failure to pass normal amounts of meconium during the first 24 hr of life. *Any one* of these observations indicates intestinal obstruction until proved otherwise.

1. *Polyhydramnios.* Amniotic fluid in excess of 1,500 to 2,000 ml is considered polyhydramnios. Twenty-five to forty percent of amniotic fluid is swallowed by the fetus and usually reabsorbed in the first 20 to 25 cm of jejunum. A high alimentary tract obstruction (e.g., esophageal atresia, pyloric atresia, duodenal atresia, high jejunal atresia) may be associated with maternal polyhydramnios.

2. *Bilious vomiting.* Bilious vomiting is *always* pathologic and must be investigated. The newborn infant's stomach usually contains less than 15 ml of clear gastric juice at birth. Greater than 18 to 20 ml of clear gastric juice or gastric juice containing bile in the newborn may signify an intestinal obstruction. Bilious vomiting may also be seen in septic infants with an adynamic ileus.

3. *Abdominal distention.* The normal contour of the newborn abdomen is round, unlike the usual scaphoid appearance of the adult; however, a distended abdomen in the neonate is pathologic. Physical findings associated with distention include visible veins on the abdominal wall due to attenuation, "bowel patterning" (visible intestinal loops with or without peristalsis), and occasionally respiratory distress caused by elevation of the diaphragm. In each instance, it is essential to obtain a recumbent and erect X-ray of the abdomen to evaluate the nature of the distention. Distention may be a result of free air (perforated

viscus), fluid (hemoperitoneum, chyloperitoneum), or distended bowel due to intestinal obstruction or adynamic ileus.

4. *Failure to pass meconium.* Normal meconium is composed of amniotic fluid, squames, lanugo hairs, succus entericus, and intestinal mucus. It is dark green or black and sticky in consistency. Failure to pass normal amounts of meconium *during the first 24 hr of life* may be pathologic. Infants with low intestinal obstruction (Hirschsprung's disease and the meconium plug syndrome) may fit into this category.

HIGH SMALL BOWEL OBSTRUCTION

High small bowel obstruction may occur at the level of the pylorus, duodenum, or jejunum in the form of atresia (complete obstruction), stenosis (partial obstruction), or volvulus (complete or partial). In the case of atresia or stenosis, the diagnosis is based on several findings. Polyhydramnios is frequently observed and should increase one's suspicion. Vomiting (with or without bile), increased gastric contents, and intolerance to feedings are uniformly observed. Resultant fluid and electrolyte disturbances are common if the diagnosis is not made promptly. Persistent or exaggerated jaundice may also occur. Duodenal atresia, in particular, is associated with Down's syndrome (trisomy 21), the confirmation of which requires appropriate chromosomal studies. Atresias may be isolated or multiple. Infants with atresia or stenosis (unassociated with other problems such as volvulus, sepsis, or other anomalies) normally present as vigorous, active babies. The physical findings are minimal, as the abdomen is usually soft, not distended, and not tender. Diagnosis is confirmed radiologically. An anterior-posterior (AP) X-ray film of the abdomen may demonstrate a large air-filled stomach without distal bowel gas—the classic double bubble (Fig. 3) of duodenal atresia—or proximal large bubbles of gas in the bowel but a scanty bowel gas pattern elsewhere (stenosis). It is impossible to differentiate large from small bowel on the basis of flat plate X-rays of the abdomen in the newborn. Therefore contrast studies are indicated when there is any question of the diagnosis. These are best performed by pediatric radiologists in an appropriate facility.

Volvulus is a surgical emergency in the newborn. It is often associated with malrotation of the intestine and is characterized by twisting of the intestine (usually the small bowel) about the mesentery. The result may be vascular compromise to the intestine with partial or complete infarction of the involved bowel. Clinical symptoms and signs may develop at any point during the newborn period or even *in utero.* Such infants become extremely ill over a short period of time, as they develop abdominal distention, tenderness, and rigidity. A metabolic acidosis is often noted, as well as other attendant complications [fluid electrolyte imbalance, respiratory distress, infection, disseminated intravascular coagulation (DIC), etc.]. Prompt diagnosis and appropriate surgical

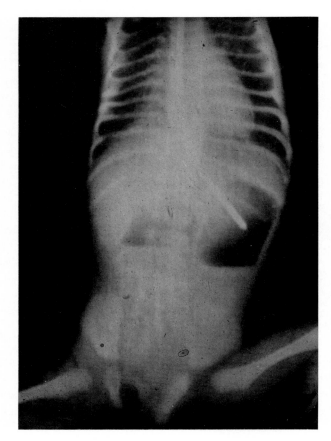

FIG. 3. "Double bubble" sign of duodenal atresia.

treatment are mandatory. X-ray findings are variable, often requiring upper or lower bowel contrast studies to confirm the presence of malrotation of the intestine and the likely presence of congenital Ladd's bands with volvulus.

LOW SMALL BOWEL OBSTRUCTION

Infants with low small bowel obstruction present with bilious vomiting and abdominal distention. Erect and recumbent abdominal radiographs demonstrate many dilated loops of bowel (Fig. 4). Because the infant colon does not show haustral markings, a barium enema is performed in low intestinal obstruction. The first enema the baby gets is the barium enema. The barium enema discerns between small and large bowel distention, determines if the colon is used or unused (microcolon) (Fig. 5) and therefore the level of obstruction (small intestinal or colonic), and evaluates the position of the cecum in regard to intestinal rotation and fixation (e.g., malrotation).

Occasionally, calcification is seen on abdominal radiographs and signifies the presence of "meconium peritonitis." This is a sign of intrauterine bowel perfora-

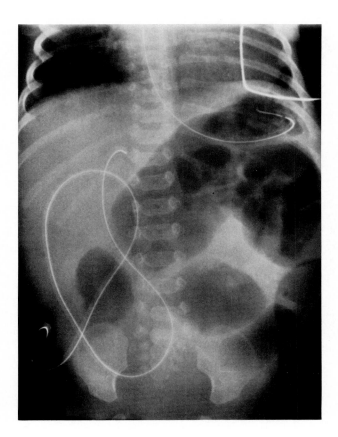

FIG. 4. Markedly dilated loops of bowel suggestive of lower bowel obstruction.

tion. The two most common causes of low small bowel obstruction are ileal atresia and meconium ileus.

Ileal Atresia

Infants with ileal atresia present with abdominal distention, bilious vomiting, and failure to pass meconium. Significant small bowel distention and many air-fluid levels (with one loop usually much larger than the others) are usually seen. The barium enema shows the unused "microcolon" (Fig. 5) limiting the obstruction to the distal small bowel.

Meconium Ileus

Meconium ileus is a unique form of congenital intestinal obstruction that occurs in 10 to 15% of infants with cystic fibrosis. A deficiency of pancreatic enzymes and an abnormality in the composition of the meconium are the factors responsible for the solid concretions which produce an obturation form of obstruction in this disorder. A careful family history is conducted when this

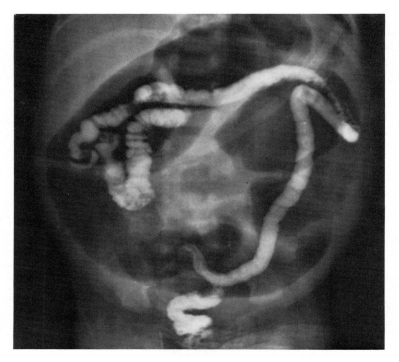

FIG. 5. Unused "microcolon" in a patient with low small bowel obstruction.

hereditary disorder is suspected. The presence of low small bowel obstruction in identical twins is almost always due to meconium ileus. These infants present with abdominal distention, bilious vomiting, and failure to pass meconium. Appropriate contrast radiographic studies may be therapeutic and diagnostic. Surgical treatment may be indicated based on the above findings.

Other less common causes of small intestinal obstruction in the newborn include intrinsic stenosis and extrinsic compression from congenital bands, bowel duplication, mesenteric cysts, and internal hernia through a mesenteric defect. In addition, one always examines carefully for the presence of an incarcerated inguinal hernia as the cause for obstruction, even during the newborn period.

COLONIC OBSTRUCTION

Causes of colonic obstruction in the neonate include meconium plug syndrome, aganglionic megacolon (Hirschsprung's disease), colon atresia, small left colon syndrome, and the various presentations of imperforate anus.

Meconium Plug Syndrome

The exact etiology of meconium plug syndrome is unknown but is thought to be due to some factor which dehydrates meconium. The patient presents with distention and failure to pass meconium. A plain X-ray of the abdomen usually shows many loops of distended bowel with some air-fluid levels. a barium enema shows a microcolon (unused) usually up to the descending or transverse colon, at which point the colon becomes dilated and copious intraluminal material (thick meconium) is observed. The barium enema is often diagnostic and therapeutic. Following instillation of the contrast material, large plugs of inspissated meconium are passed and the obstruction completely relieved. Occasionally, a second enema (usually gastrografin®) is required to prompt evacuation. If any signs of recurrent obstruction do occur, aganglionic megacolon must be considered. In addition, rarely meconium plug syndrome may be a presenting feature of cystic fibrosis, and therefore a sweat chloride test is suggested.

Hirschsprung's Disease

Aganglionic megacolon (Hirschsprung's disease) is a neurogenic form of obstruction in which there is an absence of ganglion cells in the mysenteric (Auerbach's) and submucosal (Meissner's) plexus. The absence of parasympathetic innervation results in a failure of relaxation of the internal sphincter. The disease begins at the anorectal line and (in 80% of the cases) extends proximal to the rectosigmoid. In 10% of the patients, the aganglionic segment extends proximal to the splenic flexure and may involve the entire colon and distal ileum or more proximal small bowel. Rare cases of total aganglionosis of the entire gastrointestinal tract have also been reported. The disease has a definite familial tendency. An increased association of Hirschsprung's disease and Down's syndrome has also been noted (3 to 4% of cases).

Most infants with this disorder demonstrate symptoms (Fig. 6) during the newborn period. Many (95%) fail to pass normal amounts of meconium during

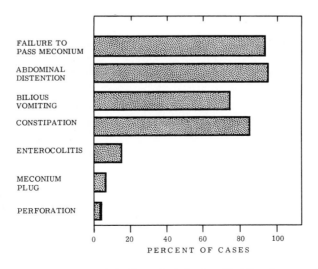

FIG. 6. Frequency of clinical findings in infants with Hirschsprung's disease.

the first 24 hr of life. These infants usually have abdominal distention and often vomit bile. Distention is often severe with dilated loops of bowel seen on the abdominal wall ("intestinal patterning"). The sigmoid colon is often palpated as a "mass." X-rays obtained in the erect and recumbent positions show many dilated loops of bowel; the barium enema *during the newborn period may look normal;* i.e., a transition zone is usually not seen. The normal infant has a bowel movement about every 4 to 6 hr and evacuates barium promptly after a contrast enema. However, neonates with Hirschsprung's disease usually retain the barium for greater than 24 hr following a contrast enema.

Occasionally, this disorder presents with the triad of abdominal distention, vomiting, and severe diarrhea alternating with constipation. This diarrhea is known as the "enterocolitis" of Hirschsprung's disease.

In obvious cases, a full-thickness rectal biopsy demonstrating absence of ganglion cells in Auerbach's plexus is the most accurate method of diagnosis. We usually obtain a mucosal aspiration biopsy (90% accurate) in questionable cases. In most instances, a partial- or full-thickness rectal biopsy is required to confirm the diagnosis; appropriate surgery is then indicated.

Colon Atresia

Colon atresia as an isolated entity (not associated with imperforate anus or cloacal extrophy) is a relatively rare anomaly. Failure to pass meconium during the first 24 hr of life, abdominal distention, and bilious vomiting are the usual clinical manifestations. These infants are usually full term and rarely have associated anomalies. Diagnosis is confirmed by a barium enema, which demonstrates a blind-ending distal end of a microcolon and dilated air-filled loops of proximal intestine.

Anorectal Anomalies

There is a wide spectrum of anal anomalies that fit the general category of anal atresia, imperforate anus, and rectal atresia. Anal atresia usually refers to an inappropriate ascent of the proctodeum, resulting in a thin, veil-like membrane covering the normal anal canal and residing within the external sphincter. Eighty-five to 90% of infants with imperforate anus and rectal atresia have an associated fistulous tract. These children frequently have a high rate of associated anomalies in other systems. A careful systems review involving other areas of the gastrointestinal tract, the cardiovascular system, musculoskeletal system, genitourinary tract, and central nervous system is carried out during early infancy to delineate these problems and initiate treatment. The detailed management of infants and children with variants of imperforate anus is beyond the scope of this short presentation regarding therapy. The operations performed on these children should be carried out by pediatric surgeons with expertise in the management of these anorectal defects. The first operation is usually the most important.

Infants who have perineal anoplasty during the newborn period will develop good external sphincter tone and have a bright outlook for developing continence. The higher the rectal atresia, the worse the potential outcome of the operation in regard to obtaining fecal continence. Long-term care and follow-up are required in such patients, and the families must be counseled not to expect the normal progression of bowel training in these children. If the pubo-rectalis sling and external sphincter are preserved at the time of the pull-through operation, most of these children have a reasonable chance of obtaining socially acceptable forms of continence. This may not be achieved, however, until 6 to 9 years of age when the child voluntarily participates in attempts to stay clean and avoid fecal odor.

ABDOMINAL WALL DEFECTS

Omphalocele

An omphalocele (Fig. 7) is a covered defect of the umbilical ring into which the intra-abdominal contents herniate. The sac is composed of an outer layer of amnion and an inner layer of peritoneum. This defect occurs in approximately

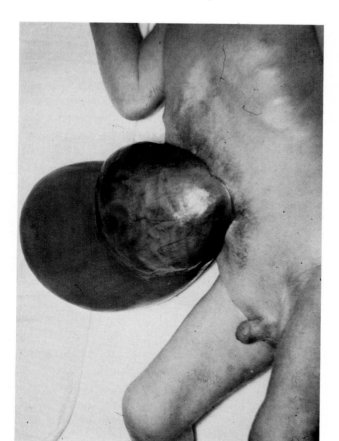

FIG. 7. Omphalocele with intestines protruding through the umbilical ring.

1/5,000 births. There is a high incidence of associated anomalies; more than 50% of cases have other serious defects involving the alimentary tract, cardiorespiratory, genitourinary, musculoskeletal, and central nervous systems. Many of these infants are premature. Others may be affected by a number of syndromes, including Beckwith-Wiedemann syndrome (gigantism, macroglossia, omphalocele or umbilical hernia, hyperactive pancreatic islet cells), and trisomy 13–15 and 16–18.

The size of the defect varies considerably, from as small as 2.0 cm to as large as 10.0 cm. The smaller the defect, the better is the prognosis. A small omphalocele may present as a small knot or discoloration at the base of the umbilical cord; in such cases, care must be taken when clamping the cord in the delivery room. The contents of the sac may include only small bowel and colon, although frequently the liver, as well as the entire gastrointestinal tract, is within the sac. Since the intestines reside in the sac and not within the abdomen, the resultant size of the abdominal cavity may be exceedingly small, making a primary repair rather difficult. In addition, malrotation is almost always present.

The emergency care of the patient includes insertion of a nasogastric tube to decompress the stomach and prevent swallowed air from resulting in bowel distention, which may interfere with an attempted repair. The intact omphalocele sac is kept covered with a sterile dressing and protected from injury. Excessively wet dressings may macerate the sac wall as well as result in temperature loss by cooling and evaporative losses. Antibiotic therapy is usually initiated (ampicillin 100 mg/kg/day and gentamicin 5 mg/kg/day). The patient's overall status is also carefully assessed in respect to his cardiorespiratory status. Because the viscera are covered by the sac, the bowel is usually normal in appearance; fluid needs are reasonably similar to those in normal newborns. The patient is transported in a thermally neutral incubator in the supine position and with a sterile dressing covering the sac and a nasogastric tube in place. Intravenous therapy is given in the form of 10% dextrose in 0.25% saline unless excessive nasogastric losses are encountered.

Prognosis in infants with omphalocele depends on the size of the defect, whether the infant is premature, if the sac ruptures (adding the dimension of potential sepsis), and the severity of associated anomalies. Mortality may be as high as 35% in the presence of the above-mentioned adverse factors.

Gastroschisis

Gastroschisis (Fig. 8) (Greek for "belly cleft") is a defect of the anterior abdominal wall just lateral to the umbilicus. The defect is almost always located to the right of an intact umbilical cord. This anomaly is associated with antenatal evisceration of the gastrointestinal tract. Unlike omphalocele, there is no peritoneal sac. The irritating effects of amniotic fluid on the exposed bowel wall result in a chemical form of peritonitis characterized by a thick edematous membrane over the bowel which is occasionally exudative in appearance. The

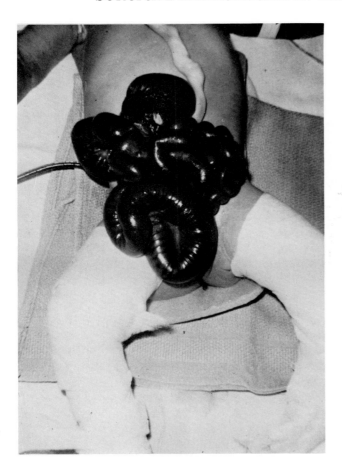

FIG. 8. Gastroschisis with the majority of the intestines protruding through the defect.

exposed viscera is often congested and foreshortened. Malrotation always accompanies this condition. In contrast to omphalocele, the incidence of associated anomalies in patients with gastroschisis is relatively infrequent. The exception to this general rule is that intestinal atresia is noted in 10 to 15% of cases. The liver is almost never eviscerated. Sexes are equally affected, and 40% of patients are either premature or small for gestational age.

Once delivered, the infant is subject to a variety of problems caused by the great increase in insensible losses related to exposure of the eviscerated bowel. Hypothermia, hypovolemia, and sepsis are the major problems to avoid. Hypothermia occurs because of increased radiant heat losses from the exposed bowel surface. There are significant "third-space" fluid deficits related to extra- and intra-abdominal sequestration of interstitial fluid. We have found it advantageous to quickly wrap the entire lower half of the infant (including the eviscerated bowel) in a sterile intestinal bag, which decreases temperature loss from the exposed viscera. In addition, sequestered fluid from the defect collects in the bag and can be measured for fluid replacement. (These plastic bags are commercially available and are found in most operating rooms.) Five percent dextrose in lactated Ringer's solution is given intravenously at a rate of 20 ml/kg over 30 to 60 min to replace initial fluid losses. Acid-base balance must be closely monitored. Metabolic acidosis is commonly observed owing to poor perfusion related to hypovolemia. A nasogastric tube is placed in the stomach to prevent air swallowing and to aspirate intestinal contents, as these babies have an associated adynamic ileus. Antibiotics (oxacillin and gentamicin) are administered to prevent secondary infection. If cyanosis or respiratory distress is noted, arterial pH and blood gases are determined, and appropriate oxygen and respiratory support initiated. Because of the often complicated nature of their care, these patients should be transferred to a tertiary neonatal intensive care facility where they can be given appropriate pediatric surgical management. With appropriate neonatal support, surgical treatment, and nutritional management, the current survival rate in these cases is 90%.

DIAPHRAGMATIC HERNIA

Congenital posterolateral diaphragmatic hernia (foramen of Bochdalek) is a defect in the developing pleuroperitoneal fold through which the viscera ascend and enter the chest—usually during the eighth to tenth week of fetal life. During this time, simultaneous development of the diaphragm, return of the bowel from the yolk sac, and differentiation of the lung buds are taking place. An imbalance of these processes may result in a defect of the pleuroperitoneal fold, with bowel entering the thorax before the diaphragm closes. The bowel in the chest occupies a space normally occupied by the developing lung and prevents normal development of the lung. The incidence is 1/2,200 births. Boys are more commonly affected than girls. The defect is on the left side in 85% of cases and on the right in 13%; it is rarely bilateral (1 to 2%).

Affected infants have no problems *in utero,* as the lungs are nonfunctional and oxygenation is provided by placental perfusion. Following delivery, however, some infants rapidly develop symptoms of respiratory distress, which may be apparent in the delivery room or may present during the first few hours of life as the gut in the chest becomes distended with swallowed air, further compressing the lung and causing a shift in the mediastinum. Hypoplasia of the ipsilateral lung is a common occurrence, and malrotation is usually present.

Mortality is higher if the symptoms become apparent early during the perinatal period. Early onset of symptoms is also directly related to the degree of pulmonary hypoplasia.

Symptoms are those that are characteristic of respiratory distress, including dyspnea, tachypnea, retractions, and cyanosis. Although respiratory distress syndrome commonly occurs in the premature infant, most babies with diaphragmatic hernia are full term. This condition is suspected in any "big" baby with respiratory distress associated with a barrel chest and a scaphoid abdomen. Heart sounds are usually heard in the right chest and are due to the shifted mediastinum. Although the disorder is frequently suspected on clinical grounds, the chest X-ray confirms the diagnosis by demonstrating intestine above the diaphragm and a mediastinal shift.

These infants demonstrate severe hypoxia and respiratory acidosis. A combined metabolic acidosis may also be present when insufficient tissue perfusion coexists with the pulmonary embarrassment. Stabilization and prompt transfer to a tertiary care facility are imperative. Infants with respiratory distress due to diaphragmatic hernia should have prompt endotracheal intubation and ventilatory support with 100% oxygen. Assisted ventilation with mask-to-face technique is avoided because it introduces a great deal of air into the gastrointestinal tract, leading to further respiratory embarrassment by distention of the bowel within the chest. Excessive pressures during ventilatory resuscitation are avoided because of the risk of contralateral pneumothorax, which almost always results in a fatal outcome. A nasogastric tube is passed to empty the stomach, preventing further distention of the alimentary tract. Serial monitoring of blood pH, pO_2, and pCO_2 is important.

The degree of pulmonary hypoplasia and/or pulmonary hypertension with right-to-left shunts directly affects survival. For infants symptomatic during the first hours of life, the mortality remains excessive (40 to 60%) despite aggressive support. Infants who present beyond 24 hr of age usually have enough cardiorespiratory reserve to survive (greater than 90%). The management of the neonate with congenital diaphragmatic hernia continues to be one of the most challenging problems in pediatric surgery.

CAVEATS

1. Infants with esophageal atresia present with a history of polyhydramnios, choking, coughing, excessive salivation, and respiratory distress.

2. The four cardinal signs of alimentary tract obstruction in the newborn include polyhydramnios, bilious vomiting, abdominal distention, and failure to pass normal amounts of meconium during the first 24 hr of life.

3. Bilious vomiting is always pathologic and requires *immediate* investigation.

4. Failure to pass meconium during the first 24 hr of life suggests the possibility of Hirschsprung's disease.

5. Recumbent and upright X-rays of the abdomen are obtained in an infant with possible bowel obstruction.

6. A barium enema cannot rule out Hirschsprung's disease in the newborn.

7. The emergency care of infants with possible bowel obstruction includes placement of a large orogastric tube for suctioning.

8. Infants with respiratory distress due to diaphragmatic hernia should have prompt endotracheal intubation and ventilatory support with 100% oxygen.

22

Seizures

The first step in the management of seizures in the newborn infant is their recognition, which is often difficult because neonatal seizures are manifested by a wide variety of signs and symptoms (Table 1). Although seizures in the newborn may manifest as generalized tonic-clonic activity, they are commonly more subtle (e.g., vasomotor changes—mottling or pallor; sudden eye opening or eye blinking; nystagmus or tonic horizontal deviation of the eyes; facial twitching; chewing, drooling, or sucking motions; and abnormal cry). Apnea or a transient change in the respiratory rate and bradycardia may represent seizures in the newborn. Other examples of seizure activity in newborn infants include tonic extension of a limb or entire body, a myoclonic jerk, clonic movements of one extremity, and episodes of limpness. The key to recognizing seizures in the newborn is a high index of suspicion with close observation of the infant.

One common problem is differentiating neonatal seizures from jitteriness in a normal newborn. Four clinical observations may help distinguish "jitters" from seizures (Table 2): (a) there is no abnormality of gaze or eye movement with jitteriness; (b) "jitters" are exquisitely stimulus-sensitive (i.e., they can be provoked by a loud noise or sudden movement), whereas seizures are not; (c) the

TABLE 1. *Neonatal seizures—types*

Apnea or transient alteration of respiratory rate
Vasomotor changes (mottling, pallor)
Sudden eye opening or eye blinking
Nystagmus or horizontal deviation of eyes
Facial twitching
Chewing or sucking motions
Drooling
Abnormal cry
Tonic-clonic movements
Tonic extension of limb or body
Myoclonic jerk
Clonic movements of one extremity
Episode of limpness

TABLE 2. *Characteristics of jitteriness*

No abnormality of gaze or eye movement
Stimulus-sensitive
Predominant movement *tremor, not clonic jerking*
Usually ceases with passive flexion

predominant movement in seizures is clonic jerking with a fast component followed by a slow return, whereas "jitters" are characterized by tremor activity, equally fast in both directions; and (d) "jitters" can be stopped by passive flexion of an extremity whereas seizures cannot.

ETIOLOGY OF SEIZURES

The next step is to determine the cause (Table 3). Metabolic disorders such as hypoglycemia and hypocalcemia are always considered in an infant with seizures. A blood glucose of less than 40 mg% in term infants or less than 30 mg% in preterm infants must be considered abnormal and treated. Hypomagnesemia (i.e., serum magnesium less than 1.5 mg%) should be considered in conjunction with hypocalcemia as hypocalcemia is often refractive to treatment until coexisting hypomagnesemia is first corrected. Electrolyte disturbances such as hyponatremia may also manifest as seizures.

TABLE 3. *Causes of neonatal seizures*

Metabolic
   *Hypoglycemia
   *Hypocalcemia
   Hypomagnesemia
   Hyponatremia and hypernatremia
   Aminoacidurias, other inborn errors of metabolism
   Hyperbilirubinemia
   Hyperthermia
   Pyridoxine (B_6) deficiency/dependency
Infection
   *Sepsis
   *Meningitis
   Encephalitis
   Congenital
*Bleeding
   Subarachnoid
   Periventricular, intraventricular
   Intracerebral, intracerebellar
   Subdural
*Developmental anomalies
*Trauma
*Asphyxia
*Polycythemia
   Drug withdrawal and toxicity

*Common causes.

Inborn errors of metabolism (e.g., the aminoacidurias) should also be considered in an infant with seizures. Characteristically, infants with inborn errors of metabolism are term and healthy at birth but develop problems a few days later—usually, but not always, after feedings have begun. Such signs include jaundice, hepatomegaly, vomiting, diarrhea, respiratory distress, lethargy, irritability, and seizures. Other metabolic causes of neonatal seizures include hyperbilirubinemia and hyperthermia.

Infectious causes of seizures in the newborn (e.g., sepsis and meningitis) must always be entertained. Other infectious etiologies include encephalitis with congenital infections, e.g., cytomegalovirus, toxoplasmosis, rubella, herpes, and syphilis.

Birth trauma and neonatal asphyxia are important causes of seizures. During a very difficult delivery a large infant may have sustained enough cerebral trauma to precipitate seizures. Infants who develop seizures secondary to neonatal asphyxia have a very poor prognosis. These infants—who are often meconium-stained, have low Apgar scores, and require extensive resuscitative efforts—begin having seizures within 8 to 24 hr after birth. In terms of prevention, careful obstetric management is needed to recognize fetal distress during labor and to identify those infants who will have difficulties during delivery. In turn, the physician must be prepared in the delivery room for aggressive resuscitation of the depressed infant to prevent further hypoxic injury. Developmental anomalies of the brain (e.g., encephalocele and cysts) also cause neonatal seizures.

Polycythemia is being increasingly recognized as a cause of seizures in infants. Polycythemia or hyperviscosity is defined as a venous (not heelstick) hematocrit reading of greater than 60 to 65%. Symptomatic infants may present with respiratory distress, cardiomegaly, lethargy, poor feeding, and irritability, as well as seizures. Hyperviscosity is frequently seen in the small for gestational age infant, the infant of the diabetic mother, and twins. Treatment of hyperviscosity in an infant consists of a partial exchange transfusion (in 5 to 20-ml increments) using fresh frozen plasma or 5% albumin in exchange for blood in order to decrease the hematocrit reading to less than 60%:

$$\frac{\text{Blood volume} \times (\text{observed Hct} - \text{desired Hct})}{\text{Observed Hct}} = \text{volume of exchange}$$

For example, if a 3.0 kg (blood volume 80 ml/kg) infant has a venous hematocrit (Hct) of 70%, the total amount of blood that should be withdrawn to reduce the hematocrit to 55% is:

$$3.0 \text{ kg} \times 80 \text{ ml/kg} \times \frac{(70\% - 55\%)}{70\%} = 240 \text{ ml} \times \frac{15\%}{70\%} = 51 \text{ ml}$$

Therefore a total of 51 ml blood should be withdrawn in 10- to 15-ml increments and replaced with the same amount of 5% protein solution. As a general rule, if the volume of blood calculated for a *full term* infant is less than 50 ml or greater than 100 ml, the calculations must be checked—they are probably in error.

Seizures can also be observed in infants experiencing drug withdrawal secondary to maternal addiction. Other signs of withdrawal include yawning, sneezing, nasal congestion, agitation, irritability, tremors, fever, sweating, respiratory distress, and gastrointestinal disturbances (poor feeding, vomiting, diarrhea). Signs of drug withdrawal may not be evident until several days of age. Treatment of these infants consists of correcting fluid and electrolyte imbalances; paregoric 5 to 8 drops q 4 hr or chlorpromazine 0.75 mg/kg q 6 hr; and controlling seizures, if present. Treatment must be continued for 20 to 45 days. Drugs implicated in withdrawal include morphine, meperidine hydrochloride (Demerol®), heroin, methadone, phenobarbital, propoxyphene hydrochloride (Darvon®), glutethimide (Doriden®), chlordiazepoxide (Librium®), pentazocine hydrochloride (Talwin®), amphetamines, and phenothiazines. It must be remembered that drug withdrawal can be seen in infants of any socioeconomic background, not just those from lower socioeconomic groups.

Although infrequent, drug toxicity can cause seizures in the newborn, usually within the first few hours of life. In mothers who have received a paracervical block or other local anesthesia, there may be sufficient transplacental passage of the local anesthetic agent (e.g., lidocaine) to produce effects on the fetus or newborn. In some cases, the agent may be accidentally injected directly into the infant's scalp with toxic effects. In addition to seizures, bradycardia is a frequent accompaniment of local anesthetic toxicity.

Intracranial hemorrhage is another important cause of neonatal seizures. Subdural hemorrhage usually occurs in large, full term infants whose delivery was traumatic. Seizures secondary to subdural hemorrhage usually occur within the first 48 hr of life. Subdural hemorrhages are now uncommon owing to improved obstetric techniques. Although subarachnoid hemorrhage, the most common type of intracranial hemorrhage, usually occurs in premature infants, it may also be seen in full term infants. The infant may be symptomatic with lethargy and irritability prior to developing seizures on the second or third day of life; however, most often the infant is healthy and asymptomatic. Fortunately, subarachnoid hemorrhage is thought to be associated with an excellent prognosis in the great majority of patients.

Prior to the development of the computerized axial tomography (CAT) scan, intraventricular hemorrhage was always thought to have an extremely poor prognosis. Seen almost exclusively in premature infants, it was thought to be the consequence of a hypoxic event. Seizures were usually noted within 24 to 48 hr of the initial insult. Preterm infants previously diagnosed as having intraventricular bleeds usually underwent catastrophic deterioration over a few hours to days with a high mortality rate. Those who did not die developed major sequelae—severe hydrocephalus and mental retardation. Use of CAT scanning, however, has demonstrated that there is a wide spectrum of intraventricular hemorrhage, ranging from mild to severe, and that intraventricular hemorrhage is much more frequent in premature and full term infants than previously suspected. Several studies have shown that many preterm infants with mild degrees of intraventricular hemorrhage are relatively asymptomatic, and a significant percentage go on to have normal development. The incidence and prognosis of intraventricular hemorrhage will be clarified further as more studies using CAT scanning and ultrasound studies in prematures become available.

In review, the more common causes of neonatal seizures include asphyxia, trauma, hypocalcemia, hypoglycemia, infection, intracranial hemorrhage, hyperviscosity, developmental anomalies, and drugs.

LABORATORY EVALUATION

The workup of an infant with seizures must be systematic (Table 4). *It is more important to diagnose and treat the cause, if possible, than simply to give phenobarbital or diphenylhydantoin sodium* (Dilantin®). A thorough history and physical examination, including transillumination of the skull, are needed. Blood is sent to the laboratory *stat* for glucose, calcium, magnesium, and sodium levels, hematocrit, and culture. A spinal tap is always done on a neonate with seizures and the spinal fluid sent to the laboratory for glucose and protein levels, a cell count, gram stain, and culture.

TREATMENT

Specific drug therapy for seizures is instituted (Table 5). Intravenous glucose $D_{10}W$ to $D_{25}W$ (2 to 4 ml/kg) is given immediately after blood is sent to the laboratory, without waiting for the results. For hypocalcemia, 10% calcium gluconate 0.5 to 2 ml/kg may be given by slow intravenous push, carefully monitoring the infusion with an electrocardiogram. Hypomagnesemia may be corrected with 3% magnesium sulfate, 2 to 6 ml i.v. by slow push, or 50% magnesium sulfate 0.25 ml/kg i.m. Intravenous antibiotics are started as soon as blood and spinal fluid are obtained for cultures.

TABLE 4. *Workup of seizures*

---

1. Minimal workup for all infants
  History and physical examination
  Transillumination
  Blood for glucose, calcium, sodium, magnesium, hematocrit, and culture
  Cerebrospinal fluid for cells, glucose, protein, culture and gram stain
  CAT scan and/or ultrasound
2. Further workup for some infants
  EEG
  Urine and blood for metabolic screen (amino acids, organic acids, ketones)
  Serum NH_3
  Skull X-ray
  Culture and titers for toxoplasmosis, rubella, cytomegalovirus, syphilis, and herpes

---

TABLE 5. *Treatment of seizures*

Drug—specific
    Glucose (D_{10-25}W 2–4 ml/kg i.v.) *immediately* after blood sample is sent to laboratory, before results come back
    Calcium gluconate 10% (0.5–2.0 ml/kg slowly i.v. with electrocardiogram)
    Magnesium sulfate 3% (2–6 ml i.v.)
    ?B_6 (pyridoxine) (20–50 mg i.v.)

Anticonvulsant therapy

	Initial intravenous	Oral maintenance
Phenobarbital	10 mg/kg (repeat if necessary)	5–10 mg/kg/day
Dilantin (infrequently needed)	10 mg/kg (repeat if necessary)	5–10 mg/kg/day

    Should monitor blood levels of both drugs. Therapeutic levels are approximately 15–25 µg/ml.

Anticonvulsant therapy (Table 5) consists of phenobarbital and, if necessary, Dilantin. Intravenous phenobarbital (10 mg/kg i.v. slow push) is used initially and may be repeated if the seizures are not adequately controlled. The maintenance dosage of phenobarbital is 5 to 10 mg/kg/day orally in divided doses. Dilantin may be added if seizures are not controlled by phenobarbital alone. An initial dose of Dilantin 10 mg/kg i.v. may be given and repeated once if necessary to stop seizures. The maintenance dosage of Dilantin is 5 to 10 mg/kg/day orally in divided doses. Blood levels should be monitored when using phenobarbital or Dilantin. Therapeutic ranges are 15 to 30 µg/ml for phenobarbital and 10 to 20 µg/ml for Dilantin. Valium 0.25 to 0.5 mg/kg i.v. slow push has been used to control seizures, but its effect lasts only 30 min, hence providing only temporary control. Other supportive measures include intravenous fluids and careful monitoring of the cardiorespiratory status.

Once the infant is stabilized, further investigation of seizures can be undertaken if the cause is still undetermined. An electroencephalogram (EEG), skull X-rays, CAT scan, ultrasound, metabolic screen (amino acids, organic acids, and ketones) of urine and blood, and cultures and titers for congenital infections may be obtained.

The outlook of neonates with seizures is dependent on the underlying cause, as well as the duration, frequency, and severity of the seizures. This is particularly true of seizures secondary to such problems as hypoglycemia, sepsis, hyperviscosity, and drug toxicity in which prompt intervention is associated with an improved outlook. Seizures secondary to asphyxia or developmental anomalies have an extremely poor prognosis. Infants with seizures secondary to hypocalcemia have greater than a 50% chance for normal development. Fifteen to 35% of infants with seizures secondary to bacterial meningitis have been normal in long-term follow-up; more recent data suggest that the chance for normal development is higher: 50 to 80%. Infants with subarachnoid hemorrhage have a very good prognosis. As stated previously, the views on prognosis of infants with intraventricular hemorrhage are changing, and the chance for normal development of such infants is no longer as dismal as formerly assumed.

CAVEATS

1. The recognition of seizures in the neonate is often difficult because of the subtle nature of the seizures.

2. Jitteriness must be differentiated from clonic seizure activity in the newborn.

3. The most important aspects in the management of neonatal seizures are the determination and treatment of the etiology of the disorder.

4. The most common causes of neonatal seizures are hypoglycemia, hypocalcemia, infection, intracranial hemorrhage, and asphyxia.

5. A partial exchange transfusion is performed when an infant has symptoms secondary to polycythemia (venous hematocrit greater than 60 to 65%).

6. Phenobarbital is the anticonvulsant of choice for the treatment of neonatal seizures.

7. The prognosis of neonates with seizures is dependent on the etiology, duration, frequency, and severity of the seizures.

23

Caring for the Family Mourning a Perinatal Death

There is little question that the birth of a baby is an emotional event, the emotions varying according to the parents and their feelings about the pregnancy. Undoubtedly, the birth of a healthy infant is the culmination of a pregnancy in which fantasies abound regarding what this child will be like. Whereas the birth of a baby can be one of the happiest moments in a family's life, the death of a newborn is traumatic and immobilizing. The effects of this family crisis are experienced for a long time.

During recent years increasing recognition is being given to the premise that the death of a newborn is as great and painful a loss as that of any close relative. As professionals involved in the care of critically ill newborns, we are also charged with the responsibility of caring for the parent and other family members. In the case of perinatal death, whether it be a stillborn baby, a baby who survives only a few hours, or one who lives several weeks, the physician, nurse, or social worker can have significant impact on the family. It is up to the individual professional whether that impact is a positive or negative one. Although the time we spend with the family may be brief, we can use this time effectively to assist them in coping with this severe loss.

IMPORTANT ASPECTS IN THE FACILITATION OF GRIEVING

The sensitivity of health professionals is a central factor in the care of a family at the time of their baby's death. Staff who are themselves uncomfortable with death have a more difficult time working with families in an effective manner. Some staff may be uncomfortable showing a dead baby to the family, permitting them to hold the baby, or providing a picture. It is imperative, however, that our personal preferences not interfere with a family's right to grieve. Although denying parents the opportunity to see their dead baby may seem a way to protect them from the pain, in reality it may merely compound the problems of coping with a perinatal death. The lack of a physical identity to mourn leaves the family with only a fantasy of what their baby was really like. With very few exceptions, the fantasized identity is far worse than what is real; e.g., the reported birth defect becomes more grotesque.

Along with seeing their dead or dying baby, parents, wherever possible, are given the opportunity to hold, or at least touch, their baby. This too can be helpful in making the baby real to the family—different from their expectations but nevertheless real. Affectional ties prior to the death have been found to relate to the grief process. Wherever possible, a picture of the infant is offered to the parents, preferably one taken prior to the baby's death; when this is not possible, one is taken after the death. A picture may be a family's only concrete remembrance of a baby who dies soon after birth. If a family has not already named their baby, they are encouraged to do so, as this too can add to the perception of the baby as real.

TALKING WITH FAMILIES AT THE TIME OF DEATH

At the time a baby dies, there are several general suggestions to bear in mind. First, a family must be informed of the death immediately. When possible, advising a family when death appears imminent can provide parents the opportunity to be present at the time of death if they so desire. If not present, they must be notified without delay. It is helpful to notify both parents together; however, realistically that is not always possible. In such cases, alternate support persons may be utilized—grandparents, aunts or uncles, or even close friends and in some cases hospital personnel who have a positive relationship with the parent.

When talking to the family, one should sit, not stand. Privacy should be assured. Although it is important to be with a family to answer questions, it is equally thoughtful to allow them some time alone with each other and, if desired, with their baby.

When discussing a baby's death and related information (e.g., funeral arrangements, emotional responses, and autopsy requests), it is suggested that, wherever possible, at least one involved health care professional be someone whom the family knows—a physician, nurse, or social worker with whom the family is familiar. If a chaplain of the appropriate faith is available, the family is informed so they may request a chaplain if they desire.

When talking with a family at the time of their baby's death, bear in mind that families are immobilized by the shock of their loss. Families are often unable to make many decisions. It is important not to ask too much of them at this time. In addition, much of what is told to families will be forgotten, reinforcing the need for follow-up.

Funerals

Rarely has a family had experience in arranging a funeral service, and so most need guidance. Often families choose a simple service, such as one at the graveside with only a few family and close friends in attendance. A service, no matter how small, provides the family with a means to "say goodbye," much as with an older person. In most cases the cost is not prohibitive. Although costs vary, a small service, including embalming and either cremation or burial with a small casket, is currently available for as little as $50. Many cemeteries have infant sections where a small plot is available for as little as $100. Although that cost does not include a gravestone, one can be added at a later time if it is not economically feasible at the time of death.

Reactions

It may be wise to prepare parents for the reactions they will experience after their baby's death. As with any death, these include the familiar stages of grieving. In addition, there are reactions specific to the loss of an infant. Mothers may at times think they feel the baby kicking *in utero*. Parents may awaken to what they, for a moment, feel is their baby crying in another room. Many parents are preoccupied with the image of their infant. To be prospectively informed may help a family understand that these are common, normal reactions—not a sign of mental disturbance.

The nature and cause of death need to be discussed. Most families, at some time, feel at least partially responsible. Nearly everyone can find something in their lives or the pregnancy that may instill a sense of guilt: ambivalence about the pregnancy, a previous elective abortion, having the baby out of wedlock, missing a day's prenatal vitamins, or taking an aspirin without a doctor's permission. It is of utmost importance that we reinforce to families, at the time of death and during follow-up, that the illness and/or death was not their fault. Well-intentioned spouses, parents or other relatives, and friends can often add to the problem with seemingly innocent comments. If extended family is available, it may be helpful to discuss this issue with them.

Communication

The importance of communication between parents cannot be overemphasized. The death of a child may result in serious marital discord for many couples only months after the death. Many families find it "easier" to avoid discussing the death of their baby, erroneously believing that if the death is not discussed the pain will lessen. Discussions of the loss of any loved one are never easy, yet to ignore the dead infant in conversation, or to try to forget, only increases and prolongs the pain.

When discussing communication and sharing, it may be advantageous to spend a brief time on the issue of the reactions of fathers. Often fathers feel they must be the strong one, the protector. One may ease this burden by letting the father know it is appropriate for him to show emotion.

Autopsies

The universal question families have when their babies die is "Why?" Of course, that is a question more easily answered for some than for others. To this end, an autopsy performed by a pathologist experienced in perinatal pathology may prove useful. Pinpointing the cause is helpful for some families, and for others there is comfort in believing that the information gathered may benefit other babies. There are families, however, who feel that their child "suffered enough already" and do not wish an autopsy. Requesting an autopsy, as well as parents' concerns and questions surrounding it, must be handled very sensitively. For instance, parents may wonder what type of incisions are made and how much they show (if an open casket service is planned), as well as the length of time an autopsy delays a funeral.

We must be aware of our responsibility to provide comfort to the family who for one reason or another does not wish an autopsy performed. For example, although it is obvious that an autopsy does not cause additional suffering for a baby, it is imperative to bear in mind the obligation of any health care professional to help the family feel comfortable with their decision. It is not appropriate to push a family into accepting the procedures. Most families, however, choose to have an autopsy performed.

Anger

When working with families at the time of the death of their infant, a common effect noted is anger. Parents may be angry at themselves or each other. They may be angry at particular medical people involved in the management of the pregnancy or the neonatal period. It is not unusual for family members to be angry with God, though they may not be willing to recognize or admit this. Being angry at someone or something else serves as a means to avoid blaming oneself, and it is important for parents to be able to ventilate some of these feelings and frustrations. It should be stressed, however, that anger is a normal part of the process, and that many families feel angry at others, including God. Having a child die seems very cruel and unfair, so there is little wonder that families question their religious beliefs.

Providing Emotional Support for Families

As a whole, it seems there is little that physicians and nurses can do to ease the pain of families who experience perinatal death. Often, staff find themselves feeling helpless, hoping to learn of some perfect statement or action that will magically erase the pain. However, it is not specifically what is said or done, but the presence of concerned and caring individuals that is remembered. There are a few comments and guidelines that parents have acknowledged as helpful (e.g., a note sent to the family's home to let them know you are thinking of them). A simple phrase "I'm sorry," or "Can I help in any way?" expresses concern and sympathy. Some comments may not be helpful for families, e.g., "It was for the best." Although that may be true in the eyes of the physician or nurse, the remark is not likely to provide comfort for the family. "You can always have other children," tends to negate the existence of the baby who died. Ignoring the baby in conversation is believed by some to be easier on the family, but it is likely that the family is thinking only of their baby. Perhaps the comment potentially least helpful to families is one often made out of a desire to comfort, "I know how you feel." Unless the staff person has had a personal experience with perinatal death, he cannot comprehend the pain of the family.

Single Parents

When the parents are unmarried, they may be as supportive to one another as married couples, or more so. Efforts should be made to include both parents. The support system of grandparents in this situation depends a great deal on their views and acceptance of the relationship. Although the emotional upset involved in an out-of-wedlock pregnancy has diminished by the time of the infant's death, there may be a greater tendency for families to feel guilty under such circumstances. Appropriate supportive counseling may be indicated.

In situations in which the baby's father is not involved at the time of birth, one must be very sensitive to the needs of the mother. She may have few support systems to help her, not only at the time of death but in the next few months as well.

Siblings

For families with other children, the death of a baby brings with it the task of informing the surviving children of the baby's death and helping them understand the loss. It is helpful to keep a few guidelines in mind when discussing siblings. Frequently parents assume that their children are too young to understand. Although a young child may not understand exactly what is wrong, most children over 2 years of age realize in their own way that something is amiss. Children, frightened by what is happening, need a simple, honest explanation. This, of course, varies with the age of the child, but it is important to tell him as soon as possible. Parents, whose own coping abilities are minimal at the time of death, may need encouragement from hospital staff regarding the importance of informing their children. In addition, parents may need the assistance of another family member, such as a grandparent. Above all, parents need to refrain from such explanations as the baby "went to sleep" or "was bad." The fantasies and insecurities resulting from such explanations can be damaging. Children need reassurance that they were in no way responsible for the death of their baby brother or sister. Children whose cognitive development has not progressed to the point that they can separate wishes and fantasies from reality may worry that they were responsible if they made jealous remarks about the baby.

Parents may wonder if their child should attend the funeral. Again, age and maturity are important factors. Some may benefit from attending, whereas others may be frightened by it. If parents choose to have their surviving children attend, someone close to them should be in attendance, as parents will likely be so caught up in their own grief that they will be unable to cope with their children's needs as well.

FOLLOW-UP

The tragedy of a perinatal death does not end when a family leaves the hospital. It is suggested that a program of follow-up be undertaken for those families. During follow-up one can accomplish the following:

1. Reinforce the information given to parents at the time of death regarding the grief process and reactions parents may experience.

2. Ensure that grieving is progressing normally and, if not, refer parents to a professional skilled in that area.

3. Discuss the autopsy report, where an autopsy was performed.

4. Assess parental communication, with encouragement to be open with one another.

5. Discuss the future, including future pregnancies.

Parents may be under subtle pressure from uncomfortable family members or friends to have another baby immediately. Parents should be encouraged to wait, preferably for a year, before deciding about another pregnancy. Data indicate that to have another infant immediately—a replacement child—may result in additional stresses and problems for families. Time is a necessary element in grieving before beginning a new life.

A review of reactions and common problems is helpful during the follow-up period because much of what was told families at the time of death will have been forgotten. This also affords parents the opportunity to discuss problems they have encountered since the death. It is helpful to reassure them that the reactions they may be experiencing (e.g., preoccupation with the dead infant) are normal.

When discussing the baby's medical problems, it is helpful to emphasize the normal aspects of the baby, as this is often comforting for families. Always refer to the baby by name, and be certain to use "he" or "she," never "it."

Parents need to be questioned about how things are going for them. It is important to *listen* to families. If a few weeks have gone by, parents should be asked if they have been out socially. If one is refusing to go out at all, it may be a sign that the grief process is not progressing. Parents may find that their friends respond differently to them now, and may be puzzled by the change in others' behavior toward them. Knowing someone else who has been through a similar experience may prove helpful. Organizations exist in various cities for parents who have suffered the death of a child, some specifically related to perinatal loss. If such an organization exists in the area where a family lives, follow-up is often an opportune time to discuss their possible participation in such a group.

Encouraging communication between parents is one of the most important aspects of follow-up. Without the encouragement of an outsider, parents may be hesitant to share their pain with each other, and may develop erroneous beliefs about the effect the death has had on the other parent.

Although various individuals involved in follow-up advocate different timetable guidelines, the most important aspect is to be certain to include follow-up as an integral part of the routine in cases of perinatal mortality. Generally speaking, a phone call within a few days, followed by one or two in-person conferences during the next several weeks, will be helpful. When parents are unable or unwilling to visit, the discussion may be by telephone. Not all families have a telephone, and in such cases a brief note including the invitation to return for a visit may be sent. In a recent study of follow-up of perinatal mortality in which there was a concentrated effort to reach all families to offer follow-up, over three-fourths of the families chose to be involved. That experience certainly serves as an indication of the need for such a program. Working with families who are suffering the loss of an infant is neither easy nor comfortable, but it is a necessary element in optimal care.

CAVEATS

1. The death of a newborn is as great and painful a loss as that of any close relative.

2. Our personal preferences must never interfere with a family's right to grieve.

3. Parents should be given the opportunity to see, touch, and hold their dying or dead infant.

4. Funerals and cemetery plots are usually available for infants for a nominal fee.

5. Parents should be prepared for the reactions they may experience after their baby's death.

6. The physician must repeatedly emphasize to the parents that the death was not their fault.

7. The parents should be encouraged to communicate their feelings to each other.

8. The infant's first name is always used when talking to the parents.

9. Siblings should be told the truth about the death.

10. A follow-up program for the parents should be an integral part of the routine management of perinatal deaths.

Part II: Procedures

Preface: Learning and Teaching Procedural Techniques

Twenty-five years ago few procedures were performed on the newborn—a "hands-off" policy was practiced—but during the past 10 to 15 years a more aggressive approach to the newborn has developed. This change in care includes the performance of numerous procedures on these small patients. Although many of the procedures are life-saving, they are all associated with some risk. Because they may result in serious complications, including death, meticulous attention to technique is necessary. Part II of this book was developed to standardize the procedures performed in our nurseries. It must in no way be interpreted that the techniques described here are the only correct methods. We do believe, however, that they represent a reasonable approach.

Learning and teaching the correct techniques for performing procedures in the newborn are difficult using conventional audiovisual aids. Although teaching these procedures in hospitalized infants seems ideal, there are significant logistical and ethical concerns to consider, especially with large groups of students, nurses, and doctors. Therefore the Section of Neonatal-Perinatal Medicine of the Department of Pediatrics and the Department of Medical Illustrations of Indiana University School of Medicine developed patient simulators. These simulators allow the teacher to demonstrate the method and then evaluate the student's technique before he performs it on actual patients.

The following simulators are currently available through Medical Plastics Laboratory, Inc., P.O. Box 38, Gatesville, Texas 76528: (a) Baby Arti, neonatal radial artery puncture; (b) Baby Umbi, neonatal umbilical artery and vein catheterization; (c) Baby Ivy, infant scalp intravenous model; (d) Baby Hippy, neonatal dislocated and dislocatable hip; (e) Baby Pee-Wee, suprapubic bladder aspiration model; and (f) Baby Stap, infant spinal tap simulator. An infant intubation model should be available in 1982.

24

Intravenous Needle Placement

Physicians and registered nurses caring for newborns should be capable of placing a peripheral intravenous (IV) needle. All premature infants less than 1,500 g or 34 weeks' gestation should have a peripheral IV started immediately after birth and continued for at least the first 24 to 48 hr of life. In addition, peripheral IVs are indicated for the administration of fluids in infants not capable of taking adequate fluids via the gastric route, administration of antibiotics in infants with sepsis or meningitis, and the prevention and treatment of hypoglycemia.

Although they are easily accessible in the newborn, it is highly undesirable to use either the umbilical artery or the umbilical vein solely for intravenous fluid therapy. Cutdowns in the newborn are rarely required. Subcutaneous injection of fluids (hypodermoclysis) is never indicated.

The materials needed for placement of a peripheral IV include: (a) a 27-, 25-, or 23-gauge butterfly infusion set; (b) 0.5-inch tape; (c) plastic medicine cup; (d) bottle of IV fluids; (e) IV fluid chamber; and (f) a continuous infusion pump.

PROCEDURE

The scalp veins are the easiest to use for placement of IVs in the newborn, but some doctors prefer the veins on the dorsum of the hands and feet. The advantages of the scalp veins include the ready accessibility of the vessels, the ease of identifying an infiltrated IV, and the minimum restraint needed.

The area is shaved clean. Arteries and veins can usually be differentiated on the scalp by the fact that arteries are more tortuous than veins, and the arteries fill from below whereas the veins fill from above. If an artery is accidentally entered, blanching occurs in the area when the fluid is infused. Should this occur, it is best to withdraw the needle and begin again.

The tubing of the 25-gauge butterfly is flushed with IV solution (Fig. 1). The wings of the butterfly are grasped between the thumb and forefinger and intro-

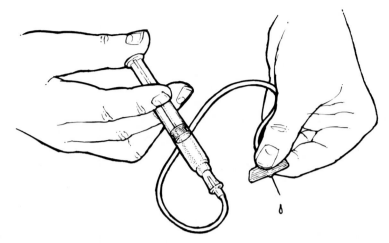

FIG. 1. The IV tubing and needle are flushed with saline solution. (Modified from Hildebrand et al.: *American Family Physician,* 21:139, 1980.)

duced beneath the skin approximately 0.5 cm distal to the anticipated site of
vessel puncture (Fig. 2).

The needle is introduced slowly toward the vessel until blood appears in the
tubing, indicating that the vessel has been punctured (Fig. 3). It is important to
proceed *very slowly* to avoid penetrating the interior and posterior walls of the
vessel. If this should happen, blood will enter the needle and tubing as the
needle is slowly withdrawn.

At this point the needle is flushed slowly with 1 to 2 ml of solution to ensure
that the IV needle is properly placed within the vein (Fig. 4). If infiltration
occurs, as reflected by a subcutaneous "lump," the needle is withdrawn and the
process repeated at another site.

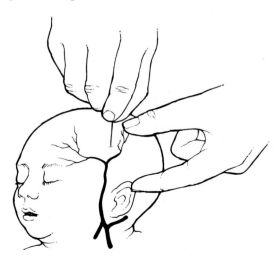

FIG. 2. The needle is introduced
approximately 0.5 cm distal to the
anticipated site of vessel puncture. (Modified from Hildebrand et
al.: *American Family Physician,*
21:139, 1980.)

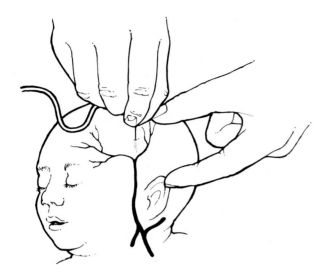

FIG. 3. The needle beneath the skin is advanced slowly until it enters the vein, which is documented by blood appearing in the tubing. (Modified from Hildebrand et al.: *American Family Physician,* 21:139, 1980.)

If infiltration does not occur with injection of 1 to 2 ml saline solution, the butterfly infusion set is taped to the infant (Fig. 5). After the butterfly wings are secured with tape, it is also helpful to tape the tubing from the butterfly set into a loop on the scalp so that it is not accidentally pulled by either the patient or his attendant. A small medicine cup can be taped over the butterfly wings and needle to protect the IV from accidental dislodgement (Fig. 6). The IV fluid set is then connected to the tubing of the butterfly set and the IV pump started.

The most important complications of peripheral IVs are infection and injection of sclerosing agents into the subcutaneous space. In newborns (especially

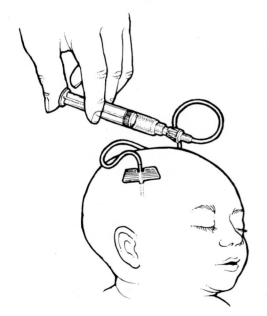

FIG. 4. Tubing and needle are flushed with 1 to 2 ml solution. (Modified from Hildebrand et al.: *American Family Physician,* 21:139, 1980).

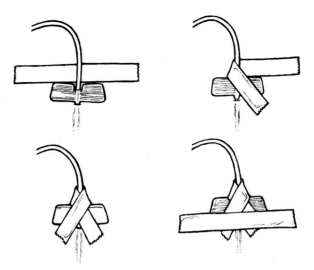

FIG. 5. One technique for taping the IV tubing. (Modified from Hildebrand et al.: *American Family Physician*, 21:139, 1980.)

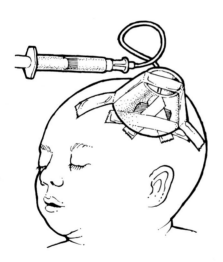

FIG. 6. A plastic medicine cup further protects the IV from accidental dislodgement. (Modified from Hildebrand et al.: *American Family Physician*, 21:139, 1980.)

prematures), this can result in necrosis and sloughing of the skin. Even 5% glucose—and particularly 10% glucose, sodium bicarbonate, or calcium—is extremely sclerosing to the tissues. Because of this, any infiltrated IV must be removed promptly and a new one started. The incidence of infection secondary to peripheral IVs with metal needles is not known. Because the "life span" of any one IV needle is fairly short (about 24 hr) in the newborn, one usually does not have to be concerned about elective removal of the needle. Meticulous attention to sterility during insertion and maintenance of IVs is important to prevent infection.

CAVEATS

1. All infants less than 1,500 g or less than 34 weeks' gestation should have a peripheral IV placed after birth.

2. Umbilical vein catheters should not be inserted solely for the purpose of infusing intravenous fluids.

3. If blanching occurs with infusion of fluids, an artery has probably been entered.

4. The most important complications are infection and infiltration with subsequent sloughing.

25

Blood Cultures

The lack of definitive clinical indicators of sepsis in the neonate and the relatively high incidence of infections at this time have led to widespread use of blood cultures in the nursery. The prenatal, neonatal, and iatrogenic factors which predispose to sepsis are discussed elsewhere in this book. Compared with many of the diagnostic procedures available to the physician, the collection of blood for culture imposes relatively little risk to the patient. Before any infant receives antimicrobials, it is imperative that cultures be obtained prior to treatment to determine the presence of sepsis and to guide in the selection of drugs. Virtually all sick infants should have a blood culture. Blood cultures may be of further benefit when used by the laboratory for tube dilution studies to determine the amount of drug necessary for bacterial inhibition and killing.

Numerous sources and techniques for obtaining blood cultures have been advocated. Limited sampling sites and a relatively small blood volume in the premature infant limit the availability of samples. Because of the greater number of organisms per milliliter of blood, a sample size of 1 ml is probably sufficient in infants. The peripheral venous stick is the most popular method of obtaining cultures but also the most difficult for those inexperienced in the care of newborn infants (Fig. 1). Alternatively, a sample may be withdrawn through the umbilical arterial or venous catheter *immediately* after sterile insertion. This, however, carries a higher incidence of false-positive results because of the greater likelihood of contamination during catheterization. Another expedient method is to obtain the culture at the time of arterial blood sampling. The area may be "prepped" as outlined, the puncture performed with a butterfly apparatus, and the initial sample sent for culture. Afterward, a heparinized tuberculin syringe may be used to obtain the blood for gas studies.

PROCEDURE

1. The puncture site is double "prepped," first with an iodine-containing solution and then with alcohol. Following completion of the procedure, all of

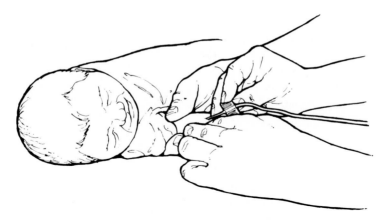

FIG. 1. Technique for drawing blood for culture by antecubital venipuncture.

the iodine solution is removed from the infant's skin in order to prevent irritation.

2. An appropriate-sized sample (½ to 1 ml for each culture) is drawn.

3. The needle which penetrated the skin is then changed. The tops of two culture bottles are "prepped" in a fashion similar to the preparation of the skin (Fig. 2) and half of the sample placed in each bottle. One bottle is vented to air

FIG. 2. Tops of blood culture bottles are wiped with iodophore solution prior to inoculation. A clean needle is attached to the syringe and 0.5 ml of blood inoculated into each bottle. One bottle is vented to air for the aerobic culture.

for the aerobic culture; the anaerobic atmosphere of the second bottle is maintained. Clotted and citrated samples are unsuitable.

Generally, a preliminary report is available within 12 to 24 hr. Significant growth should have occurred by 5 days. Diphtheroids and *Staphylococcus epidermidis* almost always represent contamination if isolated in only one inoculum. However, "contaminants" such as *Staph. epidermidis* may be pathogenic in debilitated infants.

CAVEATS

1. A blood culture is obtained from virtually all acutely sick neonates.
2. There is a high incidence of false-positive results when blood cultures are obtained from umbilical catheters.

26

Suprapubic Bladder Aspiration

The reliability of urinalysis and urine culture in infants is dependent on the method of specimen collection. True clean-catch urine samples without contamination are impossible to obtain during the neonatal period. Urethral catheterization is not only unreliable because of contamination from colonization of the urethra and prepuce, but it may also induce bladder infection. Since its introduction in 1959, suprapubic bladder aspiration has proved to be an efficacious and safe method for urine collection. Any neonate or infant being evaluated for septicemia should have a suprapubic bladder aspiration for urinalysis and culture.

Numerous studies have documented the problems of contamination with clean-catch urine collection. In a study of 162 asymptomatic neonates, Newman[1] reported in 1967 that 64% of bag urine specimens were positive for 100,000 bacterial colonies per milliliter. Other investigators have cited similarly high contamination rates. In contrast, Pierog[2] found bacterial growth in only 6 of 283 infants studied by suprapubic bladder aspiration. Three of these represented true infections, whereas the other three were probably contaminated; the false-positive rate was thus 1%.

What are the potential adverse effects? In a review of the literature, 4,985 cases of suprapubic bladder aspiration were found to be reported, with a total of 11 complications. Ten additional individual cases of complications of bladder aspiration have been reported. Overall, the complication rate is on the order of 0.2%, whereas the success rate for the procedure is approximately 90%. The reported complications of suprapubic bladder aspiration are listed in Table 1. Most of these complications are caused by performing the procedure in the presence of a known contraindication. The most obvious, and common, mistake is performing this procedure on an infant with an empty bladder. A dry diaper for 1 to 3 hr prior to the procedure is required. Because of decreased urine production, dehydration is an obvious contraindication to suprapubic aspira-

---

[1]Newman et al. Pyuria in infancy, and the role of suprapubic aspiration of urine in diagnosis of infection of urinary tract: *British Medical Journal*, 2:277, 1967.
[2]Pierog et al. Incidence of bacteriuria in high risk neonate: *New York State Journal of Medicine*, 75:2152, 1975.

TABLE 1. *Reported adverse effects associated with suprapubic bladder aspiration*

Effect	No. of cases
Microscopic hematuria	Very frequent
Gross hematuria	9
Suprapubic hematoma	1
Bowel perforation	5
Perforation of abdominal organs	1
Death	1

TABLE 2. *Contraindications to suprapubic bladder aspiration*

Empty bladder
Dehydration
Abdominal distention
Organomegaly
Abdominal anomalies
Genitourinary anomalies
Hemorrhagic disorders

tion. Other major contraindications include abdominal distention, organomegaly, genitourinary and abdominal anomalies, and hemorrhagic disorders (Table 2).

PROCEDURE

1. The infant is checked to see that he has not voided during the previous hour. This is done either by noting the presence of a dry diaper or by applying a urine collection bag to the infant for a known period prior to aspiration.

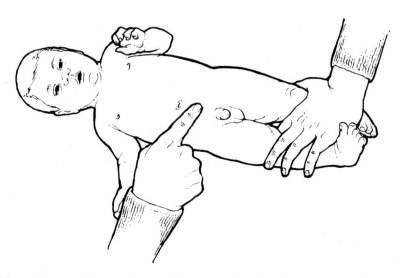

FIG. 1. The bladder is palpated prior to performing the needle aspiration.

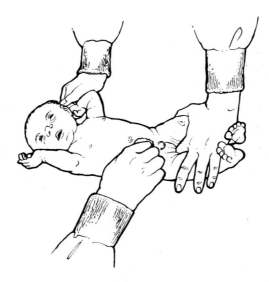

FIG. 2. The suprapubic area is scrubbed while an assistant immobilizes the infant.

2. An assistant is necessary to immobilize the infant.

3. The bladder is palpated (Fig. 1), although in neonates it may not be possible to feel the bladder. The suprapubic area is scrubbed with an antiseptic solution (Fig. 2).

4. The assistant may help prevent the infant from voiding by pinching the proximal penile urethra in the male (Fig. 3) or by inserting a finger in the rectum of the female and compressing the urethra anteriorly against the pubis.

5. Aspiration is performed with a suitable needle and syringe (e.g., 3-cm 21-gauge needle on a 3- to 10-ml syringe).

6. Puncture is performed 1.0 to 1.5 cm above the symphysis pubis in the midline (Figs. 4 and 5). (There is often a skin crease in this location.) The needle

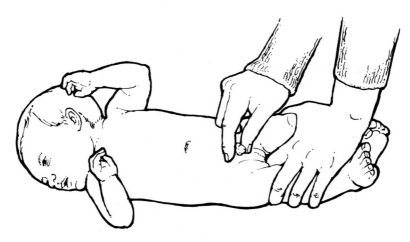

FIG. 3. The proximal penile urethra may be compressed by an assistant to prevent voiding during the procedure.

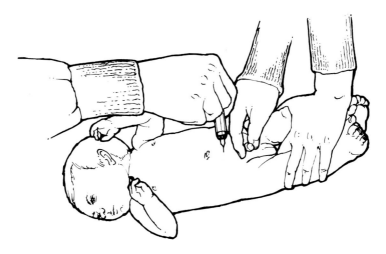

FIG. 4. Bladder aspiration is performed 1.0 to 1.5 cm above the symphysis pubis. The needle is directed perpendicular to the table and inserted 1 to 2 cm until the bladder is aspirated.

is inserted perpendicular to the examining table or angled slightly (10°) toward the head, to a distance of 1 to 2 cm, at which point a slight decrease in resistance may be felt, indicating that the bladder has been penetrated.

7. Urine is aspirated and the needle withdrawn. Gentle pressure is applied over the puncture site until any bleeding stops.

8. If no urine is obtained, the needle is withdrawn. Aimless probing or repeated attempts are *not* warranted.

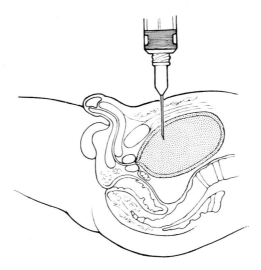

FIG. 5. Cross-sectional view of the abdomen showing insertion of the needle into the bladder.

9. The syringe with urine may be capped and sent on ice directly to the laboratory for urinalysis and bacteriologic studies.

The most common *mistakes* when performing a suprapubic tap are: (a) failure to wait until the bladder is full (dry diaper); (b) insertion of the needle too close to the pubis; and (c) insertion of the needle angled toward the feet, rather than perpendicular to the table or angled slightly toward the head. The bladder is an abdominal organ in the newborn; if the needle is inserted too close to the pubis or angled toward the feet, the bladder is frequently missed.

CAVEATS

1. "Clean-catch" urine specimens are generally useless in the neonate.

2. The contraindications to suprapubic bladder aspiration are an empty bladder (dry diaper), dehydration, serious abdominal pathology, and hemorrhagic disorders.

3. The needle is inserted 1 to 1.5 cm above the symphysis pubis perpendicular to the table or angled slightly toward the head.

27

Blood Transfusions

INDICATIONS FOR BLOOD TRANSFUSION

The transfusion of blood in the newborn should be performed judiciously and with caution, as there are well-documented hazards (Table 1). Therefore the decision to transfuse an infant is made on the basis of specific indications in a specific situation.

The etiology of hypovolemic shock in the delivery room may be related to tears of fetoplacental vessels, fetal-maternal transfusion, twin-to-twin transfusion, placenta previa, abruptio placenta, partial cord occlusion, and inappropriate elevation of the infant after delivery with loss of blood back to the placenta.

Infants with hypovolemic shock may have tachypnea, pallor, poor perfusion of peripheral vessels (poor filling of blanched skin), tachycardia, normal to low

TABLE 1. *Blood transfusion—potential complications*

Bleeding complications
　Overheparinization
Vascular complications
　Embolization
　Thrombosis
　Skin slough at infusion site
Cardiac complications
　Arrhythmias
　Volume overload
Metabolic complications
　Hyperkalemia
　Acidosis
　Others
Infectious complications
　Bacteremia
　Cytomegalovirus
　Hepatitis
Other complications
　Mismatched blood

arterial blood pressure, and decreased central venous pressure. Together the symptoms may mimic the respiratory distress syndrome. As perfusion becomes more compromised, a progressive metabolic acidosis develops. The hematocrit is not a reliable guide to hypovolemic shock, as it may be normal for a peroid of time following acute blood loss.

The following is recommended for management of acute blood loss (Table 2). Rapid volume replacement with whole blood over a short span of time (5 to 15 min) is ideal. Most hospitals have O Rh⁻ available in the blood bank, and this can be used for an emergency blood transfusion in the delivery room without crossmatching. However, if the blood is over 5 days old, the plasma potassium may be elevated to dangerous levels. If the need for blood is apparent prior to actual delivery and the placenta is not contaminated, blood can be aspirated from the umbilical cord before the placenta is delivered and transfused into the infant (Table 3). A heparinized 20-ml syringe with a 20-gauge needle is used. Heparin is drawn into the syringe to coat the barrel, after which the remaining heparin is expelled except for that remaining in the hub of the needle. The umbilical cord is "prepped" with an antiseptic solution (e.g., tincture of iodine). The umbilical vein (largest vessel) is penetrated and 20 ml blood obtained. This blood can be given directly to the infant, through either the umbilical or a peripheral vein, for correction of acute blood loss. Do not use this source of blood if there is any possibility that the placenta might be contaminated or if the placenta has already separated from the uterus prior to collection (which may raise thromboplastin levels and increase the risk of clotting).

If an O Rh⁻ donor is available, blood can be obtained for an emergency transfusion without crossmatching. Except when there is a known maternal-fetal blood incompatibility, blood may also be obtained from the mother and given to the infant. If packed cells are used (hematocrit 70 to 90 vol %), the cells are diluted with fresh frozen plasma, Plasmanate, or 5% albumin. If none of these is readily available, normal saline or a 5% protein solution may be used.

Replacement is at a rate of 10 to 20 ml/kg over a short time span. If the infant remains in shock, another transfusion of this amount may be given. It

TABLE 2. *Acute blood loss*

---

1. Replacement—rapid
   a. Give whole blood 10 to 20 ml/kg; repeat if necessary.
   b. Monitor clinical response.
      Blood pressure.
      Peripheral skin perfusion.
      Color—change from pallor to "pink."
      Resolution of tachycardia, tachypnea.
2. If whole blood is not available, then give
   a. Packed red cells reconstituted with fresh frozen plasma, Plasmanate, or 5% albumin (ratio approximately 5 ml packed cells to 3 ml plasma) to increase the hematocrit to 40 to 50 vol%.
   b. Fresh frozen plasma 10 to 20 ml/kg, Plasmanate, or 5% albumin until blood is available.

TABLE 3. *Placental blood*

1. Indications to draw placental blood
   a. Abruptio placentae, placenta previa, other possible fetal hemorrhage.
   b. Severe intrauterine asphyxia.
2. Procedure
   a. Prepare sterile 20-ml syringe with 20-gauge needle containing 0.1 ml heparin (1,000 units/ml).
   b. Immediately upon clamping and cutting the umbilical cord, sterilize cord with tincture of iodine and draw 20 ml blood from the umbilical vein.
   c. Use blood as indicated; discard after 30 to 60 min.

must be remembered, however, that the normal newborn blood volume is only 85 to 100 ml/kg. The heart rate, blood pressure, and clinical response are monitored. The pallor should disappear, and peripheral perfusion should improve.

CIRCULATORY STATUS

The circulatory status of an infant is best followed by measuring blood pressure, serum sodium, urine output and specific gravity, and pH with base deficit, and by noting the skin color (Table 4). Low systemic blood pressure (see Chapter 15) may be associated with sepsis, hyaline membrane disease (HMD), asphyxia, cardiac disease, or hypotension due to blood loss. The appropriate treatment of hypotension depends on the etiology.

If not corrected, hypotension with impaired perfusion may cause acidosis, hypoxia, and organ damage. Brain hypoxia may cause mental retardation or other neurologic impairment. Necrotizing enterocolitis, as well as acute tubular necrosis of the kidneys, may be the result.

Replacement of blood in the newborn infant depends a great deal on clinical judgment. The guidelines listed in Table 5 must be used *only if the clinical situation warrants* blood replacement. In infants with cardiac decompensation, blood must be given cautiously. It may be wise to give packed red cells or perform a partial exchange transfusion to raise the hematocrit. If vascular decompensation is not due to hypovolemia, then vasopressors or appropriate measures other than blood transfusion may be indicated. Table 6 details formulas to help determine the quantity of blood to give.

TABLE 4. *Parameters to follow*

Blood pressure	Urine	Blood	Others
Doppler Transducer	Output Specific gravity	Serum sodium pH (metabolic acidosis) BUN	Clinical—skin perfusion Central venous pressure

TABLE 5. *Indications for blood replacement in neonatal unit*

1. Accumulated blood loss in acutely sick infant equals 10 to 15% of blood volume with hematocrit (Hct) less than 50%. (*Caution:* This may contribute to hyperbilirubinemia and necessitate exchange transfusion.)
2. Hct less than 40 to 45% postdelivery in sick infant.
3. Hct less than 40 to 45% in HMD or other pulmonary and cardiac decompensation.
4. Hct less than 40 to 45% in persistent fetal circulation.
5. Hct less than 40 to 45% in cyanotic heart disease.
6. Hct less than 40% in infant <1,250 g with episodes of bradycardia or apnea.
7. Hct less than 25% in growing premature or term infant without distress.
8. Hct less than 40% in infant with patent ductus arteriosus which is likely to be symptomatic (infant <1,250 g)
9. Hct less than 40% in bronchopulmonary dysplasia (BPD) if unstable.
10. Hct less than 30% in BPD if stable.

TABLE 6. *Blood replacement*

1. Formula to raise the hematocrit:

$$\frac{80\text{ml}}{\text{kg}} \times \frac{\Delta\text{Hct}}{\text{Hct PC}} \times \frac{\text{wt(kg)}}{} = \text{ml packed cells to give patient.}$$

Usually give approximately 7 to 10 ml/kg.

2. Formula to raise the hemoglobin:

$$\frac{3\text{ml packed cells}}{\text{kg body wt}} \times \text{body wt (kg)} = \text{ml packed cells to give patient.}$$

Increases hemoglobin by 1 g.

3. Do not give more than 10 ml packed cells/kg at any one time except in acute blood loss with hypovolemia.

4. Hematocrit of packed red blood cells varies from 70 to 90%.

TECHNIQUE OF BLOOD TRANSFUSION

In an emergency, the umbilical vein is readily accessible and can be easily catheterized. A peripheral route (see Chapter 24) may also be employed, although in the presence of impaired perfusion peripheral veins may be difficult to cannulate.

Unless the infant has a marginal cardiac status, the blood can be "pushed" in over 10 to 15 min by the physician or nurse. A pump may be used, although extensive extravasation with resultant tissue slough can occur if the baby is not closely observed.

An appropriate filter to remove large particulate matter should be used before transfusing blood. *Do not* attempt to infuse blood through a filter (0.22 μm) intended for removing bacteria or other small particles, however. In order to prevent rouleaux or microthrombus formation in the transfused blood, normal saline is used to clear the intravenous line of all medications and glucose.

Vital signs are monitored during the transfusion. If a transfusion reaction occurs, the transfusion is discontinued immediately, the remaining blood saved for evaluation by the blood bank, and the infant treated appropriately. Such reactions are extremely rare in the newborn.

CAVEATS

1. The hematocrit cannot be used to evaluate the degree of *acute* blood loss.
2. The circulatory status of an infant is best followed by blood pressure, serum pH, urine output and specific gravity, and skin color and capillary filling.
3. During emergencies in the delivery room, blood may be obtained from an O Rh⁻ donor, the mother, or the placenta.

28

Exchange Transfusions

During recent years there has been a dramatic change in the indications for exchange transfusion in the newborn infant. This change is due to a number of factors, including the decreased frequency and severity of Rh sensitization, the improved survival of the very low birth weight infant, improved management of disseminated intravascular coagulopathy, and the earlier, more frequent recognition of such problems as neonatal polycythemia. One may expect further alterations in the indications for, and applications of, exchange transfusion for the newborn baby in the future.

Current general indications for exchange transfusion in the newborn are outlined in Table 1. Although each of these general indications may constitute adequate grounds for considering a complete or partial exchange transfusion, they should be applied flexibly to the individual clinical situation. The very few absolute indications for exchange transfusions which do exist were reviewed in Chapter 9.

TECHNIQUE OF EXCHANGE TRANSFUSION

Before reviewing the specific protocol for exchange transfusion, some of the basic aspects of newborn care important to any infant for whom exchange is being considered will be re-emphasized. First, it is imperative to determine the etiology of the problems for which the infant is being exchanged. For example, in the presence of hyperbilirubinemia or disseminated intravascular coagulopathy (DIC), an adequate evaluation for the possibility of underlying sepsis with institution of appropriate antibiotic therapy may be warranted. Second, meticulous attention must be paid to the general aspects of newborn management, including adequate hydration, maintenance of normal temperature, prevention of hypoglycemia, and avoidance of hypoxemia and/or acidosis. In the presence of clinical jaundice, it is always important to consider other appropriate modalities which may lower the bilirubin level or decrease the rate at which it is rising before embarking on an exchange transfusion. For example, in addition to

TABLE 1. *Indications for exchange transfusion*

---

1. *Complete two-volume exchange transfusion*
    a. Prevention of kernicterus and correction of hyperbilirubinemia, regardless of cause
    b. Removal of red blood cell antibodies and platelet antibodies
    c. Correction of DIC
    Controversial
    d. Removal of toxins, e.g., local anesthetic agents or other drugs, ammonia, amino acids
    e. Treatment of overwhelming sepsis refractory to conventional therapy
    f. Treatment of sclerema
2. *Partial exchange transfusion*
    a. Partial packed cell for correction of severe anemia
    b. Partial plasma for correction of hyperviscosity/polycythemia

---

adequate hydration, frequent stooling may be stimulated by using small glycerin suppositories to reduce the enterohepatic circulation, or phototherapy may be used as indicated.

Once the decision has been reached to proceed, a number of steps must be taken prior to beginning the exchange. It is useful to review all laboratory tests that are planned at the initiation of the exchange transfusion. It may indeed be helpful to draw up a complete list of all appropriate tests to be performed. Further, it must be ascertained that the appropriate blood has been ordered from the blood bank for the exchange transfusion. For a complete two-volume exchange transfusion, fresh heparinized or citrate phosphate dextrose (CPD) anticoagulated blood less than 72 hr old is mandatory. If possible, notification of the blood bank 6 to 12 hr prior to the anticipated time of exchange transfusion is helpful. If the blood bank does not have access to fresh blood less than 72 hr old, then the unit of blood they do have may be packed, the plasma drawn off, and the packed cells reconstituted with fresh frozen plasma to a hematocrit of 40 to 55%. This is done to prevent marked aberrations in electrolyte content, particularly elevated potassium levels. Blood which is less than 72 hr old and available for exchange transfusion may be semipacked in the blood bank to a hematocrit of 40 to 55%. Further, the blood bank should routinely send an aliquot of the blood to be used for exchange transfusion for potassium determination prior to sending the unit to the nursery. Although this often entails an additional delay of 45 to 60 min, this precaution is recommended when time permits. If the blood has a potassium level greater than 7 to 10 mEq/liter, the blood should not be used for exchange transfusion. The volume of blood requested should be at least twice the estimated infant's blood volume plus an additional 50 ml required for filling the blood warmer (which is lost in the setup for the exchange transfusion). The estimated blood volume of an infant is 80 to 100 ml/kg. The group and type of blood used is noted in Table 2.

Once the blood is ordered and the laboratory tests are enumerated, the infant is prepared for the exchange transfusion. First, the area in which the exchange is to be done is prewarmed and the radiant warmer turned on with the servo control probe in place. Appropriate monitoring of the infant's heart rate, elec-

TABLE 2. *Group and type of blood for exchange transfusion*

Indication	Blood group	Rh type	Crossmatched against
Rh incompatibility	O or same as infant	Negative	Mother's or baby's serum
ABO incompatibility	O or same as mother	Same as infant	Mother's or baby's serum
Hyperbilirubinemia (unexplained)	Same as infant	Same as infant	Mother's or baby's serum

trocardiogram (ECG), and temperature is maintained throughout the exchange process. Adequate oxygenation and hydration with sufficient glucose intake are ensured prior to beginning the exchange transfusion. A feeding tube is passed into the infant's stomach and the stomach contents removed prior to exchange. The tube is then left in place to maintain open drainage during the entire procedure.

The usual route for exchange transfusion is via a central umbilical venous catheter. Recent reports indicate that continuous exchange transfusion by infusing blood into the umbilical venous catheter (or other venous line) and extracting blood via an umbilical arterial catheter is a safe and efficacious method of total exchange transfusion.

After restraining the infant and ensuring that the baby can be observed following sterile draping, a polyvinyl catheter is inserted into the umbilical vein (see Chapters 7 and 31). A No. 8 French (for babies greater than 2 kg) or a No. 5 French (for babies less than 2 kg) catheter prefilled with isotonic solution and attached to a three-way stopcock and syringe is recommended. The umbilical venous catheter is inserted until the tip is in the inferior vena cava (through the ductus venosus) and below the right atrium or proximal to the portal sinus. The catheter is almost always in the inferior vena cava if it can be introduced beyond 8 cm in the premature infant or 11 cm in the term infant without meeting resistance. However, if resistance is encountered, the catheter is withdrawn to approximately 3 cm for the premature infant and 5 cm for the term baby, at which point blood return should be adequate. The catheter is fixed firmly in place using a silk purse-string suture. The exchange transfusion is then performed with the following aliquots as tolerated: 1,000 to 1,500 g baby, 5 ml; 1,500 to 2,000 g baby, 10 ml; 2,000 to 2,500 g baby, 15 ml; and greater than 2,500 g baby, 20 ml. An exchange transfusion performed in this manner by the isovolumetric method achieves the following blood replacement: one-volume exchange, 63% of original cells replaced; two-volume exchange, 86% of original cells replaced; and three-volume exchange, 95% of original cells replaced. In this connection, it should be noted that bilirubin moves quickly between extravascular and intravascular compartments. For this reason more bilirubin is removed from the infant during a two-volume exchange than was originally present in the circulation, while at the same time plasma concentrations fall only 40 to 55%. The reduction in serum bilirubin is particularly small during an early exchange transfusion. The equilibration between intra- and extravascular compartments is almost instantaneous so that little is gained by doing exchange transfusions very slowly. The ideal duration of an exchange is approximately 50 to 70 min. During the exchange transfusion, it is important that an assistant record the volumes of blood exchanged and the times throughout the entire procedure. It is usually recommended that a balanced exchange (same total volume infused as is withdrawn) be performed.

Close attention must be paid to the infant's heart rate and perfusion status throughout the exchange procedure, watching for signs of vascular compromise or volume overload. If an infant deteriorates abruptly during an exchange transfusion, it is imperative to stop the exchange immediately and attempt to determine the cause of the deterioration. Further, for a baby who has significant cardiorespiratory embarrassment, it is important to do an arterial blood gas determination prior to and 15 to 20 min after beginning an exchange transfusion, with the oxygen concentration or ventilator settings adjusted accordingly. The use of calcium gluconate is not recommended as a routine practice during the exchange transfusion.

At the completion of the exchange transfusion, it is important to apply a purse-string suture around the umbilical vein or an umbilical tape around the umbilical cord. While removing the catheter, the tape or purse-string suture is tightened to prevent the possibility of air embolus during the inspiratory phase of the infant's respiration. Such an embolus is usually preventable; if missed, it can be fatal. The umbilical vein is then tagged with a small loop of suture next to it for easy identification in the event of repeated exchange transfusions. It is also helpful to draw a diagram of the location of the umbilical vein in the progress notes of the chart. A complete procedure note is written in the chart to document the entire procedure as well as any attendant complications.

Diagnostic studies normally performed prior to and after an exchange transfusion for hyperbilirubinemia are listed in Table 3. In the case of hyperbiliru-

TABLE 3. *Pre- and postexchange diagnostic studies*

1. Immediately pre-exchange
   Hematocrit
   Total protein/albumin
   Sodium, potassium
   Bilirubin (direct and indirect)
2. Immediately postexchange
   Hematocrit
   Sodium, potassium
   Type and crossmatch
   Bilirubin (direct and indirect)
   pH
   Platelet count
   Dextrostix
3. At 3 to 4 hr postexchange
   Bilirubin (direct and indirect)
   Total protein/albumin
   Dextrostix q 2 hr × 3
   Platelet count

binemia, repeat fractionated bilirubin studies are obtained every 4 to 6 hr or as the rate of rise of the bilirubin level indicates. Routine platelet counts are obtained every 12 hr for at least 24 hr after an exchange transfusion, as thrombocytopenia commonly follows this procedure.

PARTIAL EXCHANGE TRANSFUSION

Partial exchange transfusions are utilized for increasing or reducing the hematocrit to a normal range. In the presence of polycythemia (central or venipuncture hematocrit greater than 60 to 65%) a partial plasma exchange transfusion may be indicated, particularly in the presence of cardiopulmonary or neurologic symptoms. The exchange is performed technically in the same manner as a two-volume exchange. However, the infant's blood is replaced with a 5% protein solution instead of donor blood. To calculate the amount of infant blood which must be replaced in order to reduce the hematocrit (Hct) to a desired range, the following formula may be used:

$$\text{Volume to be exchanged} = \frac{\text{beginning Hct} - \text{desired Hct}}{\text{beginning Hct}} \times 85 \text{ ml/kg} \times \text{weight}$$

For example, should a 3-kg baby with a *heelstick* hematocrit of 78% and a *central venipuncture* hematocrit of 68% have symptoms indicating the need for partial exchange, the following calculation is performed to reduce the central hematocrit to approximately 50%.

$$\text{Volume to be exchanged} = \frac{68\% - 50\%}{68\%} \times 85 \text{ ml/kg} \times 3 \text{ kg}$$
$$= \text{approximately 68 ml}$$

The exchange is then performed by withdrawing appropriate aliquots of the infant's blood (10, 15, or 20 ml at a time) via an umbilical venous catheter and replacing each aliquot with an equal volume of 5% protein solution to a total of 68 ml. A similar calculation may be performed when a partial exchange transfusion with packed red blood cells is performed to raise the hematocrit of an acutely ill, severely anemic baby. Caution must be used in this circumstance so as not to overload the infant, as abruptly raising the hematocrit may cause extravascular fluid to enter the vascular compartment and produce pulmonary edema.

COMPLICATIONS

Exchange transfusions have certain attendant risks and complications. In general, the mortality rate of exchange transfusions is directly related to the severity of illness in the baby and the experience of the personnel performing the procedure. In vigorous, otherwise healthy babies, the mortality rate is less than 1% when performed by skilled individuals. In a large series of exchange

TABLE 4. *Complications of exchange transfusion*

Infections
Electrolyte abnormalities
Cardiac arrhythmias and ECG changes
Perforations of vessels, peritoneum, or bowel
Spontaneous hemorrhage
Hypervolemia or shock
Citrate intoxication
Thrombocytopenia
Serum hepatitis
Air embolization
Acidosis or alkalosis
Hypoglycemia
Hypothermia
Massive hemolysis caused by old exchange blood
Transient ileus
Necrotizing enterocolitis

transfusions reported in the literature, the mortality rate in clinically unstable infants was 2.8%, in infants with kernicterus 33%, and in hydropic babies 75%. Complications occasionally encountered are listed in Table 4.

The cardiac arrhythmias include tachycardia, bradycardia, atrioventricular (A-V) block, and alterations in the T-wave or QT, PR, and ST segments. They may be related to a variety of problems which include hyperkalemia, hypocalcemia (associated with the citrate anticoagulant), abrupt changes in circulating blood volume, hypothermia, and acidosis.

In summary, exchange transfusion is a technique with a variety of clinical applications. It is most frequently used for the treatment of hyperbilirubinemia and the prevention of kernicterus. When performing an exchange transfusion, it is imperative that the procedure be done under optimal conditions by an experienced team with appropriate monitoring of the baby throughout. The attendant risks of complete two-volume exchange transfusions are significant and include the possibility of death. However, such complications may be minimized through meticulous attention to all aspects of the procedure and appropriate management of the infant before, during, and after the exchange.

CAVEATS

1. Blood used for exchange transfusion should be less than 72 hr old.

2. If the potassium level of the exchange blood is ≥ 7 to 10 mEq/liter, the blood should not be used.

3. The infant must have continuous heart rate monitoring during the exchange transfusion.

4. If the infant's condition deteriorates during an exchange, the procedure is stopped and the cause of the deterioration determined.

5. The complication rate of exchange transfusion is directly related to the severity of illness in the baby and the experience and expertise of the personnel performing the procedure.

29

Intubation

Endotracheal intubation by the oral or nasal route is always performed under controlled conditions. With the exception of the infants at risk for meconium aspiration (see Chapter 7) and those with a diaphragmatic hernia, the airway can usually be maintained and respiration supported with a resuscitation bag and mask. As with any procedure, intubation must not further jeopardize the infant's clinical status.

PROCEDURE

1. The following equipment is needed (Fig. 1):
   a. Laryngoscope with a straight size 0 blade for premature and newborn infants, or a straight size 1 blade for older infants.
   b. Endotracheal tubes in a variety of sizes ranging from 2.5 mm internal diameter for small prematures (less than 1,000 g) to 3.5 mm internal diameter for full-term infants. Cole tubes are useful for emergency orotracheal intubation in the delivery room.
   c. McGill forceps for nasotracheal intubation or a stylet for orotracheal intubation.
   d. Resuscitation bag, mask, and oxygen.
   e. Sterile suction equipment and gloves.
   f. Xylocaine jelly to lubricate the tube.
   g. Tape and benzoin to fasten the tube.
2. The infant's heart rate is monitored electronically, the monitor beep being audible for continuous surveillance.
3. Body temperature is maintained by placing the infant under a warmer.
4. Oxygenation is maintained before and after the procedure with oxygen and a resuscitation bag, and during the procedure by administering oxygen over the face.
5. Gastric contents are aspirated.
6. The nasopharynx is suctioned.

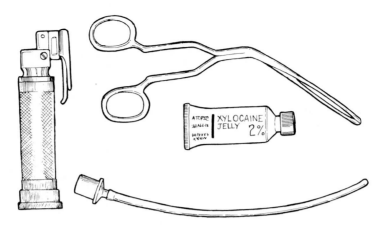

FIG. 1. Equipment necessary for nasotracheal intubation, in clockwise order beginning at the top: McGill forceps, xylocaine jelly, endotracheal tube with adapter, and laryngoscope with straight blade.

7. The infant is ventilated with 100% oxygen for several breaths with a resuscitation bag prior to intubation.
8. Intubate:
   a. The laryngoscope is held between the thumb and index finger of the left hand (Fig. 2). After insertion of the blade, the third and fourth fingers are used to elevate the chin, and the fifth finger to apply pressure over the hyoid bone to bring the larynx more directly into view.

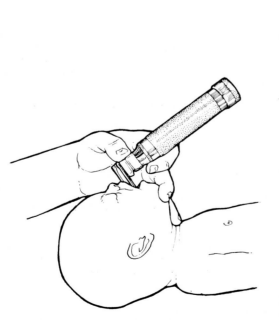

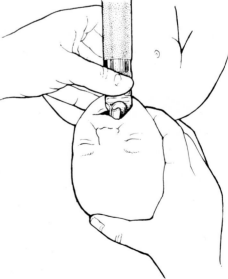

FIG. 3. Laryngoscope is inserted into the right-hand side of the mouth and the tongue retracted toward the left with a sweeping motion.

FIG. 2. Position for holding the laryngoscope.

b. The infant is positioned supine *without* hyperextension of the neck.

c. The laryngoscope blade is inserted through the right side of the mouth (Fig. 3). The larynx is visualized by gentle elevation and sweeping of the blade to the left to remove the tongue from the field of vision. The tip of the blade is inserted into the vallecula (the pouch above the epiglottis).

d. With elevation of the tip of the blade, the vocal cords may be visualized. The orotracheal tube is introduced through the right corner of the mouth and passed through the cords (Fig. 4). The barrel of the laryngoscope blade is used for visualization, not as a guide for the tube. For nasotracheal intubation the tube is passed through the nares into the pharynx prior to visualization of the cords (Fig. 5). When the cords are seen, the tip of the tube is advanced with the McGill forceps (Fig. 6).

e. The tube is positioned with the 2-cm mark at the vocal cords in a 1-kg premature infant and to 3 cm in a full-term infant (Fig. 7).

f. The lettering at the mouth or nares is checked as an indicator of position.

g. The infant is ventilated and breath sounds auscultated bilaterally. If the breath sounds are unilateral, the tube is slowly pulled back while listening until the sounds are equal. With unilateral breath sounds the tube has probably passed the right mainstem bronchus.

h. The tube is secured with 0.5-inch tape and benzoin.

i. A chest X-ray is obtained to determine tube position. The proper location of the tube on X-ray is above the carina but below the clavicles.

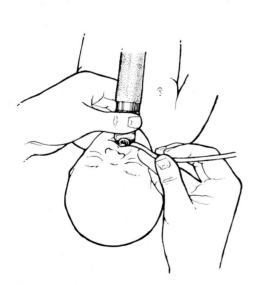

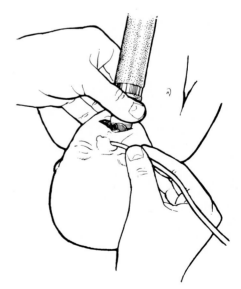

FIG. 4. Endotracheal tube is inserted through the right-hand corner of the mouth—*not* down the laryngoscope blade.

FIG. 5. For nasotracheal intubation the tube is inserted through the nostril into the pharynx prior to visualization of the cords.

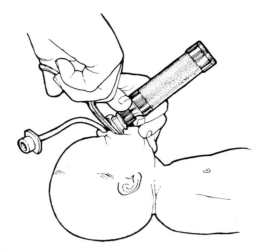

FIG. 6. The tube is advanced with the use of McGill forceps.

FIG. 7. Graduated markings are used for positioning.

9. Once again, the infant needs close monitoring throughout this procedure. All attempts must cease if bradycardia (heart rate less than 100) or cyanosis occurs. The infant is stabilized prior to repeat attempts.

PROCEDURAL PITFALLS

A few errors in the intubation procedure account for most failures. The most common fault is the tendency to overextend the neck. Although helpful in the older child or adult, in the newborn the resting position of the head is preferred. There is also a tendency to insert the laryngoscope blade too far. Usually in this instance the orifice of the esophagus is visualized. This opening appears more horizontal than the trachea, and the glistening white vocal cords cannot be seen. Gentle retraction of the blade allows visualization of the cords.

Another common error in intubation is malpositioning the tube, in either a mainstem bronchus or the esophagus. As a result, atelectasis, deterioration of arterial blood gases, and worsening of the clinical condition may be observed. Careful auscultation prior to anchoring the tube and close attention to prevention of tube slippage may prevent such problems. Other complications and side effects of intubation are summarized in Table 1.

TABLE 1. *Complications and side effects of endotracheal intubation*

Malposition of tube
   Mainstem bronchus
   Esophagus
   Perforation of trachea or pharynx
Occlusion of tube
   Kinking
   Plugging—due to secretions or blood
Accidental extubation
Long-term consequences
   Inflammation, granuloma formation, and stenosis of cords and trachea
   Nasal septal erosion
   Erosion and stenosis of nares
   Erosion of palate and gingiva (cleft palate, dental damage)
Other
   Infection
   Eliminates grunt (zero end-expiratory pressure)
   May contribute to bronchopulmonary dysplasia
   Potential for pneumothorax, pneumomediastinum, or subcutaneous air dissection

KITTEN TEACHING MODEL

Because of the lack of realism in teaching intubation on rubber models, we have used anesthetized 4-month-old kittens as an effective means to teach the technique. The kitten is given 40 mg ketamine into the triceps muscle. The duration of anesthesia is approximately 60 min. Intubation is performed with a 3-mm endotracheal tube, stylet, and a No. 1 laryngoscope blade. This procedure offers the advantages of anatomy, secretions, and intact laryngeal reflexes similar to those in the neonate, and vocal cord spasm that is more pronounced than in the neonate.

CAVEATS

1. In most cases, an infant can be adequately ventilated and oxygenated with bag and mask ventilation.

2. If an infant has bradycardia or cyanosis during the intubation attempt, bag and mask ventilation is instituted.

3. The barrel of the laryngoscope blade is used for visualization of the larynx, not as a guide for the tube.

4. The most common mistake is the tendency to overextend the infant's neck.

5. Another common error in intubation is malpositioning the tube in the esophagus or in a mainstem bronchus.

30

Techniques of Obtaining Arterial Blood

One of the most important laboratory tests in the evaluation and monitoring of an infant with respiratory distress is determining the arterial blood gas values. Frequent blood gas analyses and correlation of results with the patient's clinical condition are essential for safe and effective care. This is especially true with the high-risk neonate whose cardiopulmonary system is subject to continuous change. In the care of any sick newborn requiring supplemental oxygen, it is imperative that the arterial partial pressure of oxygen (pO_2) be monitored to prevent damage from either hypoxia or hyperoxia. If inadequate oxygen is administered, hypoxia may cause pulmonary vasoconstriction; the resultant increased right-to-left shunting across the foramen ovale and ductus arteriosus leads to further hypoxia and metabolic acidosis. In addition, permanent hypoxic damage to tissues may result in cerebral palsy, mental retardation, renal damage, and congestive heart failure. In the premature infant with jaundice, the risk of brain damage secondary to elevated bilirubin levels is increased by hypoxia. Excessive oxygen administration, on the other hand, may increase the risk of oxygen toxicity to the lungs (bronchopulmonary dysplasia) and the eyes (retrolental fibroplasia).

SOURCES OF ARTERIAL BLOOD

For all these reasons, arterial blood gas analysis is extremely important in neonatal respiratory care. Monitoring arterial blood gases in newborns presents technical difficulties, especially in small, premature infants. Possible sites of blood sampling include: (a) radial, brachial, temporal, dorsal pedal, and posterior tibial arteries; (b) umbilical arteries; and (c) capillaries ("arterialized"). Femoral arteries are not used for obtaining blood samples.

Umbilical artery catheters (see Chapter 31) are frequently used, but there are many serious potential complications. Because of the possibility of adverse side effects, most physicians prefer to remove the catheters early even though the infant may still require supplemental oxygen. Furthermore, attempts to insert an umbilical artery catheter are not always successful, even in the hands of the most experienced physician. Recent reports of success with transcutaneous electrodes suggest that such instruments may provide an alternative to umbilical catheterization. These advances, however, will not replace the need for intermittent arterial samples.

RADIAL ARTERY PUNCTURE

The radial artery puncture (Table 1) is one of the most frequently used methods for obtaining intermittent arterial samples from neonates. Before this procedure is attempted, it is important that one be aware of the anatomy of the arteries and nerves of the wrist (Fig. 1). Only the radial artery is used for arterial puncture in order to preserve the collateral circulation to the hand via the ulnar artery. Some neonatologists advocate performing punctures and catheterization of the ulnar artery, but we prefer not to do this in order to maintain collateral supply to the hand—even though those investigators who use the ulnar artery have reported no impairment to the circulation to the hand. The median nerve in the midline and the ulnar nerve near the ulnar artery are areas to be avoided when doing punctures.

When preparing for radial puncture, a tuberculin syringe is first heparinized. All remaining heparin and air are then ejected from the syringe. The amount of heparin remaining in the neck of the syringe and the hub of the needle is adequate to anticoagulate the sample; excess heparin may result in inaccurate pH and pCO_2 determinations owing to dilution of the blood sample.

The radial artery is palpated just proximal to the transverse wrist creases to feel the pulsations (Fig. 2). The infant's wrist and hand are grasped in your left hand (if right-handed). The area is then cleansed with alcohol. Some physicians advocate the use of subcutaneous lidocaine to decrease the pain. With a hep-

TABLE 1. *Radial artery puncture*

---

1. Heparinize a 25- or 26-gauge needle on a tuberculin syringe. (All heparin and air is expelled from the syringe. Heparin left in the hub of the needle and the neck of the syringe is adequate for anticoagulation.)
2. Palpate the radial artery.
3. Hold the wrist and hand of the infant with your free hand.
4. Cleanse the area with alcohol.
5. Infiltrate the subcutaneous area with 1% lidocaine (0.2 to 0.3 ml).
6. Penetrate the skin at approximately a 30° to 45° angle (Fig. 3).
7. Aspirate after penetration of the skin. If blood appears, the radial artery has been punctured.
8. If resistance is met, withdraw the needle slowly, staying beneath the skin, and repeat the procedure.
9. After 0.3 ml blood is obtained, withdraw the needle and apply pressure for at least 5 min to prevent bleeding.
10. Note the source of blood and FiO_2 on patient record.

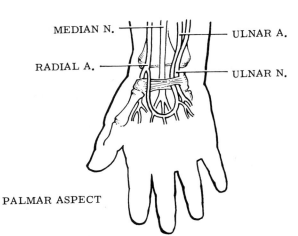

FIG. 1. Anatomy of the wrist. (From Kisling and Schreiner: *Respiratory Care,* 22:1977.)

arinized tuberculin syringe and a 25- or 26-gauge needle, the skin is penetrated at a 30° to 45° angle (Fig. 3). While pulling on the plunger of the syringe, the needle is pushed slightly deeper until the radial artery is punctured or until resistance is met (Fig. 4). In infants it is necessary to provide continuous suction on the plunger of the syringe. One can be sure that the radial artery is punctured when blood appears in the hub of the needle.

There is some controversy as to whether the needle should be bevel up or bevel down when doing a radial artery puncture in the newborn. We believe it does not make any difference. The artery is so small in the newborn that only a

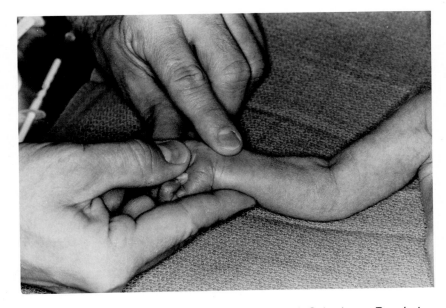

FIG. 2. Palpating the radial artery. (From Kisling and Schreiner: *Respiratory Care,* 22:1977.)

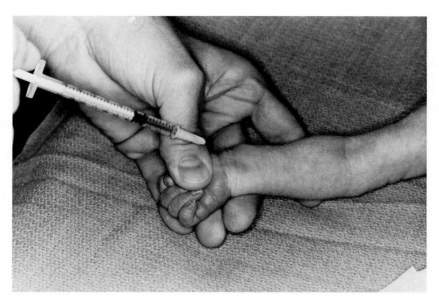

FIG. 3. Insert needle under the skin at a 30° to 45° angle.

part of the needle opening is actually within the arterial lumen. There are other methods of radial artery puncture; e.g., some prefer using a 25-gauge scalp vein butterfly needle connected to a syringe.

If resistance (Fig. 4) is met while pushing the needle deeper, the needle is slowly withdrawn staying beneath the skin, and the procedure repeated. After a 0.3-ml sample of blood is obtained, the needle is withdrawn and a pressure dressing applied for 5 min or longer to stop the bleeding.

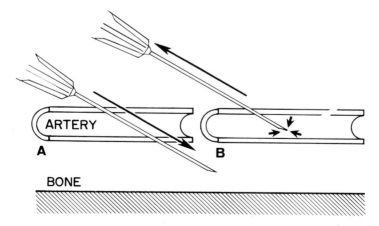

FIG. 4. If resistance is met, it usually indicates contact with bone. Withdraw the needle slowly; if the needle has traversed both walls of the artery, blood is obtained as the needle is slowly withdrawn into the arterial lumen.

The complications of radial artery puncture include infection, hematoma formation, and nerve damage; however, with the use of proper technique (as described above), the complication rate is extremely low. Probably the most important complication of radial artery or any peripheral arterial puncture in the newborn is that the baby may start to cry before blood is obtained, thus changing the pO_2 and pCO_2 from that present in the quiet state. If it takes more than a few seconds to obtain the arterial blood and the infant is crying, the procedure is stopped and tried again later.

"CAPILLARY" STICKS

Many physicians, nurses, and respiratory therapists are not experienced in the technique of arterial puncture. In addition, there is an obvious limit to the number of times that extremely small vessels can be successfully aspirated by a needle. Because of the limitations of these blood sampling techniques, capillary or "arterialized" blood has been used in the past. These samples are usually obtained from the heel. Many studies have compared the pH, pCO_2, and pO_2 of capillary and arterial samples, and the results have been highly variable. Most studies showed a good correlation of the pH and pCO_2 between the arterial and capillary sample when the patient has a normal blood pressure. Unfortunately, the vital measurement of pO_2 is not equally reliable by both procedures. Essentially all reported studies indicate that the capillary pO_2 is poorly correlated with the actual arterial pO_2, particularly when the latter is greater than 60 mm Hg. For example, a capillary pO_2 of 60 may reflect an arterial pO_2 of 60 to 160 mm Hg. In any given case, however, it is not known how close the capillary value is to the arterial value. Relying on capillary pO_2 measurements in an acutely sick infant is therefore fraught with serious potential risk. At least one study suggests that "capillary" blood obtained from finger- and toesticks is more reliable than heelsticks for pO_2 determination.

Many sources of error in such samples could contribute to the observed variations. Inadequate warming of the extremities, undue squeezing of the heel resulting in venous contamination, and exposure of the blood to ambient oxygen concentrations have been implicated as causes for the repeated discrepancies. In sick, young, premature infants receiving supplemental oxygen, it is mandatory that the arterial pO_2 be followed accurately. If the capillary samples are used without adequate documentation of a good correlation to arterial pO_2, there is a considerable risk of exposing the infant to either hypoxia or hyperoxia for prolonged periods with the concomitant risk of developing brain damage secondary to the former or retrolental fibroplasia secondary to the latter.

To perform a heelstick properly (Table 2), it is necessary to be familiar with the anatomy of the heel (Fig. 5). Since the posterior tibial artery is located on the medial aspect, heelsticks are performed on the lateral aspect of the heel. A 3-mm lancet is used, never a scalpel blade. The infant's foot is wrapped with a warm, not hot, towel or diaper for 3 min, and then the heel is cleaned with

TABLE 2. *Heelstick procedure for obtaining capillary blood samples*

1. Warm the foot with a warm diaper (not hot) if sample is for blood gases.
2. Heparinize a capillary tube.
3. Use only a 3-mm lancet—not a scalpel blade!
4. Clean the heel with alcohol.
5. Avoid bruised or edematous areas.
6. Use the lateral aspect of the heel.
7. Puncture the heel one time.
8. Collect 0.3 ml blood.
9. Send the sample to the laboratory.
10. Apply pressure to the puncture site after blood is obtained.

alcohol. The skin is punctured with a lancet on the lateral portion of the foot just anterior to the heel (Fig. 6). Only one stab is usually necessary. Never slash at the heel. The first drop of blood is discarded and then the blood is allowed to flow freely into a heparinized capillary tube (Fig. 7). The tip of the tube is placed as near the puncture site as possible to avoid exposing the blood to environmental oxygen. Collecting air in the tube is to be avoided, as is excessive squeezing of the foot, as tissue damage may result and the pO_2 may be artificially lowered. A 0.3-ml volume of blood is collected in the capillary tube and the blood then aspirated into a heparinized tuberculin syringe. A dry pressure dressing is applied to the puncture site.

Improperly done, heelsticks can cause lacerations, infection, and scarring. These complications are rare when the procedure is performed by trained persons. The most important potential error associated with heelstick blood gases is that of false information, which may result in the infant's exposure to improper amounts of supplemental oxygen. Heelstick blood gas values are never used: (a) during the first 24 hr of age; (b) when the infant is hypotensive; (c) when the heel is markedly bruised; or (d) when there is evidence of peripheral

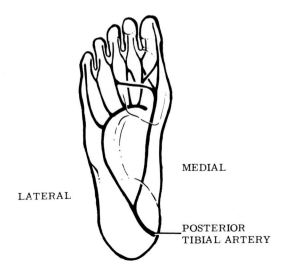

LATERAL

MEDIAL

POSTERIOR
TIBIAL ARTERY

FIG. 5. Arterial anatomy of heel. (From Kisling and Schreiner: *Respiratory Care*, 22:1977.)

vasoconstriction. In addition, when the capillary pO_2 is over 60 to 70 mm Hg, one cannot be sure that values obtained by heelstick correlate with the arterial pO_2. In the latter instances, either an arterial pO_2 must be obtained or the FiO_2 is decreased and another blood gas obtained.

In summary, capillary samples provide a reliable means for obtaining pH and pCO_2 determinations in most newborns. However, the inherent variability in pO_2 measurements from heelstick samples preclude their use for effectively monitoring the need of an infant for supplemental oxygen. This is particularly true for the premature or acutely ill baby, where the risks of hypoxemia or hyperoxemia may be augmented by unreliable pO_2 determinations.

CAVEATS

1. When caring for a sick newborn who requires supplemental oxygen, it is imperative to monitor the arterial pO_2.

2. The most important complication of a peripheral arterial puncture is that the baby may start crying and the pO_2 and pCO_2 may not accurately reflect the unstressed pO_2 and pCO_2 values.

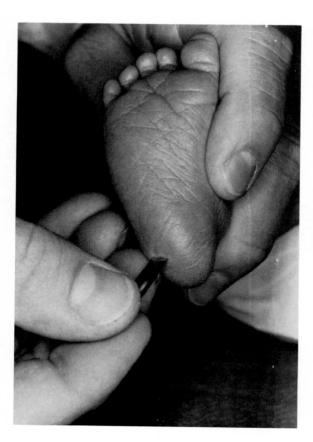

FIG. 6. The heelstick is performed on the lateral aspect of the heel. (From Kisling and Schreiner: *Respiratory Care,* 22:1977.)

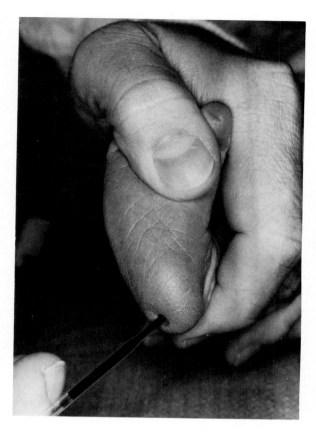

FIG. 7. Blood is allowed to flow into the capillary tube, avoiding air bubbles. (From Kisling and Schreiner: *Respiratory Care,* 22:1977.)

3. Heelsticks are a poor means of monitoring the pO_2 and are never used during the acute phase of the illness.

4. The most important complication of heelstick blood gases is the erroneous information concerning the pO_2 value obtained.

31

Umbilical Artery Catheterization

Umbilical artery catheterization is a useful procedure in the care of infants who require frequent arterial blood gas or blood pressure assessment. Additionally, medication and parenteral fluids may be infused by this route, although special precautions must be taken as push medications have been associated with a high incidence of complications. In spite of their usefulness, one must be aware of, and watchful for, potential complications of umbilical lines.

EQUIPMENT

All equipment should be assembled prior to catheterization to be sure of its availability and working condition. Supplies and equipment are as follows (1 through 8 are shown in Fig. 1):

1. Line fluids usually consist of $D_{10}W$ with electrolytes. Some physicians also add 1 unit heparin/ml fluid (theoretically to prevent clotting in the catheter).
2. Fluid chamber.
3. IV tubing.
4. Infusion pump.
5. Filter (0.22 μm).
6. Short length of IV tubing.
7. Three-way stopcock.
8. 3.5 or 5.0 French umbilical artery catheter.
9. 3-0 Silk suture on an atraumatic needle.
10. Heparinized saline 10 ml for flush (1 unit sodium heparin/ml fluid).
11. Surgical cap, mask, gown, and gloves.

PROCEDURE FOR CATHETERIZATION

1. The infant is placed under a radiant warmer and all four extremities restrained (Fig. 2). The skin temperature is maintained at 96.5°F by a servo-control mechanism. Oxygen is administered as needed, and the beep on the cardiac monitor must be audible.

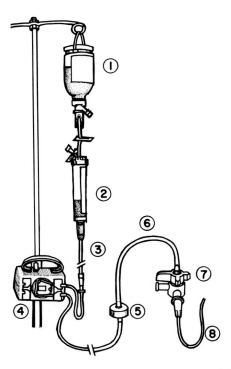

FIG. 1. Umbilical artery catheter material.

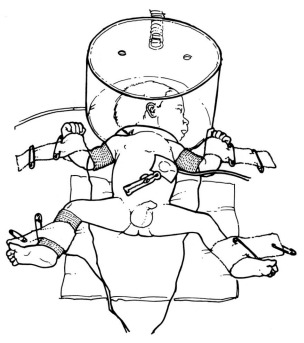

FIG. 2. The infant is properly re-strained and the heart rate moni-tored continuously.

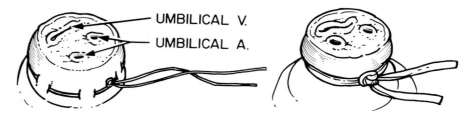

FIG. 3. A purse-string suture or umbilical tape around the base of the cord provides hemostasis.

2. The umbilicus is scrubbed with a bactericidal solution for 5 min. Remember to clean off iodine-containing preparations after the procedure to avoid skin irritation. Avoid pooling of liquid at the infant's side, as this has been associated with blistering while under a radiant warmer.

3. The operator must wear a surgical cap and mask, perform a 5-min scrub, and put on a surgical gown and gloves using aseptic technique.

4. The umbilicus is draped in a sterile fashion, leaving the head exposed for clinical observation.

5. To provide hemostasis and to anchor the line after placement, a 3–0 silk purse-string suture is placed at the junction of the skin and the cord (Fig. 3). Alternatively, a constricting loop of umbilical tape in the same position may be utilized. The cord may then be cut 3 to 4 mm from the skin and the vessels identified. The vein is the largest vessel with a relatively thin wall and large lumen. Two arteries with thicker walls and smaller lumens are usually present.

6. The cord is grasped with two curved hemostats near the selected artery. This provides clear visualization and stabilization of the vessel. Using the curved Iris forceps, the artery may be gently dilated (Fig. 4).

7. A previously prepared 3.5 or 5.0 Fr. umbilical artery catheter may then be introduced (Fig. 5). A 3.5 Fr. catheter is usually recommended for infants less

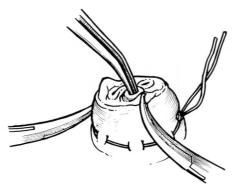

FIG. 4. Dilating the umbilical artery with curved Iris forceps.

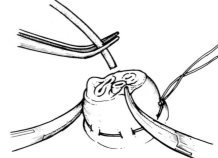

FIG. 5. Introduction of a catheter into a dilated artery.

than 2 kg and a 5.0 Fr. for those greater than 2 kg. The catheter is prepared by cutting off a portion of the larger, tapered end and inserting either an 18-gauge stub adapter for the 5.0 Fr. or a 20-gauge adapter for the 3.5 Fr. catheter. This should then be attached to the three-way stopcock and the air cleared from the line by flushing with saline solution.

8. On insertion of the catheter, tension is placed on the cord in the cephalad direction and the catheter advanced with *slow, constant* pressure toward the feet (Fig. 6). Resistance is occasionally felt at 1 to 2 cm—the junction of the artery and the fascial plane. Resistance is overcome by *gentle* sustained pressure and rotation of the catheter between the thumb and forefinger. If the catheter passes 4 to 5 cm and meets resistance, this generally indicates that a false passage through the vessel wall has occurred. Occasionally, the perforation is bypassed by attempting catheterization with the larger 5 Fr. catheter. If the second catheter enters a false passage, further attempts with that vessel are usually unsuccessful.

9. If a low (L_3–L_4) position is desired, the catheter may be advanced 7 to 8 cm in a 1-kg premature or 12 to 13 cm in a full term infant. Once sterile technique is broken, the line may not be advanced. Therefore it is preferable to position the catheter too high and withdraw as necessary according to the abdominal X-ray. After positioning, the catheter is tied with the previously placed suture (Fig. 7) and then taped to the abdominal wall as illustrated in Fig. 8. An X-ray is obtained and the catheter repositioned, if necessary, at the lower border of the L_3 vertebra. Some physicians prefer to place the catheter high (above the diaphragm). There are no data to support either preference.

X-rays of an arterial catheter (Fig. 9) show the catheter proceeding from the umbilicus down toward the pelvis, making an acute turn into the internal iliac artery and proceeding toward the head into the bifurcation of the aorta, and then up the aorta slightly to the left of the vertebral column. On lateral view the umbilical artery catheter is posterior. An umbilical venous catheter (Fig. 10)

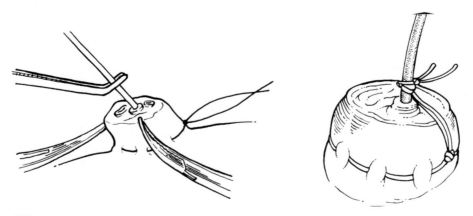

FIG. 6. The catheter is advanced in the caudal direction.

FIG. 7. The suture placed around the base is tied to the catheter.

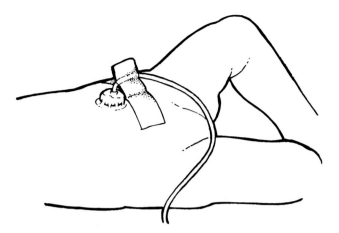

FIG. 8. The tape is pleated above and below the catheter.

proceeds directly toward the head without making the downward loop. On lateral view the catheter is in the anterior position until it passes through the ductus venosus.

UMBILICAL ARTERY CATHETERIZATION FAILURES

Studies have demonstrated that most umbilical artery catheter attempts fail because the catheter perforates the arterial wall approximately 1 cm below the umbilical stump where the umbilical artery curves toward the feet. In this in-

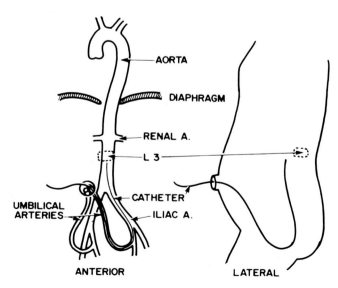

FIG. 9. The umbilical artery catheter makes a loop downward before heading in the cephalad direction.

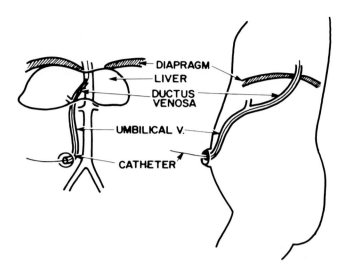

FIG. 10. An umbilical vein catheter is directed in the cephalad direction and remains anterior until it passes through the ductus venosus into the inferior vena cava.

stance, the catheter is advanced in the extraluminal space and resistance is met at 4 to 6 cm. Many people mistakenly think that the catheter cannot be advanced past the 5 to 6-cm mark because of arterial spasm at that point. However, this is not the case. We have found that the following three maneuvers make it possible to avoid perforating the umbilical artery wall in 95% of umbilical artery catheterizations.

1. It is most important that the catheter be advanced slowly. When slight obstruction is met at about 1 cm, the catheter is advanced very gently with even, steady pressure, not intermittent jabs. The catheter must never be forced through this obstruction at 1 cm because it will likely perforate the wall. This is probably the most important aspect of avoiding an unsuccessful umbilical artery catheterization.

2. Because the artery curves toward the feet, the umbilical stump is held with a curved clamp and pulled toward the head so that the catheter is inserted in as straight a direction toward the feet as possible, rather than having to negotiate the curve at 1 to 2 cm below the stump.

3. The tip of a 5.0 Fr. catheter has a blunter end than a 3.5 Fr. umbilical artery catheter. Therefore if the first catheterization with a 3.5 catheter fails, we suggest using a 5.0 Fr. catheter for the other artery.

We have found that with these three maneuvers, umbilical artery catheterizations are successful in over 95% of attempts.

CATHETER CARE

1. If a low position is desired, the catheter is withdrawn to the lower edge of L_3. No catheter is advanced once sterile technique has been broken.

2. If the catheter becomes plugged, fails to function properly, or there is blanching or discoloration of the buttocks, heels, or toes, the catheter is *removed at once.* NEVER FLUSH AN OBSTRUCTED ARTERIAL LINE.

3. To avoid confusion, pre-existing bruising of the lower extremities (secondary to breech presentation, etc.) is outlined with a felt marker. Heelsticks are avoided to prevent further bruising which might be confused with vascular compromise.

4. When the catheter is to be removed, it is withdrawn slowly to 3 cm and left 5 to 10 min without infusion to allow spasm of the artery to occur so as to prevent bleeding. The stump is observed for oozing for 10 min after catheter removal.

5. Blood is obtained in the following manner: using a sterile tuberculin syringe, the fluid is slowly aspirated from the tubing (Fig. 11). After the first blood is obtained, 0.5 ml is withdrawn (Fig. 11A). This is set aside on a sterile surface (4 × 4 gauze) for reinfusion later. Using another 1-ml heparinized syringe, 0.3

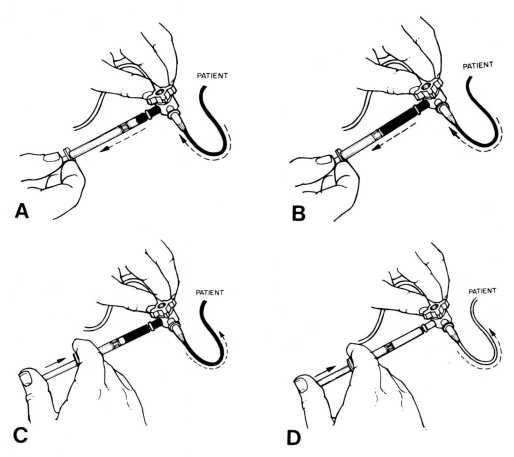

FIG. 11. Technique of withdrawing blood from an umbilical artery catheter (see text for details).

ml blood is withdrawn for pH, pCO_2, and pO_2 analysis (Fig. 11B). The fluid previously withdrawn is reinfused (Fig. 11C). The line is flushed with approximately 0.3 ml of flush solution so that no blood remains in the line, and this syringe is left attached to the stopcock until the next sample is drawn (Fig. 11D). Be sure that all connections are tight.

6. An accurate record of fluid infused (including flush solution) and blood removed is kept on all infants with umbilical artery catheters.

7. A disposable 0.22-μm filter is included to prevent infusion of air or particulate matter.

8. To replace an occluded catheter, the catheter is withdrawn to 3 cm and 5 to 10 min allowed to pass for spasm of the artery to occur (lack of pulsations alone is not helpful). "Prep" and drape before withdrawing catheter fully so that the new catheter may be immediately inserted into the same arterial lumen.

CATHETER COMPLICATIONS

Although the incidence of major complications is low in most medical centers where this procedure is in common use, umbilical catheterization is not without risk. The incidence of major complications varies with the expertise of the physician or nurse who inserts the catheter and the personnel caring for it. Complications include hemorrhage, infection, thromboembolic phenomenon (especially to kidneys, gastrointestinal tract, and lower extremities), vasospasm, air embolism, vessel perforation, electrical hazards, peritoneal perforation, hypertension, and possible effects of plasticizers. It is very important that technique in the insertion and maintenance of catheters be meticulous.

CAVEATS

1. The only indication for an umbilical artery catheter is the need for frequent arterial blood sampling or blood pressure monitoring.

2. Most failures are secondary to perforation of the arterial wall at approximately 1 cm below the umbilical stump.

3. It is very important that the catheter be advanced slowly.

4. The catheter is advanced very slowly and in as straight a direction toward the feet as possible.

5. Never flush an obstructed arterial line.

6. In order to prevent serious complications, meticulous attention must be paid to the technique of insertion and maintenance of the catheter.

32

Lumbar Puncture

Lumbar puncture (LP) is an important part of the complete workup of any newborn suspected of sepsis. In addition, an LP may be valuable in the evaluation of infants for intracranial bleeding. Any infant with symptoms suggestive of meningitis (seizures, intractable vomiting, etc.) must have an LP performed. The equipment required for an LP is simple and readily available (Table 1) as either a locally packaged LP tray or a commercial pediatric LP setup.

PROCEDURE

1. A skilled assistant immobilizes the infant in either the lateral decubitus or sitting posture (Figs. 1 and 2). The infant is held so the spine is maximally arched in the anterior-posterior axis but absolutely straight laterally (fetal position). Care is taken to ensure that respiration is not compromised. *The assistant must pay close attention to the infant's clinical status during the entire procedure.* Unrecognized cyanosis is a common complication.

2. Next, the physician localizes the L_3-L_4 intervertebral space. This is usually the interspace which intersects a line connecting the posterior-superior portion of the iliac crests (Fig. 3). During a difficult or traumatic tap, it is often beneficial to move cephalad one interspace.

3. The physician scrubs his hands and puts on gloves.

4. The infant's back is scrubbed, first with an iodophore solution and then with alcohol. The area of the puncture is the first area cleansed, and then the remainder of the back scrubbed in a concentric circular pattern (Fig. 4); the infant's back is draped with sterile towels.

TABLE 1. *Equipment for LP*

Alcohol 70%, iodophore solution, and 2 × 2 inch gauze pads
Sterile gloves and two sterile towels
Spinal needle, 22 to 25 gauge, 1 to 1.5 inch, with a stylet
Three sterile test tubes with caps

FIG. 1. The lateral decubitus position for performing an LP. Note that the infant's back is maximally arched, yet parallel to the table surface.

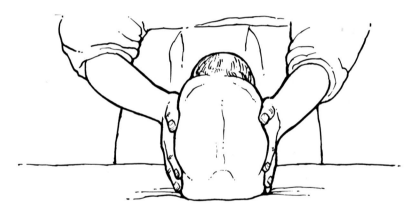

FIG. 2. Upright position for LP.

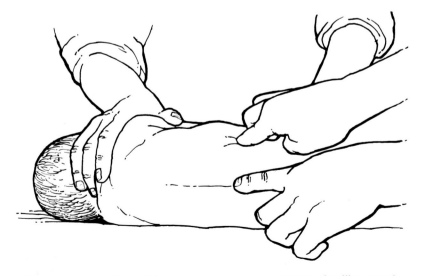

FIG. 3. Localization of the L$_3$–L$_4$ interspace between the iliac crests.

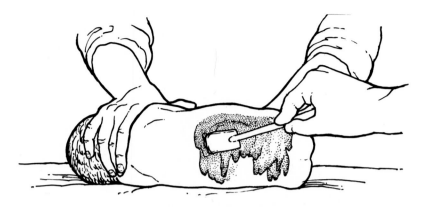

FIG. 4. The site for LP is "prepped" with a concentric circular scrubbing pattern.

5. The needle is directed cephalad, toward the umbilicus but perpendicular to the lateral axis of the spine (Fig. 5).

6. The needle is advanced 1 to 1.5 cm until a "pop" or decrease in resistance is felt, although this may be quite attenuated in the newborn. The stylet is removed to visualize cerebrospinal fluid (CSF). This may take 15 to 30 sec with the infant at rest. If no fluid is obtained, the stylet is replaced and the needle once again cautiously advanced. If the spinal canal is traversed and bone encountered, bleeding from the anterior venous plexus almost always occurs, resulting in bloody CSF (traumatic LP).

7. Once CSF is visualized, a three-way stopcock and manometer may be attached to obtain a CSF pressure, but this is not usually done in newborn infants.

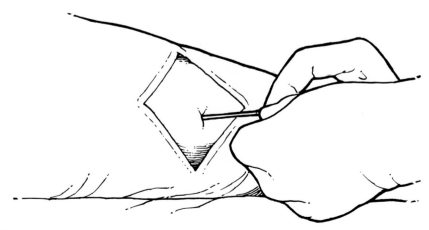

FIG. 5. Needle is aimed toward the umbilicus but perpendicular to the lateral plane of the back.

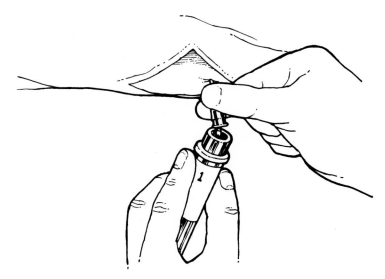

FIG. 6. CSF is collected in three labeled test tubes.

8. CSF (0.5 to 1.0 ml) is allowed to drip into each of three sterile test tubes (Fig. 6). These are then sent to the laboratory for the following tests:

    a. Tube 1—glucose and protein

    b. Tube 2—culture, sensitivity, and gram stain

    c. Tube 3—red blood cell count (RBC), white blood cell count (WBC) and differential

A serum glucose is done prior to the LP for comparison with CSF glucose.

9. The stylet is replaced and the needle withdrawn.

PROCEDURAL PITFALLS

A number of minor alterations in technique may be responsible for the success or failure of an LP. It is essential to have the infant immobilized and positioned with the spine straight in the transverse axis. In addition, the infant must be arched into the fetal position to maximally widen the interspinous spaces. The needle is inserted into the interspace, without lateral deviation. Last, and most important, the needle is advanced slowly with close attention to the "pop" felt when the dura is penetrated. The most common cause of a traumatic LP is overadvancement of the needle with penetration of the venous plexus on the anterior side of the spinal canal. When this occurs, a repeat attempt one interspace higher or lower may yield clear fluid.

INTERPRETATION OF CSF RESULTS

The analysis of CSF is multifaceted; however, all findings must be considered collectively. The sample collected in tube 1 is sent to the laboratory for glucose and protein determinations. There is some controversy concerning the normal values for these studies. Generally, a normal value for CSF glucose is two-thirds of the serum level, and this is usually true for term and premature infants. A decrease is usually found with infection. Protein values are more variable; in premature infants during the first week of life, the protein averages 180 mg% as compared to 117 mg% in full term infants. These values decrease to 117 mg% and 74 mg%, respectively, by the fourth week of life in the premature and full term infant. CSF protein generally rises with infection.

The second tube of CSF may be sent for culture and gram stain. Although the gram stain is frequently overlooked, it is valuable for the rapid detection and identification of the pathogenic organism. Although nonspecific, information as to the type of organism (rods versus cocci) and gram staining properties (gram positive or negative) may assist in the preliminary diagnosis and selection of antimicrobials. Since LPs are performed under sterile conditions, any growth is considered pathogenic.

The third and final specimen of CSF is used for RBC, WBC, and differential. The mean WBC count in CSF is 3 to 6 WBC/mm³ in premature and full term infants during the first 4 weeks of life (normal range 0 to 50 WBC/mm³). Unless a central nervous system (CNS) hemorrhage has occurred, the CSF RBC count is zero under ideal circumstances. It has been suggested that xanthochromia may be used for differentiation of a traumatic LP (acute event) from blood secondary to CNS bleeding. However, this yellow discoloration of the CSF is a nonspecific finding which may be due to blood breakdown products or other pigments. Clinical indicators of a traumatic LP are: (a) clotting of the fluid or clots mixed with CSF; (b) the finding of blood mixing with CSF at the needle hub; or (c) clearing of the CSF during the procedure. Diagnosis of a CNS bleed on the basis of CSF results is difficult, and correlation with the clinical status and other diagnostic modalities (e.g., CAT scan, ultrasound) is indicated.

COMPLICATIONS

Although brainstem herniation has been reported in older children with papilledema at the time of LP, this complication is uncommon in the neonate because the open fontanelles disperse pressure. Spinal epidermoid tumors have been reported years after an LP was performed with an open spinal needle (without a stylet)—theoretically caused by displacement of a core of epidermis into the spinal canal by the open end of the needle. The most common untoward result is a traumatic LP. Although of little direct consequence to the patient, it confuses the interpretation of CSF results.

CAVEATS

1. LP is an important part of the complete septic workup of a newborn.
2. An assistant must pay close attention to the infant's clinical status during an LP to detect evidence of respiratory compromise.

3. The normal CSF white blood cell count and protein concentrations are higher in the newborn than during later infancy and childhood.

4. The gram stain is valuable in the rapid detection and preliminary identification of the pathogenic organism.

5. The yellow discoloration of CSF in the newborn cannot be used to indicate intracranial hemorrhage.

33

Treatment of Pneumothorax: Aspiration and Chest Tube Placement

Pneumothorax is a common cause of respiratory distress in newborn infants. Spontaneous pneumothorax occurs in 0.5 to 2% of all newborns. This disorder occurs even more frequently in infants with hyaline membrane disease and aspiration pneumonia, and after resuscitation. The use of positive-pressure respirators and continuous positive airway pressure (CPAP) may further increase the incidence (Table 1).

The pathophysiology of pneumothorax (Table 2), pneumomediastinum, and pneumopericardium begins with hyperinflation of alveoli. In spontaneous pneumothoraces, this alveolar hyperinflation may be due to the high intrathoracic pressures generated during the first extrauterine breaths. At the time of birth a combination of factors—including uneven ventilation, poor compliance of the lung, high viscosity of lung fluid, and high surface tension—results in intra-alveolar pressures as high as 40 to 100 cm water with the first gasp by the infant. Subsequently the alveoli may rupture, allowing air to escape under a pressure gradient into the interstitium (Fig. 1) and advance along the perivascular spaces in the lung. The air continues to dissect along the perivascular spaces toward

TABLE 1. *Predisposing factors*

Resuscitation
Aspiration (blood, mucus, meconium)
Continuous positive airway pressure
Respirator therapy
Endotracheal tube down right mainstem bronchus
Hyaline membrane disease
Pneumonia
Congenital lobar emphysema
Hypoplastic lungs (e.g., Potter's syndrome, diaphragmatic hernia)

TABLE 2. *Pneumothorax pathophysiology*

Increased intra-alveolar pressure
↓
Alveolar rupture
↓
Interstitial air
↓
Dissection of air along perivascular spaces toward root of lung
↓
Rupture into pleural space, mediastinum, pericardial space

the hilum and may rupture into the mediastinum producing a pneumomediastinum, through the visceral pleura resulting in a pneumothorax (Fig. 2), or into the pericardial space resulting in a pneumopericardium (Fig. 3). In addition, the air may dissect into the peritoneal cavity causing a pneumoperitoneum.

DIAGNOSIS

The symptoms of a pneumothorax in the newborn (Table 3) include tachypnea, retractions, cyanosis, grunting, irritability, and tachycardia or bradycardia. The breath sounds may be decreased on the ipsilateral side, although the absence of this sign never rules out a pneumothorax. The heart sounds may be shifted to the contralateral side, and there may be enlargement of the hemithorax. Impairment of cardiac output may result in hypotension and metabolic

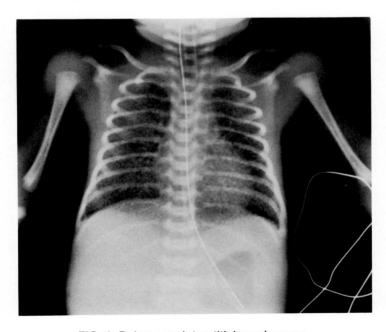

FIG. 1. Pulmonary interstitial emphysema.

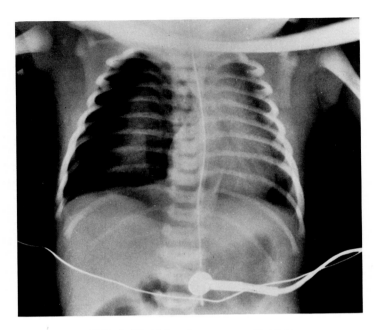

FIG. 2. Right tension pneumothorax.

acidosis. Arterial blood gases may show hypoxia and hypercapnia. The clinical diagnosis of a pneumothorax is frequently difficult, and it is impossible to rule out a pneumothorax by clinical examination. Therefore a chest X-ray is mandatory in any infant with respiratory distress.

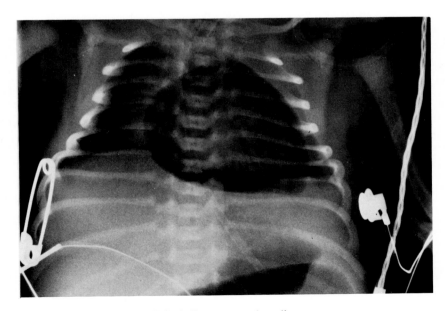

FIG. 3. Pneumopericardium.

TABLE 3. *Symptoms and signs of pneumothorax*

Tachypnea
Apnea
Retractions
Grunting
Cyanosis
Irritability
Tachycardia, bradycardia
Decreased pO_2
Increased pCO_2
Metabolic acidosis
Fighting the respirator
Increased ventilator inspiratory pressure with volume ventilator
Decreased breath sounds
Shift of heart sounds
Chest bulge
Hypotension

Recently transillumination of the chest with a high-intensity fiberoptic light has provided an additional means of prompt diagnosis of a pneumothorax. However, appropriate application and interpretation of this technique require extensive experience. Although we have such an instrument available in the unit, we believe it cannot replace the chest X-ray, nor is treatment instituted solely on the basis of transillumination except when the infant's condition precludes waiting for the X-ray.

Because the infants are in a supine position, in many cases the pneumothorax collects anteriorly. In these situations, it may be difficult to diagnose the pneumothorax by an anterior-posterior chest X-ray because lung markings may still be visible extending to the chest wall. Increased lucency of one hemithorax always suggests the possibility of an anterior pneumothorax. Diagnosis is best confirmed by a *lateral decubitus* X-ray with the hyperlucent hemithorax in the superior position (Fig. 4).

Air in the subpulmonary area and over the apex of the lung may be the earliest sign of a pneumothorax. A frequently confusing radiographic finding is the medial stripe sign (Fig. 5), which may be associated with a pneumothorax or pneumomediastinum. Skin folds and the border of the scapula may mistakenly suggest a pneumothorax. Again, the best method of confirming a pneumothorax is to obtain a lateral decubitus X-ray.

TREATMENT

There are a number of modes of therapy for a pneumothorax. In term infants with only mild respiratory distress, 100% inspired oxygen may be used for a few hours, with the pneumothorax resolved utilizing the principle of nitrogen washout. This treatment is *never* used in premature infants or as the sole means of therapy for infants in moderate to severe distress.

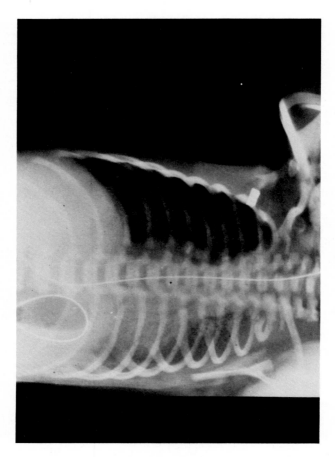

FIG. 4. Left lateral decubitus X-ray in a patient with an anterior right pneumothorax. Note how the air layers out to define the pneumothorax clearly.

In an infant who is critically ill with a pneumothorax suspected clinically, diagnostic and therapeutic thoracentesis is performed immediately (before obtaining an X-ray). This may be life-saving in certain situations. A No. 23 scalp vein needle may be used to aspirate the pneumothorax in such emergencies. The needle, connected to a stopcock and a 20-ml syringe, is inserted into the chest in the anterior axillary line (Fig. 6) with the needle passing over the superior edge of the third or fourth rib. While the needle is advanced into the chest, negative pressure is applied to the plunger of the syringe. This technique may be used to relieve a pneumothorax until support personnel arrive. If an error in diagnosis is made and there is, in fact, no pneumothorax present, this technique rarely induces one. As the blood supply runs along the inferior border of the superior rib, the needle is passed along the superior aspect of the rib to avoid hemorrhage resulting from passage of the needle through this vascular area.

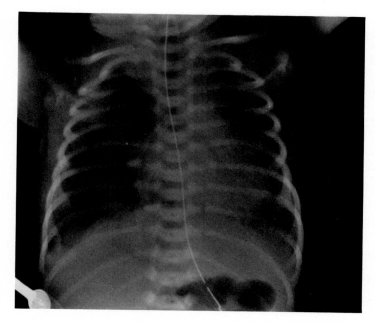

FIG. 5. Air along the right side of the heart which could be confused as either a pneumothorax or pneumomediastinum. A lateral decubitus differentiates the two.

A medium-sized intracath may be used as a temporary chest tube by inserting the catheter in the same position as described above. After removal of the needle, the catheter may be connected to either a stopcock and syringe for aspiration of the pneumothorax or to intravenous infusion (IV) tubing, which in turn may be connected to an underwater drainage. This procedure may serve as

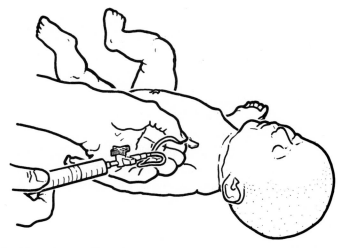

FIG. 6. Aspiration of a pneumothorax with a scalp vein needle, stopcock, and syringe.

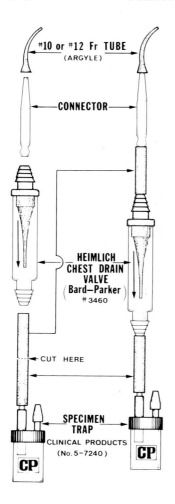

FIG. 7. Heimlich flutter valve system for transporting an infant with a chest tube.

a temporizing measure to relieve a pneumothorax until personnel experienced in the placement of chest tubes are available. For transport of infants or if no underwater seal is available, the Heimlich flutter valve (Fig. 7) may be connected to the chest tube.

CHEST TUBES

An 8 Fr. or larger tube is used; when draining purulent material or blood, a larger (10 to 12 Fr.) tube is necessary. Additional equipment (Table 4) includes sterile instruments, an infant-sized underwater seal drainage system, sterile connector, suture with curved needle, plastic tubing, tape, chest tube clamp, and surgical light.

Sterile technique is essential. The person performing the procedure and his assistant wear a sterile gown, cap, mask, and gloves; observers wear caps and masks.

TABLE 4. *Chest tube tray equipment*

Small scissors
Fixation forceps with teeth
Small curved mosquito
Straight mosquito
Needle holder
Drape with hole
Scalpel with No. 15 curved blade

Adequate lighting is essential. The infant's heart rate must be monitored, and adequate oxygenation, ventilation, and warmth provided. Appropriate intervention is necessary if these fundamental physiologic parameters are abnormal.

The infant's extremities are restrained (Fig. 8) with the arms positioned away from the chest. The anterior chest wall on the side in which the tube is to be inserted is carefully prepared as for any surgical procedure. A 3- to 5-min scrub is recommended.

After infiltration with 1% xylocaine, an incision of approximately 0.3 to 0.4 cm is made lateral to the nipple or in the anterior axillary line. A purse-string suture is then placed around the incision. Care is taken not to traumatize the areola or breast tissue.

The tip of the tube (8 to 12 Fr.) is grasped with a small curved hemostat (Fig. 9). The hemostat is then placed through the incision, point down, perpendicular to the plane of the chest and advanced with a rotary "screwing" type motion into the pleural cavity through the interspace superior to the level at which the skin incision was made (Fig. 10). A fair amount of force is required to accomplish this, even in small premature babies.

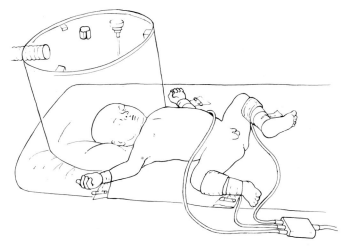

FIG. 8. Infant is properly restrained, in oxygen, and monitored.

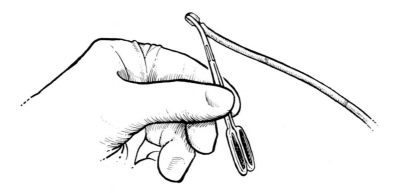

FIG. 9. Tip of chest tube grasped with a small curved hemostat.

Once the pleural cavity is entered, the hemostat blades are separated and the tube is advanced between them into the chest for a length of about 5 cm, being certain that all holes of the tube are within the thoracic cavity. After the hemostat is removed, the purse-string suture is then tightened and tied. This prevents leakage of air around the incision. The ends of the suture are then tied around the chest tube itself to prevent the tube from being pulled (Fig. 11). After an antibiotic ointment is applied to the incision area, the tube is carefully secured with benzoin and tape.

The tube is then connected to the underwater seal drainage bottle and the water level observed for fluctuation with respiration. If this is absent, the chest tube is probably obstructed or improperly placed. A common error is placement of the tube in the subcutaneous tissue rather than in the intrapleural space.

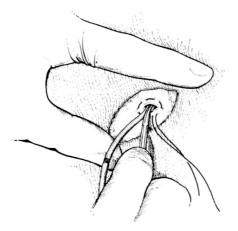

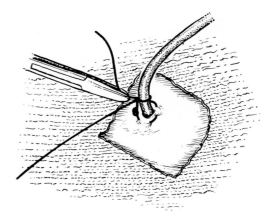

FIG. 10. Pressure is applied on hemostat perpendicular to the plane of the chest.

FIG. 11. Chest tube is secured with a suture.

A chest X-ray is obtained immediately to determine placement and its effectiveness in reinflating the lung. A lateral chest X-ray (Fig. 12) is helpful to determine whether the tube is placed anteriorly or posteriorly; many pneumothoraces accumulate anteriorly as the patient is in the supine position.

If the infant is on a ventilator or if the pneumothorax persists and proper placement is assured, the chest tube is connected to a continuous suction of about 5 to 10 cm water. Occasionally it is necessary to increase the suction to approximately 20 cm water. If negative pressure is applied to the chest tube and continuous bubbling results, one of two problems may be present: (a) there may be a large rent in the visceral pleura, i.e., the pneumothorax is so large a chest tube cannot drain the air fast enough; or (b) more likely, there is a leak in the system, e.g., one hole of the chest tube may be outside the chest (Fig. 13) or there may be a loose connection within the chest tube system.

In a few instances of pneumothorax in the newborn, even a large chest tube is not adequate for drainage because of a large tear in the visceral pleura. In these cases, surgical intervention with an open thoracostomy and suturing of the tear may be required.

Complications of Chest Tubes

One of the most serious complications of chest tube placement is perforation of the lung. The diagnosis of perforated lung is suspected when a pneumothorax does not resolve despite proper placement of the chest tube. These infants usu-

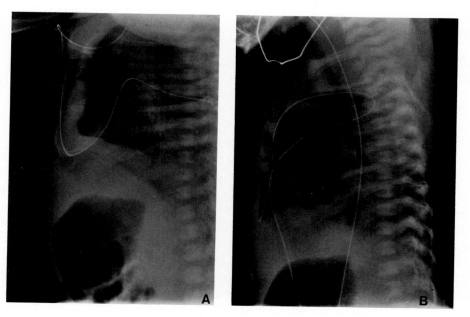

FIG. 12. Tip of chest tube in posterior **(A)** and anterior **(B)** position.

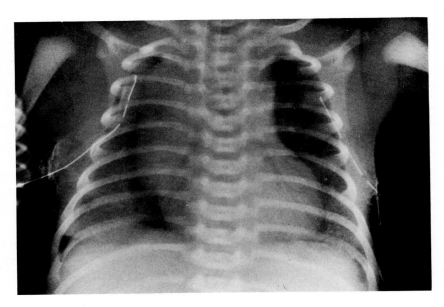

FIG. 13. Left chest tube with hole outside the thoracic space.

ally show continuous bubbling in the chest tube bottle. A recent report of a 35% incidence of lung perforation when a trocar was used to introduce the tube suggests that such instruments should not be used for placement of chest tubes in neonates. When placement of a chest tube does result in this complication, surgical therapy with an open thoracostomy and suturing the leak in the lung may be indicated.

Teaching Chest Tube Insertion

Teaching physicians and nurses the technique of chest tube placement in actual patients is difficult because of the urgency of the situation. We use the cat for training purposes, and others have used the rabbit with equal success.

The cats are sedated with intramuscular ketamine hydrochloride (40 to 60 mg in the deltoid muscle). All four extremities are restrained. After the chest is shaved, sterile soap is applied and a surgical drape placed. We found it necessary to place the tube in the middle to anterior axillary line in the sixth to ninth intercostal space *in the cat,* since failure to penetrate the intercostal muscle frequently results when attempts are made more anteriorly or superiorly.

We found the cat model ideal for teaching house officers, community physicians, and nurses the proper technique of aspiration and chest tube placement. It allows the instructor time to answer questions and carefully discuss the procedure while it is in progress. This is obviously not possible during an emergency with an infant.

Care and Maintenance of Chest Tubes

Each hour the nurse notes the presence of fluctuation or bubbling in the chest tube bottle or tubing. Generally a chest tube placed for a pneumothorax drains very little fluid, whereas a chest tube placed postoperatively has more drainage. With small tubes in small infants, the intrapleural pressure may not be strong enough to cause fluctuations in the drainage bottle, but fluctuation is noted in the tubing at the chest wall. The presence of fluctuation in the bottle or the tubing indicates that the holes of the chest tube are patent and within the intrapleural space. The presence of bubbling in the chest tube drainage bottle indicates that the chest tube is, in fact, removing air from the intrapleural space. A chest tube may be fluctuating (i.e., the holes are patent and within the intrapleural space) yet not functioning to drain the pneumothorax. This may be because: (a) the pneumothorax has accumulated anteriorly because the infant is in the supine position and the tip of the chest tube has been placed posteriorly; or (b) the pneumothorax may be accumulated in the subpulmonic area, whereas the chest tube holes are in the apical area. Therefore it is helpful to turn the infant frequently and note the change in bubbling within the chest tube bottle.

Pleur-evac drainage systems (Krale; Division of Deknatel, Inc.) (Fig. 14) are frequently used in the newborn intensive care unit. The water in the blue ("suction control chamber") area is connected to the suction. The depth of the water determines the centimeters of water suction. Bubbling in this area does *not* indicate drainage of air from the chest. The pink area ("water seal chamber") of the Pleur-evac is connected to the baby. Bubbling in this area reflects drainage of air from the chest. Fluctuation of water in the pink area of the system means that the hole of the chest tube is patent and in the intrapleural space. However, if suction is applied to the system, the suction causes the water level in the pink area to fluctuate, even if the chest tube is plugged.

In general, a chest tube placed for treatment of a pneumothorax must never be clamped, especially if the chest tube is still draining air from the intrapleural space. Clamping the chest tube results in accumulation of air within the intrapleural space and typical symptoms and signs of pneumothorax.

Chest Tube Removal

The chest tube is left in place until bubbling has not been observed for 24 hr. If the infant is on a ventilator, chest tubes are usually left in for longer periods.

The tube is clamped, the baby's clinical condition closely monitored, and an X-ray obtained shortly thereafter to identify a possible recurrence. If a pneumothorax persists, the clamp is removed and the tube left patent for at least another 24 hr. If the lung remains inflated, the tube may be removed 12 to 24 hr after it has been clamped. The tube is withdrawn rapidly and aseptically. Pressure is applied to the incision with gauze coated with an appropriate antibiotic ointment or Vaseline to prevent entrance of air through the chest tube incision.

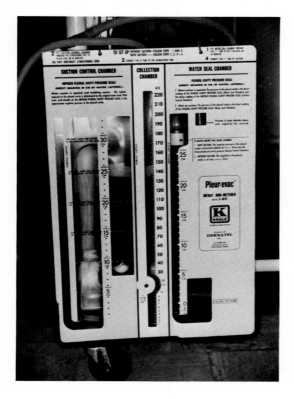

FIG. 14. Pleur-evac drainage system.

The gauze is then taped in place. A chest X-ray is obtained immediately after withdrawal of the tube to check for recurrence.

CAVEATS

1. The clinical diagnosis of a pneumothorax is frequently difficult; it is impossible to rule out a pneumothorax by clinical examination.

2. A chest X-ray is mandatory in any infant with respiratory distress to exclude the possibility of a pneumothorax.

3. A hyperlucent hemithorax suggests the possibility of an anterior pneumothorax.

4. Whenever there is a question concerning the possibility of a pneumothorax on a chest X-ray, diagnosis is best confirmed by a lateral decubitus X-ray with the questionable side in the superior position.

5. If an infant is severely ill and a pneumothorax is suspected clinically, diagnostic and therapeutic thoracentesis is performed without waiting for an X-ray.

6. Hyperoxygenation (100% O_2) must never be used to treat a pneumothorax in a premature infant.

7. Trocars are never used for chest tube placement in the neonate.

Part III: Appendix

Normal Nursery Admission Orders

Initial Care: Observation Nursery

1. Vitamin K_1 1 mg i.m. and silver nitrate 1% to eyes in delivery room.
2. *Admission:* Axillary temperature, heart rate, respiratory rate, color. If temperature less than 35.7°C (96.4°F), place under warmer. *At 1 hr:* vital signs, blood pressure, Dextrostix, hematocrit. *Thereafter:* Routine vital signs q 1 hr until stable with temperature of 36.4° to 37°C (97.6° to 98.6°F).
3. Bathe with clear water when stable. Initial cord care per protocol.
4. Weight, length, occipital frontal circumference, gestational age. Record time of first urine and meconium.
5. Offer D_5W at 4 hr of age.
6. Transfer to regular nursery after first feeding, if stable.

Daily Care

1. Axillary temperature, resting heart rate and respiratory rate, b.i.d.
2. Weight, skin care with clear water, cord care per protocol; record intake and number of voids and stools.
3. Feed five to seven times per day, 20 cal/ounce formula or breast milk. Breast-fed infants may have D_5W or sterile water after nippling; all babies may have water or D_5W on demand.
4. Extended time with mother if she wishes.

"General Care"

1. Phenylketonuria (PKU) test third through fifth day if feeding well or PKU test instructions on discharge.
2. Bilirubin, Dextrostix, hematocrit, as needed, per nurse.
3. Trim nails as needed.
4. Aspirate gently with bulb syringe for mucus, as needed.
5. Call nearest physician in any emergency.
6. Call infant's doctor according to "notification guidelines."
7. T_4 dot test.

Admitting Orders for Special Care Infants to Observation Nursery

1. Admit to observation nursery. Diagnosis _____.

2. Notify physician of infant's presence and reason for admission.
3. Place under radiant warmer with servo control to maintain abdominal skin temperature at 97°F or 36°C.
4. Temperature, heart rate, respiratory rate on admission; then every hour × 2; then every 2 hr until stable. After stable, temperature, heart rate, and respiratory rate before feedings.
5. Blood pressure on admission. Call physician if rechecked systolic blood pressure is less than 40 mm Hg and infant is in distress.
6. Dextrostix on admission. If Dextrostix is ever less than 40 mg% or if infant is at risk of hypoglycemia, refer to nursing guide for hypoglycemia.
7. Hematocrit on admission. Notify physician if duplicate hematocrit is less than 45%. If duplicate is greater than 65%, refer to nursing guide for hyperviscosity syndrome.
8. Suction with bulb syringe or DeLee catheter as needed.
9. Routine newborn care.
   a. Crede procedure.
   b. Vitamin K_1 1 mg i.m.
   c. Skin and cord care per nursing guidelines.
   d. Weight, length, occipital frontal circumference, gestational age.
10. Offer D_5W at 4 to 6 hr or earlier if indicated by low Dextrostix (if low, refer to hypoglycemia protocol) or apparent hunger. Feed infant approximately 5 ml/kg and gavage if indicated. Do not feed infants who have a respiratory rate greater than 60/min without physician's order.
11. Use O_2 as needed to relieve cyanosis or in infants with respiratory distress. Notify physician and monitor O_2 concentration. Further changes will be based on blood gases.
12. Determine bilirubin level on any infant appearing jaundiced. Refer to *Jaundice: Nursing Guide* before calling physician.
13. Release to regular nursery after 24 hr, unless ordered otherwise by physician. Resume regular nursery orders upon release.

Admitting Orders to Special Care Nursery

1. Admit to SCN. Diagnosis: _____

   _____.

2. Notify physician of infant's presence and reason for admission.
3. Place infant under radiant warmer or in isolette with servo control to maintain axillary skin temperature at 97°F (36°C).
4. Cardiac monitor.
5. Oxygen monitor if O_2 being used. If O_2 being used, the concentration ordered is checked and recorded every 2 hr. Use O_2 as needed to relieve cyanosis or in an infant with respiratory distress. Notify physician.
6. Temperature, heart rate, respiratory rate on admission; then every hour × 4; then every 2 hr until stable. After stable, temperature, heart rate, and respiratory rate before each feeding.
7. Blood pressure on admission. Call physician if rechecked systolic blood pressure is less than 40 mm Hg and infant is in distress.
8. Dextrostix on admission and every hour × 4. If Dextrostix ever less than 40 mg%, or if infant is at risk of hypoglycemia, refer to *Hypoglycemia: Nursing Guide.*
9. Hematocrit on admission. Notify physician if duplicate hematocrit is less than 45%. If duplicate is greater than 65%, refer to *Hyperviscosity Syndrome: Nursing Guide.*
10. Suction with bulb syringe or DeLee catheter as needed.
11. Routine newborn care.
    a. Crede procedure.
    b. Vitamin K_1 1 mg i.m.
    c. Skin and cord care per nursing guidelines.
12. Offer D_5W at 4 to 6 hr or earlier if indicated by low Dextrostix (if low, refer to hypoglycemia protocol) or apparent hunger. Feed infant approximately 5 ml/kg and gavage if indicated. Do not feed infants who have a respiratory rate greater than 60/min without physician's order.
13. Determine bilirubin level on any infant appearing jaundiced. Refer to *Jaundice: Nursing Guide* before calling physician.

Umbilical Artery Catheter Orders

1. X-ray of abdomen to check position of umbilical artery catheter.
2. Fluids: _____
3. No heel- or toesticks.
4. Call physician for cyanosis, blanching, or mottling of lower extremities; hematuria; bleeding from umbilicus; or blood backup in catheter.
5. Do not flush arterial line when blood cannot be aspirated.
6. Change IV system (bottle, tubing, filter, stopcock) every 24 hr.
7. Blood pressure transducer for continuous mean blood pressure monitoring.
8. Keep accurate record of blood withdrawn for laboratory studies.
9. Flush line after blood sampling with 0.3 ml normal saline.

Exchange Transfusion Orders

1. Monitor skin temperature during entire procedure. Keep at 36° to 37°C (96.8° to 98.6°F).
2. Heart monitor to be on audio during entire procedure.
3. Dextrostix immediately before and after procedure and q 2 hr × 3 or more frequently as needed post-exchange. Call physician if less than 40 mg%.
4. Aspirate stomach contents prior to exchange.
5. Use neonatal exchange transfusion blood warmer.
6. Send pre-exchange blood for hematocrit, bilirubin (direct and indirect), total protein, albumin, sodium, and potassium.
7. If infant is receiving supplemental oxygen, increase FiO_2 by 10%; determine arterial blood gas values 20 min after completion of exchange.
8. Exchange blood with plasma potassium greater than 10 mEq/liter is not used unless specifically ordered by physician.
9. Agitate blood q 15 min to avoid settling of red blood cells.
10. Obtain arterial blood gas values midway through procedure if infant is requiring oxygen.
11. Send immediate postexchange blood for hematocrit, platelets, sodium, potassium, bilirubin (direct and indirect), pH, and type and crossmatch.
12. Resume pre-exchange orders unless otherwise indicated.
13. At 3 to 4 hr after exchange, determine bilirubin (direct and indirect), total protein, and platelet count.

Intubation Procedure Note

The indication for intubation was _____
_____. At _____ *(time)*, the
infant had a pO_2 _____, pCO_2 _____, and pH _____ on FiO_2 _____.
(Oral, Nasal) tracheal intubation with a _____ mm endotracheal tube was
performed *(with, without)* complications. Chest X-rays showed the tip of the
endotracheal tube to be *(at, above, below)* the carina. The endotracheal tube
(was, was not) repositioned to lie *(at, above, below)* the carina.

Chest Tube Procedure Note

The patient was diagnosed as having a pneumothorax *(with, without)* tension on the *(left, right)* side at _____ *(time)*. At this time the patient was on _____% oxygen with pO_2 _____, pCO_2 _____, and pH _____. The chest was cleansed with _____ for _____ minutes and draped with sterile towels. A _____ catheter was inserted in the _____ intercostal space and sutured in place. The catheter was then connected to an underwater seal and _____ cm of negative pressure. Chest X-ray after placement of the chest tube showed that the pneumothorax *(was, was not)* resolved. The patient tolerated the procedure *(with, without)* complications.

Lumbar Puncture Procedure Note

The lumbosacral area was "prepped" with _____ for _____ minutes and draped. A _____ needle was inserted into the _____ intervertebral space. _____ ml of *(clear, xanthochromic, bloody)* CSF was obtained. The procedure was performed *(with, without)* complications. Cell count: WBC _____; RBC _____; corrected WBC _____; CSF protein _____; CSF glucose/blood glucose ratio _____/_____; gram stain _____.

Umbilical Arterial Catheterization Procedure Note

The periumbilical area was cleansed with _____ for _____ minutes and draped with sterile towels. A No. _____ French Argyle end hole umbilical artery catheter was inserted into the umbilical artery *(with, without)* complication. X-ray of the abdomen revealed the tip of the catheter to be at the _____ vertebra. The catheter *(was, was not)* repositioned to lie at the level of the _____ vertebra. The estimated blood loss was _____ ml. The infant tolerated the procedure *(with, without)* complications.

Exchange Transfusion Procedure Note

Exchange No. _____

Hematocrit of unit of blood _____ %

Potassium of unit of blood _____ mEq/liter

The indication for exchange transfusion is _____ _____. The periumbilical area was cleansed with _____ for _____ minutes and draped with sterile towels. A No. _____ French side hole umbilical vein catheter was inserted _____ cm into the umbilical vein *(with, without)* complications. The patient's heart *(was, was not)* continuously monitored during the entire procedure. _____ ml of blood with _____ anticoagulant were used in the exchange in _____ ml increments. Calcium gluconate *(was, was not)* administered during the procedure. Total duration of the exchange transfusion was _____ minutes. The infant tolerated the procedure *(with, without)* complications.

Pre-exchange		*Post-exchange*	
Total bilirubin	_____	Total bilirubin	_____
Direct	_____	Direct	_____
Indirect	_____	Indirect	_____
Total protein	_____	Sodium	_____
Albumin	_____	Potassium	_____
Sodium	_____	Platelets	_____
Potassium	_____	pH	_____
Hematocrit	_____		

Jaundice: Nursing Guide

INFANTS ESPECIALLY AT RISK

1. Rh incompatability
2. ABO incompatability
3. Premature infants
4. Septic infants
5. Infants with hyperviscosity
6. Infants with large cephalohematomas or extensive bruising

PROCEDURE

1. Obtain a blood sample for a bilirubin determination from any infant who appears jaundiced.
2. Have the following information when calling the physician.
   a. Infant's age in hours and any significant history or physical findings.
   b. That a total bilirubin determination with direct and indirect fractions is being performed in the laboratory.
   c. Hematocrit and total protein values.
   d. Mother's blood type and Rh factor.
   e. Infant's blood type, Rh, and direct Coombs results.

Hypoglycemia: Nursing Guide

INFANTS AT RISK

1. Diabetic progeny
2. SGA infants
3. Premature infants
4. Rh infants (severe)
5. Infants with hyperviscosity
6. Any severely stressed infant
7. Infants with infections

Routine determinations for infants at risk are done each hour for 4 hr, then q 4 hr × 5, then q 12 hr × 3.

PROCEDURE

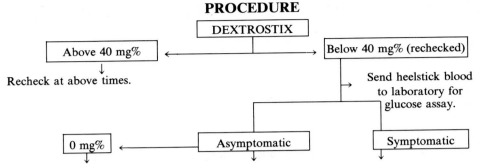

DEXTROSTIX

| Above 40 mg% | | Below 40 mg% (rechecked) |

Recheck at above times.

Send heelstick blood to laboratory for glucose assay.

| 0 mg% | Asymptomatic | Symptomatic |

0 mg%

1. Call physician
2. Try to feed infant orally or gavage unless otherwise contraindicated.
3. Set up $D_{25}W$ and IV as in symptomatic infants.

Asymptomatic

1. Feed $D_{10}W$ or formula 5 ml/kg per gavage or orally if infant sucks vigorously.
2. Check Dextrostix in 0.5 hr.
3. If no rise or does not tolerate feedings, call physician and set up $D_{10}W$ and infusion pump for IV placement.

Symptomatic

1. Call physician immediately.
2. Have prepared:
   a. $D_{50}W$ diluted with sterile H_2O to $D_{25}W$ and scalp vein set-up.
   b. Set up IV with $D_{10}W$ and infusion pump for IV placement.

Hyperviscosity Syndrome: Nursing Guide

INFANTS AT RISK

1. SGA
2. Diabetic progeny
3. Twins
4. Infants of eclamptic mothers
5. Infants of mothers with chronic disease
6. Infants with intrauterine asphyxia
7. Postmature infants

PROCEDURE

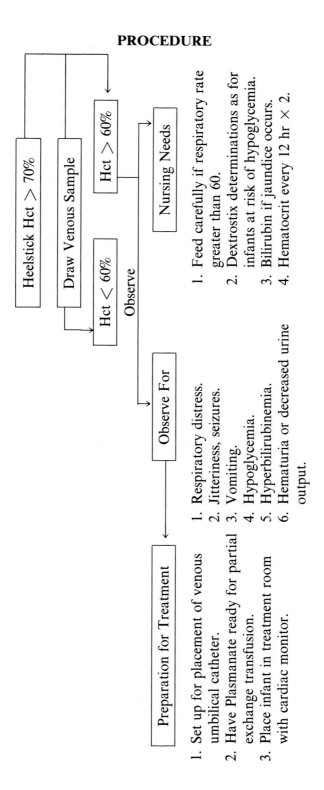

Heelstick Hct > 70%

Draw Venous Sample

Hct > 60% → Nursing Needs

Hct < 60% → Observe

Nursing Needs

1. Feed carefully if respiratory rate greater than 60.
2. Dextrostix determinations as for infants at risk of hypoglycemia.
3. Bilirubin if jaundice occurs.
4. Hematocrit every 12 hr × 2.

Observe For

1. Respiratory distress.
2. Jitteriness, seizures.
3. Vomiting.
4. Hypoglycemia.
5. Hyperbilirubinemia.
6. Hematuria or decreased urine output.

Preparation for Treatment

1. Set up for placement of venous umbilical catheter.
2. Have Plasmanate ready for partial exchange transfusion.
3. Place infant in treatment room with cardiac monitor.

Indiana University Hospitals
Indianapolis, Indiana

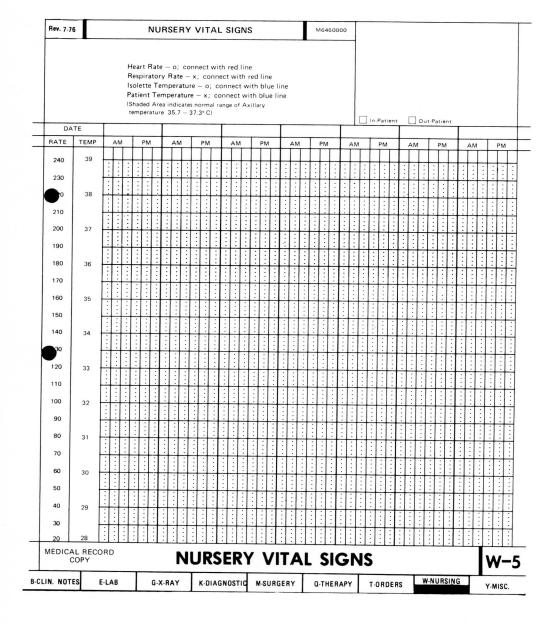

| Rev. 7-76 | NURSERY VITAL SIGNS | M6460000 |

Indiana University Hospitals
Indianapolis, Indiana

Rev. 7-75	NURSERY WEIGHT CHART	

☐ In-Patient   ☐ Out-Patient

Date
Hosp. Day
(Gms)
00
80
60
40
20
00
80
60
40
20
00
80
60
40
20
00
80
60
40
20
00
80
60
40
20
00
80
60
40
20
00
Wt. (Lbs. Oz.)
Wt. Kg. (Gms)

INTAKE
| I.V. cc |
| I.V. cal. |
| P.O. cc |
| P.O. cal. |
| Total cc |
| Total cal. |
| Total cc/kg. |
| Total cal./kg. |

OUTPUT
| Urine |
| Stool |
| Total |

MEDICAL RECORD COPY

NURSERY WEIGHT CHART   W—10

| B-CLIN. NOTES | E-LAB | G-X-RAY | K-DIAGNOSTIC | M-SURGERY | Q-THERAPY | T-ORDERS | W-NURSING | Y-MISC. |

| Rev. 9/75 | | | NEWBORN INTENSIVE CARE FLOW SHEET | | M6457410 | | | | | | | | | | | | | |

Actions and Observations
Procedures   Date_____

(Sign at end of shift)

TIME	BLOOD PRESSURE	APNEA BRADYCARDIA		BLOOD WHOLE PACKED	I.V. #1			I.V. #2			REPLACEMENT	FORMULA P.O./GAVAGE	Aspirate	Amt. fed	EMESIS	URINE	S.G.	PROT./SUGAR	GASTRIC HEMATEST	STOOL HEMATEST	CHEST	BLOOD OUT
					Left Add	Tot.	Amt.	Left Add	Tot.	Amt.												

24 HOUR TOTALS:

Indiana University Hospitals
Indianapolis, Indiana

PRESSURE		RATE		TIME		Flow	Pop Off	ALARM SETTING		Sat.	FiO₂		Mode		BD		1000's Plat	Na		Ca		Dextros		BILI		Hct
Insp																										
Exp	Pat Mach	Insp	Exp		VOL	Flow Rate	TEMP	Hi	Low	Source	PO₂	PCO₂		pH		Bun	K	CO₂		Sugar		Uncong	Tot.		T.P.	

I.V.'s #1 _____
    #2 _____

Replacement #1_____
        #2_____
        #3_____

Formulas #1_____
     #2_____
     #3_____

ACTIONS
I —Instillation of saline (trachea)
S —Suction
PD —Postural Drainage

ACTIVITY
++ —Spontaneously Active
+ —Active when stimulated
− —Unresponsive
T —Twitchy
C —Convulsion
Ir —Irritable

CHEST TUBE DRAINAGE
F —Fluctuating
B —Bubbling
S —Serous
SS —Serosanguineous
R —Bright Red

BLOOD GAS SOURCE
UA—Umbilical Artery Catheter
R —Right Radial or Brachial Stick
L —Left Radial or Brachial Stick
T —Temporal Artery Stick
C —Capillary (Heel)
V —Vein
RC —Radial Artery Catheter
TC —Temporal Artery Catheter

COLOR
P —Pink
W —Pale
D —Dusky
M —Mottled
B —Blue
J —Jaundice

O₂ MODE
H —Hood
I —Isolette
N —Nasal Prongs
E —ET tube

STOOLS
B —Brown
Y —Yellow
G —Green
Mc —Meconium
S —Seedy
M —Mushy
F —Formed
L —Liquid
Lo —Loose
Mu —Mucoid
W —Water ring

Ventilator #_____

MEDICAL RECORD COPY

NEWBORN INTENSIVE CARE FLOW SHEET

W-4

B-CLIN. NOTES	E-LAB	G-X-RAY	K-DIAGNOSTIC	M-SURGERY	Q-THERAPY	T-ORDERS	W-NURSING	Y-MISC.

History Sheet for Transport to Riley Hospital Special Care Nursery

Registration Information

Date of Transfer _____

Infant's Name _____

Sex ___ Male ___ Female

Transferring Diagnosis _____

_____

Mother's Name _____

Father's Name _____

Home Address _____

Phone No. _____

Other means of reaching parents (father's phone at work, relatives, neighbors)

_____

Name of Hospital _____

City/County _____/_____

Date of Birth _____

Time of Birth _____ a.m.   p.m.

Birth Weight _____

Estimated Due Date _____

Mother's Employer _____

Father's Employer _____

Employer's Phone _____

Insurance _____

Physician who delivered infant _____   Office phone_____

Physician who will care for infant after discharge from   Office phone _____
Riley Hospital _____

Physician who referred baby to Riley (if different from   Office phone _____
above) _____

Maternal History

Age	_____	Gravidity	_____	Height	_____
Race	_____	Parity	_____	Delivery Weight	_____
Marital Status	_____	Aborta	_____	Pregnancy Weight Gain	_____
Blood Group	_____				
Rh	_____				

Past Obstetric History

Birth date of Previous Infant	Birth Weight	Gestational Age	Sex	Type of Delivery	Complications

Present Obstetric History

Complications of Pregnancy

_____ Placenta Previa
_____ Abruptio Placenta
_____ Pre-eclampsia/Eclampsia
_____ Hypertension
_____ Diabetes Mellitus
_____ Infection _____ (Specify)
_____ Other _____

Medications During Pregnancy
According to Trimester

1st	*2nd*	*3rd*
_____	_____	_____
_____	_____	_____
_____	_____	_____
_____	_____	_____

Fetal monitoring	*(Current Pregnancy)*		*Most Recent Value*	*Date*
_____ Estriol	yes	no	_____	_____
_____ Ultrasound	yes	no	_____	_____
_____ L/S Ratio	yes	no	_____	_____
_____ Fetal ECG	yes	no	_____	_____
_____ Amniocentesis	yes	no	_____	_____
_____ Fetal Scalp pH	yes	no	_____	_____
Other _____				

Labor and Delivery Record

	Date	Time	(circle)		
Onset of Labor			a.m. p.m.	spontaneous	Placenta Wt. _____
Rupture of Membranes			a.m. p.m.	induced	Abnormalities

_____
_____

Type of Delivery
_____ Vaginal
_____ C-Section
   _____ Emergency
   _____ Elective
   _____ Repeat

Presentation
_____ Head
_____ Breech
_____ Transverse
_____ Shoulder
_____ Other _____
_____

Operation
_____ Version
   _____ external
   _____ internal
_____ Forceps
   _____ high
   _____ mid
   _____ low

Abnormalities of Amniotic Fluid
_____ Meconium stained
_____ Foul smelling
_____ Oligohydramnios
_____ Polyhydramnios
_____ Other _____

Complications of Labor
_____ Excessive bleeding
_____ Cephalopelvic disproportion
_____ Prolonged labor
_____ Fetal distress
_____ Prolapsed cord
_____ Other _____

Postpartum Complications
_____ Bleeding
_____ Infection _____
_____
_____ Other _____
_____

Medications During Labor

Anesthesia

Local	Regional	General	Other

_____
_____
_____

INFANT HISTORY

Apgar: _____ 1 min   % O_2 required to keep infant pink _____ %

_____ 5 min   Axillary temp. _____ Isolette temp. _____

Resuscitation

_____ bag _____ mask _____ intubation

Results of most recent laboratory tests

Blood sugar   _____

% of oxygen   _____

pH   _____

pO_2 _____

pCO_2 _____

Other _____

_____

_____

Medications given

Vitamin K _____

$AgNO_3$ _____

_____

Feedings

Was infant ever fed?_____

If so: When was last feeding? _____

What formula? _____

How much? _____

Problems _____

_____

_____

Signature of Individual Completing Form

Subject Index

A

Abdomen, 25-26
Abdominal distension, 26
Abdominal mass, 26
Abdominal wall defects, 191-194
ABO hemolytic disease, 81
Acidosis, 140-142
   and newborn transport preparation, 158
   treatment, 65-66
Acrocyanosis, 16
Air Shields Isolette, 112
Airway obstruction, 91
Alcoholism, and breast feeding, 51
Alimentary tract obstruction, 184
Ames Reflectance Meter, 70
Amniotic bands, 29
Anemia, 99, 143
Anencephaly, 19
Anesthesia bag, 119-120
Anomalies
   anorectal, 190
   developmental, 198
Antibiotics, and breast feeding, 50
Anus, 27
Apgar scores, and infant resuscitation, 60-61
Apnea
   causes of, 128-130
   investigative approach, 131-132
   patient monitoring, 130-131
   treatment, 132-136
Arrhythmia, cardiac, 92
Arterial blood, techniques of obtaining
   capillary sticks, 246-248
   radial artery puncture, 243-246
   sources, 242-243
Arthrogryposis, 29
Asphyxia, 163, 198
Aspiration
   meconium, 95-96
   and newborn transport preparation, 157
   in pneumothorax, 26
Atresia
   choanal, 22, 91
   colon, 190
   esophageal, 182-185
   ileal, 187

B

Barlow maneuver, 29
Beckman D2 oxygen analyzer, 113-114
Beckman OM-10 oxygen analyzer, 115
Bilirubin metabolism, 76-77; *see also*
   Hyperbilirubinemia
Birth trauma, and seizures, 198
Bladder, extrophy of, 27
Blood studies, and fluid balance, 170
Blood transfusions
   circulatory status, 228
   indications for, 226-228
   technique, 229-230
BMI oxygen analyzer, 115
Body measurements, 16
Body weight, and fluid balance, 169
Bowel habits, 13
Bowel obstruction
   high small bowel obstruction, 185-186
   and jaundice, 78
   low small bowel obstruction, 186-188
   and newborn transport preparation, 160
Brachial arches, 24
Bradycardia, 128
Breasts
   enlarged, 24
   in gestational age assessment, 32
Breast feeding, 5, 12
   advantages, 48-50
   breast care, 53-54
   disadvantages and contraindications,
     50-52
   engorgement, 53, 54
   immunity and, 49
   infections, 54
   and jaundice, 51, 77
   lactation suppression, 54-55
   milk duct obstruction, 54

Breast feeding (*contd.*)
  milk production stimulus, 52
  nutrition during, 55
  nutritional composition of, 49
  positioning, 53
  prenatal instruction, 52
  schedule, 52-53
  supplementation, 55-56

C

Caffeine, in apnea, 134-135
Calcium gluconate, in respiratory problems, 143
Capillary sticks, 246-248
Caput succedaneum, 19
Cardiorespiratory disorders, and apnea, 129-130
Cardiorespiratory system, examination, 25
Cascade humidifier, 108-109
Cataracts, 20
Catheterization, *see* Umbilical artery catheterization; Umbilical vein catheterization
Caudal regression syndrome, 74
Central nervous system disorders, and apnea, 130
Cephalohematoma, 19
Cesarean section, 163
Chest, 24
Chest tubes, 270-276
  care and maintenance, 275
  complications, 273-274
  procedure note, 285
  removal, 275-276
  teaching insertion, 274
Childproofing home, 13
Chloride requirement, 173
Circumcision, 11
  advantages and disadvantages, 5
  care, 13
Cleft palate, 22
Colonic obstruction, 188-191
Colorado Intrauterine Growth Chart, 31, 42
Computerized axial tomography, 199-200
Conjunctivitis, 20
Continuous positive airway pressure (CPAP), 144
Coombs test, 9, 78, 79, 82
Cornea, clouding of, 20
Cow's milk allergy, 50
Crying, 12
Cyanosis, 86

D

Death, perinatal, 203-209
Delivery room management, 6-8
Dextrostix®, 9, 70, 72
Diabetic pregnancies, *see* Infants of diabetic mothers
Diaper rashes, 13
Diaphragm disorders, 98
Drug(s)
  and breast feeding, 50-51
  intake
    and jaundice, 78
    and kernicterus, 85
    and respiratory distress, 87-88
  therapy and seizures, 200
  toxicity and seizures, 199
  withdrawal and seizures, 199
Dwarfism, 29
Dysplasia, bronchopulmonary, 104

E

Early neonatal care, 9-11
Ears
  examination of, 20-21
  in gestational age assessment, 32, 34-35
  low-set, 21
  malformation of, 21
Edema, 17
Electrolyte balance
  chloride, 173
  potassium, 173
  sodium, 172-173
Electrolyte disturbances, and seizures, 197
Emotional disability, and breast feeding, 51
Encephalocele, 19
Enterocolitis, necrotizing (NEC)
  clinical signs, 177
  laboratory test, 176, 177
  management, 176-180
  predisposing factors, 175
  prognosis, 180-181
  surgery for, 178, 180
Epinephrine, and newborn resuscitation, 66
Epstein's pearls, 22
Erythema toxicum, 17
Exchange transfusions, 231-236
  complications, 235-236
  in hyperbilirubinemia, 83
  orders, 283
  partial exchange transfusion, 235

Exchange transfusions (*contd.*)
   procedure note, 288
Extremity recoil, and gestational age assessment, 40
Eyes, 19-20
Eyetone Reflectance Colorimeter, 70

F
Family care
   at birth, 11-12
   discharge interview, 12-14
   and perinatal death, 203-209
   prenatal visit, 3-6
   and transfer of critically ill newborn, 160-161
Feeding, *see* Nutrition
Feet, positional abnormalities, 28
Fibroplasia, retrolental, 102-104
Fingers, 28
Fluid management
   fluid balance assessment, 169-172
   and respiratory problems, 139-140
   water requirement, 166-169
Fluoride, 56

G
Gastroschisis, 26, 192-194
Genitalia
   examination of, 26-27
   in gestational age assessment, 36
Gestational age
   charting, 40-41
   estimating, 31-41
   large for gestational age infants, 31
      problems, 41, 43
   small for gestational age infants, 31
      problems, 41, 43
Glossoptosis, 23
Goiters, 24
Group B β-hemolytic streptococcus (GBBS)
   infections, 149-153
      early-onset, 151
      late-onset, 151
      treatment, 151-152
Grunting, and respiratory distress, 87

H
Harlequin sign, 18
Head, 18-19

Health promotion, 13
Heart defects, congenital, 123
Heart disease, congenital, 97
Heart failure, congestive, 74
Heart murmurs, 25
Heat loss, 44
Hemangiomas, 18
Hematologic disorders, 99
Hemolytic disease, and jaundice, 77
Hemorrhage
   intracranial, 199
   subconjunctival, 20
Hepatitis, and breast feeding, 51
Hernia, 98
   diaphragmatic, 194-195
   and newborn transport preparation, 159
Hiccups, 12
Hip dislocation, 28-29
Hirschsprung's disease, 189-190
Hope I manual resuscitator, 116-117
Hope II resuscitation bag, 118-119
Hyaline membrane disease, 91-94
Hydrocele, 26
Hydrocephalus, 19
Hyperbilirubinemia
   and breast feeding, 51
   in infants of diabetic mothers, 74
   and respiratory problems, 143
   therapy, 82-83
Hypercoagulability, 75
Hyperglycemia, 72
Hyperthermia, 45, 138
Hyperthyroidism, 97
Hypertonia, 30
Hyperviscosity syndrome, 292, 293
Hypervolemia, 99
Hypocalcemia, 73
Hypoglycemia, 98
   causes, 70-71
   definition, 70
   and diabetic pregnancies, 73-75
   diagnosis of, 69-70
   early screening procedures, 9-10
   and newborn transport preparation, 156
   nursing guide, 290, 291
   prognosis, 73
   in respiratory problems, 142-143
   signs and symptoms, 69
   treatment, 71-73
Hypomagnesemia, 197
Hypospadias, 26

Hypotension, 65
Hypothermia, 6, 45, 101, 138, 139
Hypothyroidism, 78
Hypotonia, 30
Hypoxia, 101-102
　　and persistent fetal circulation, 124
　　treatment, 65

I

IL oxygen analyzer, 115
IMI oxygen analyzer, 115
Inborn errors of metabolism, and seizures,
　　198
Infants of diabetic mothers (IDM)
　　complications in, 73-75
　　jaundice and, 78
Intensive care flow sheet, 296, 297
Intravenous fluids, and newborn transport
　　preparation, 156
Intravenous needle placement, 213-217
Intubation, 237-241
　　kitten teaching model, 241
　　and newborn resuscitation, 63
　　procedure note, 284
　　procedural pitfalls, 240

J

Jaundice
　　bilirubin metabolism, 76-77
　　and breast milk feeding, 51
　　causes of, 77-78
　　diagnostic approach, 77-80
　　hyperbilirubinemia therapy, 82-83
　　kernicterus, 84-85
　　nursing guide, 289
　　physiologic, 80
　　Rh and ABO incompatibility and, 81-
　　　82

K

Kernicterus, 84-85

L

Laboratory workups
　　apnea, 132
　　bacterial sepsis, 148-149
　　early newborn period, 9-10
　　hypoglycemia, 70

jaundice, 78-80
necrotizing enterocolitis, 177
prenatal care, 3-4
respiratory distress, 90
seizures, 200
Lactation, *see* Breast feeding
Lanugo, 17
Lesions, infectious, 18
Lingula frenulum, 22
Liver disease, and jaundice, 77
Lumbar puncture
　　complications, 262
　　interpretation of CSF results, 261-
　　　262
　　procedure, 258-261, 286
Lung disorders, 91-97

M

Macroglossia, 24
Malformations, congenital, 74
Maternal-infant interaction, early neonatal
　　period, 11-12
Meconium ileus, 187-188
Meconium plug syndrome, 188-189
Meconium staining, 17-18
　　management of, 66-67
Meningomyelocele, 28
Metabolic disorders
　　and apnea, 29
　　and jaundice, 77
　　and seizures, 197
Micrognathia, *see* Short jaw
Milia, 13, 17
Mongolian spot, 17
Mouth, 22-24
Musculoskeletal system, 28-30

N

Nails, hypoplastic, 30
Naloxone, 65
Nasal continuous positive airway pressure
　　(CPAP), 134
Nasal flaring, and respiratory distress, 87
Nasal septal cartilage, dislocation, 22
Neck, 24
Necrotizing enterocolitis, *see* Enterocolitis
Neonatal bacterial sepsis
　　bacterial etiology, 146
　　clinical signs, 147
　　GBBS infections, 149-153

Neonatal bacterial sepsis (*contd.*)
    laboratory tests, 148-149
    predisposing factors, 146-147
    treatment, 149
Neurologic examination, 30
Neuromuscular disorders, 98
Nevus flammeus, 17
Nipples
    in gestational age assessment, 32
    supernumerary, 24
    wide-spaced, 24
Nose, 22
Nursery
    admission orders
        normal, 279
        special care, 280, 281
    procedures, 11
    vital signs chart, 294
    weight chart, 295
Nutrition
    breast feeding, *see* Breast feeding
    early neonatal period, 10
    formula, 55, 58
    premature infant, 56-58
    and respiratory problems, 142-143
    solid foods, 56

O

Ohio incubator, 112
Omphalocele, 26, 191-192
    and newborn transport procedures,
        158
Oral contraceptives, and breast feeding, 51
Ortolani test, 29
Oxygen, *see also* Oxygenation
    administration, 104-106
        in respiratory problems, 137-138
    analyzers, 113-115
    blenders, 120
    deficiency, 101-104
    and emergency transport preparation, 100-
        101
    excess, 101-104
    heating, 107-108
    hoods, 111-112
    humidification, 108-109
    incubators, 112
    masks, 109
    resuscitators, manual, 116-119
Oxygenation
    and emergency transport preparation, 157

and newborn resuscitation, 63
Oxytocin, and jaundice, 78

P

Parenthood, psychologic aspects, 5, 11-12,
    13-14
Penlon bag, 119
Persistent fetal circulation (PFC), 97
    clinical profile, 122-123
    differentiation from congenital heart
        disease, 123
    disturbances in, 124, 125
    pathophysiology, 123-125
    stress factors and, 124
    therapy, 125-127
Petechiae, 18
Phototherapy, in hyperbilirubinemia, 83
Physical examination
    abdomen, 25-26
    anus, 27
    body measurements, 16
    cardiorespiratory system, 25
    chest, 24
    ears, 20-21
    eyes, 19-20
    genitalia, 26-27
    head, 18-19
    mouth, 22-24
    musculoskeletal system, 28-30
    neck, 24
    neurologic examination, 30
    nose, 22
    observations, 16
    skin, 16-18
Physician-parent interview
    discharge, 12-14
    prenatal, 3-5
Pierre-Robin anomaly, 23
Pneumomediastinum, 97
Pneumonia, 94-95
Pneumothorax
    chest tube placement, 270-276
    diagnosis, 265-267
    and newborn transport preparation,
        158
    pathophysiology, 265
    predisposing factors, 264
    treatment, 267-270
Polycythemia, 99
    in infants of diabetic mothers, 74-75
    and jaundice, 78

Polycythemia (*contd.*)
    and seizures, 198
Postterm infants, 41
Potassium requirement, 173
Preauricular tags, 21
Premature infant, *see also* Gestational age;
    Very low birth weight infant
    and diabetic births, 74
    feeding, 56-58
        breast feeding, 57
        formula, 58
        guidelines, 57
    incubator regulation and, 46
    problems in, 41
    and retrolental fibroplasia, 103-104
    temperature regulation, 44, 45
Prenatal care, 3-5
Priscoline ®, 127
Procedures
    arterial blood, obtaining, 242-249
    blood transfusions, 226-230
    exchange transfusions, 231-236
    intravenous needle placement, 213-217
    intubation, 237-241
    lumbar puncture, 258
    in pneumothorax
        aspiration, 268
        chest tube insertion, 269-276
    suprapubic bladder aspiration, 221-225
    umbilical artery, catheterization, 250-257
Prune belly syndrome, 26
Pulmonary hypertension, persistent, *see*
    Persistent fetal circulation

R
Reflexes, and apnea, 130
Respiratory distress, 94
    clinical findings, 86-87
    diaphragm disorders, 98
    heart disorders, 97
    hematologic disorders, 99
    history and physical exam, importance,
        87-90
    infections, 99
    laboratory workup, 90
    lung disorders, 91-97
        infection, 94-95
        meconium aspiration, 95-96
        other pulmonary disorders, 97
        transient tachypnea, 94
    metabolic disorders, 98
    thorax disorders, 97

upper airway obstruction, 91
Respiratory problems, *see also*
    Respiratory distress
    acidosis, 140-142
    amelioration of primary disorder, 137
    assisted ventilation, 144
    bilirubin, 143
    fluid balance and circulation, 139-140
    nutrition and, 142-143
    oxygen administration, 137-138
    temperature stabilization, 138-139
Resting posture, and gestational age
    assessment, 39
Resuscitation
    acidosis and, 65-66
    asphyxia and, 59, 60
    epinephrine and, 66
    equipment, 60
    hypotension and, 65
    infant evaluation, 60-61
    intubation and, 63
    meconium-stained infant, 66-67
    oxygenation and, 63
    technique, 61-66
    umbilical vein catheterization, 66
    ventilation and, 63
Resuscitators, manual, 116-119
Retractions, and respiratory distress, 87
Rh incompatibility, 81-82
Rho Gam ®, 82
Rib cage malformation, 24
Rickets, 51

S
Sacral dimple, 28
Scaling, skin, 16
Screening procedures, neonatal, 9-10
Seizures
    anticonvulsant therapy in, 201
    characteristics, 196-197
    etiology, 197-200
    laboratory evaluation, 200
    treatment, 200-202
    types, 196
Sephadex test, 82
Sepsis, *see also* Neonatal bacterial sepsis
    and apnea, 129
    and breast feeding, 51
    in infants of diabetic mothers, 75
    and jaundice, 79
    and newborn transport proteins,
        160

Shock, and newborn transport preparation, 157
Short jaw, 23, 91
Skin
    care, 13
    examination, 16-18
Sneezing, 12
Sodium bicarbonate, in metabolic acidosis, 141-142
Sodium requirement, 172-173
Sole crease, and gestational age assessment, 37-39
Spitting up, 12
Stool loss, 167
Suprapubic bladder aspiration, 221-225
Surgical emergencies
    abdominal wall defects
        gastroschisis, 192-194
        hernia, diaphragmatic, 194-195
        omphalocele, 191-192
    alimentary tract obstruction, 184-185
    colonic obstruction
        anorectal anomalies, 190-191
        colon atresia, 190
        Hirschsprung's disease, 189-190
        meconium plug syndrome, 188-189
    esophageal atresia and TEF, 182-184
    high small bowel obstruction, 185-186
    low small bowel obstruction, 186-188

T
Tachycardia, 87
Tachypnea, 86-87, 94
Teeth, 24
Temperature regulation
    and apnea, 128-129
    disadvantages of newborn and, 45-46
    equipment, 46
    heat loss methods, 44
    and neonatal stabilization, 9
    and newborn transport preparation, 156
    in respiratory problems, 138-139
    thermal environment, 44-45
Theophylline, in apnea, 134-135
Thermal environment, 44-45
Thermal stability, see Temperature regulation
Thermal stress, 101
Thorax disorders, 97
Thrombosis, renal vein, 75
Tissue turgor, in fluid balance assessment, 169

Tongue, 24
Torticollis, 24
Tracheo-esophageal fistula (TEF), 91, 182-185
    and newborn transport preparation, 159-160
Transfusions, see Blood transfusion; Exchange transfusion
Transport, critically ill newborn
    criteria for transport, 160-161
    family care, 160-161
    history sheet for, 298-300
    infant preparation, 155-160
        acidosis, 158
        aspiration prevention, 157
        bowel obstruction, 160
        esophageal atresia, 159
        gastroschisis, 159
        hernia, diaphragmatic, 159
        hypoglycemia, 156
        intravenous fluids, 156
        omphalocele, ruptured, 159
        oxygenation/ventilation, 157
        pneumothorax, 158
        sepsis, 160
        shock, 157
        temperature, 156
        tracheo-esophageal fistula, 159
    return to nursery of origin, 161
Tris-hydroxymethylaminomethane (THAM), 141, 142
Tuberculosis, and breast feeding, 51
Turner's syndrome, 17

U
Umbilical artery catheterization
    catheter care, 255-257
    catheter complications, 257
    equipment, 250
    failures, 254-255
    orders, 282
    procedure, 250-254, 287
Umbilical vein catheterization, 66
Umbilicus, 13
Urine studies
    specific gravity, 170-171
    urine loss, 167
    urine output, 167

V
Ventilation, 63, 144, 157

Ventilation (*contd.*)
    and resuscitation, 63
    in respiratory problems, 144
    and transport preparation, 157
Venturi masks, 110-111
Vernix, 17
Very low birth weight infant, *see also*
      Premature infant
    asphyxia and Apgar score, 163
    delivery, 163
    intrapartum management, 162-163
    prenatal management, 162-163

    resuscitation and stabilization, 163-165
Vitamin E therapy, 105
Vitamin supplementation, 12

W
Water loss, insensible, 166-167
Weaning, 55

Y
Yawning, 12